PROBLEMS OF CAPITAL FORMATION
IN UNDERDEVELOPED COUNTRIES
AND
PATTERNS OF TRADE AND DEVELOPMENT

RAGNAR NURKSE

Problems of Capital Formation
In Underdeveloped Countries

AND

Patterns of Trade and Development

OXFORD UNIVERSITY PRESS
New York

Problems of Capital Formation in Underdeveloped Countries, first published 1953;
Patterns of Trade and Development, first published 1961
First issued as an Oxford University Press paperback, 1967
This reprint, 1970
Printed in the United States of America

CONTENTS

Problems of Capital Formation in Underdeveloped Countries, vii

Index, 159

Patterns of Trade and Development, 163

Index of Authors, 227

PROBLEMS OF CAPITAL FORMATION
IN UNDERDEVELOPED COUNTRIES

PREFACE

The greater part of this book is a revised version of six lectures which I gave in Rio de Janeiro in July and August 1951 as a guest of the Brazilian Institute of Economics under the chairmanship of Professor Eugenio Gudin. A Portuguese translation of these lectures, with English and French summaries, appeared in the quarterly *Revista Brasileira de Economia*, December 1951.

I have incorporated a paper read at a symposium on ' Growth in Underdeveloped Countries' at the Boston meeting of the American Economic Association on December 29th, 1951, published in the *American Economic Review, Papers and Proceedings*, May 1952. I am indebted to Professors Arthur R. Burns, J. Marcus Fleming and Gottfried Haberler for some detailed criticism of this paper, which I have tried to take into account in the present fuller version.

Some of the material that has gone into this book was delivered before the Société d'économie politique in Cairo in April 1952 as part of a lecture programme of the National Bank of Egypt, on the initiative of Professor N. Koestner, chief of the bank's research department, and was printed by the bank for limited private distribution.

Even though the text has been revised and largely re-written, all traces of the lecture form in which the bulk of it first took shape can scarcely have been removed. The treatment is of necessity selective and cannot claim to give a balanced picture. Nor is this in any sense a piece of research. It is an attempt, on a small scale, to make use of economic theory as well as specific observation, with a view to elucidating some of the basic conditions of progress in the poorer two-thirds of the world. If it can stimulate discussion and contribute to a clearer perception of the troublesome problems with which it deals, the book will have served its purpose.

R. N.

New York,
July, 1952.

CONTENTS

PREFACE, v

INTRODUCTION, 1

I The Size of the Market and the Inducement to Invest, 4

The Vicious Circle of Poverty, 4
Weakness of Investment Incentives, 5
The Theory of Development and the Idea of Balanced Growth, 11
Determinants of the Size of the Market, 17
Balanced Growth and International Specialization, 20
The Traditional Pattern of Foreign Investment, 24

II Population and Capital Supply, 32

Excess Population in Densely Settled Countries, 32
The Saving Potential Concealed in Rural Underemployment, 36
Population Growth and Capital Requirements, 47
The Case of Sparsely Populated Areas, 49
The Two Cases Compared, 54

III The Standard of Living and the Capacity to Save, 57

A New Theory of Consumption and Saving, 58
Growing Awareness of Advanced Living Standards, 61
Effects on the Propensity to Save, 65
Effects on the Balance of Payments, 70
The Defeatist Solution: Economic Isolation, 75
International and Interregional Income Transfers, 77

IV External Sources of Capital, 82

Direct Business Investments, 82
International Loans and Grants, 89
The Significance of the Terms of Trade, 97

V Commercial Policy and Capital Formation, 104

Infant Protection and Infant Creation, 104
Effects of Import Restrictions on Money Income and Saving, 109
Effects on the Pattern of Investment, 116
The Rationale of Luxury Import Restrictions, 117

VI   Recent Trends in the Theory of International Capital Movements, 120

Classical and Neo-Classical Theory, 120
Capital Exports and the Income Approach, 123
Foreign Investment as an Economic Stimulant, 126
The Real Case for Foreign Investment, 129
The Problems of the Return Flow, 131

VII   Action on the Home Front, 140

External and Domestic Sources, 140
The Role of Public Finance, 142
Social Overhead Capital, 152
Individual Effort: The Groundwork, 154

Index, 159

PROBLEMS OF CAPITAL FORMATION IN UNDERDEVELOPED COUNTRIES

INTRODUCTION

BEFORE we take up our first topic, let me make a few preliminary remarks about the general theme of capital formation. This subject lies at the very centre of the problem of development in economically backward countries. The so-called 'underdeveloped' areas,[1] as compared with the advanced, are underequipped with capital in relation to their population and natural resources. We shall do well to keep in mind, however, that this is by no means the whole story. Economic development has much to do with human endowments, social attitudes, political conditions—and historical accidents. Capital is a necessary but not a sufficient condition of progress.

The subject of capital formation has many ramifications, of which only a few can be singled out for consideration here. My selection will inevitably be arbitrary in some degree. The topics chosen will be of a general character. I therefore beg the reader not to expect anything like a systematic treatise, nor anything specifically related to any particular country. While the discussion will deal with problems which many of the poorer nations have in common, we must remember that different countries all have their special circumstances, into which a general survey such as this cannot possibly enter.

Among the topics selected for review are some international aspects of the problem of capital formation in the less developed countries. In fact, I may be criticized for devoting more attention to the international aspects than is warranted by their true relative importance. I myself believe that the note to be stressed above all is that of self-help; yet only about half the time is the spotlight in this book turned on the domestic scene. My excuse is that a fuller account of domestic problems would soon lead into local

---

[1] The term is not entirely satisfactory, but it has passed into general use and will be adopted in this book to cover the group of 'low-income countries' shown in the table on p. 63, below, and explained in the accompanying text.

details, for which I have neither the time nor the competence, and that the international aspects are of special interest in both the United States and the United Kingdom.

The meaning of ' capital formation ' is that society does not apply the whole of its current productive activity to the needs and desires of immediate consumption, but directs a part of it to the making of capital goods : tools and instruments, machines and transport facilities, plant and equipment—all the various forms of real capital that can so greatly increase the efficacy of productive effort. The term is sometimes used to cover human as well as material capital : it can be made to include investment in skills, education and health—a very important form of investment. I would prefer, however, not to take up matters relating to cultural, social and demographic conditions, partly because of the great diversity of those conditions, but mainly because of my lack of knowledge in these fields. I would rather limit the discussion, on the whole, to the accumulation of material capital.

The essence of the process, then, is the diversion of a part of society's currently available resources to the purpose of increasing the stock of capital goods so as to make possible an expansion of consumable output in the future. It is on this basic feature of capital accumulation that our attention will be centred. Certain aspects of the process will be treated as subsidiary. Thus the technological side of capital formation will be almost entirely neglected. When the stock of capital increases, naturally the technical form of it changes. Imagine a group of workmen building a road, each of them equipped with a dollar's worth of capital, namely, with a shovel. Now if capital per head were increased to, say, one thousand dollars, so that each could have a thousand dollars' worth of equipment to work with, it would be senseless to give each worker a thousand shovels. Some of them at least would now get, say, a tractor or a small truck to work with. Capital changes its concrete shape with the capital-intensity of production. This change in the technical appearance of equipment is what usually strikes the layman most. It is no doubt an interesting and important phenomenon, but for us it is merely an engineering aspect of the increase in the stock of real capital. We shall generally take it for granted without further discussion.

We should only remember that there may be important technical discontinuities in the physical shape which capital may assume as and when production becomes more capitalistic.

What is commonly known as 'technical progress' can mean two things. First, and quite frequently, it refers to the construction of more and better instruments of production and to the utilization, for this purpose, of a greater share of the existing store of technical knowledge. The store of knowledge may remain unchanged, and yet we may have 'technical progress' in the sense of a greater application and embodiment of it in material objects. The other sense of the term is that in which technical knowledge increases without any change in the form or quantity of capital goods. An advance in technical knowledge in the abstract may be of no economic relevance if there is no capital in which to incorporate it and with which to take advantage of it in the process of production. Leaving aside the engineering aspect of capital formation, we shall proceed on the assumption—a quite realistic assumption for the less developed countries—that there is a great fund of technical knowledge in the world which could be applied advantageously to the productive process if only the economic resources were available to make use of it.

There will be more to say on financial than on technological matters, but the financial aspect too is one that will be pushed into the background by our concern with the 'real,' or non-monetary, problems of accumulation. A detailed discussion of financial mechanics would involve us in questions of financial organization and institutions, which show considerable—and sometimes only accidental—differences from country to country, and are not always of basic importance.

So much for what is *not* on our agenda. Now we must see what *is*.

CHAPTER I

THE SIZE OF THE MARKET AND THE INDUCEMENT TO INVEST

OUR first topic has to do with the inducement to invest, such as it presents itself to the individual investor or entrepreneur. It is concerned, in other words, with the conditions that determine the demand for capital for use in the productive process. The dichotomy between demand and supply, so dear to economists, is fully applicable to the forces that govern the accumulation of capital. Capital formation is not entirely a matter of capital supply, although this is no doubt the more important part of the problem. The later chapters will deal with a number of points on the supply side. But there may be a snag on the demand side as well, and this I propose to take up first.

THE VICIOUS CIRCLE OF POVERTY

In discussions of the problem of economic development, a phrase that crops up frequently is ' the vicious circle of poverty.' It is generally treated as something obvious, too obvious to be worth examining. I hope I may be forgiven if I begin by taking a look at this obvious concept.

It implies a circular constellation of forces tending to act and react upon one another in such a way as to keep a poor country in a state of poverty. Particular instances of such circular constellations are not difficult to imagine. For example, a poor man may not have enough to eat; being under-fed, his health may be weak; being physically weak, his working capacity is low, which means that he is poor, which in turn means that he will not have enough to eat; and so on. A situation of this sort, relating to a country as a whole, can be summed up in the trite proposition : ' a country is poor because it is poor.'

Perhaps the most important circular relationships of this kind are those that afflict the accumulation of capital in economically backward countries. The supply of capital is governed by the ability and willingness to save; the demand for capital is governed by the incentives to invest. A circular relationship exists on both sides of the problem of capital formation in the poverty-ridden areas of the world.

On the supply side, there is the small capacity to save, resulting from the low level of real income. The low real income is a reflection of low productivity, which in its turn is due largely to the lack of capital. The lack of capital is a result of the small capacity to save, and so the circle is complete.

On the demand side, the inducement to invest may be low because of the small buying power of the people, which is due to their small real income, which again is due to low productivity. The low level of productivity, however, is a result of the small amount of capital used in production, which in its turn may be caused at least partly by the small inducement to invest.

The low level of real income, reflecting low productivity, is a point that is common to both circles. Usually the trouble on the supply side receives all the emphasis. The trouble there is certainly obvious and serious, and some aspects of it will be thoroughly gone into later. But the possible block on the demand side, once one becomes aware of it, is also fairly obvious, though it may not be so serious, or so difficult to remove, as the supply deficiency.

Besides, let us remember that capital is not everything. In addition to the circular relationships that plague the capital problem, there are, of course, matters of unilateral causation that can keep a country poor; for instance, lack of mineral resources, insufficient water or barren soil. Some of the poorer countries in the world to-day are poor partly for such reasons. But in all of them their poverty is also attributable to some extent to the lack of adequate capital equipment, which can be due to the small inducement to invest as well as to the small capacity to save.

WEAKNESS OF INVESTMENT INCENTIVES

It may at first be surprising to hear that there can be anything wrong on the demand side of the problem of capital formation in underdeveloped countries. Can there be any deficiency in the demand for capital ? Are not the backward areas, almost by definition, greatly in need of capital for the efficient use of their labour and for the exploitation of their natural resources ? Is not the demand for capital in these areas tremendous ? It may well be; and yet in terms of private incentives to adopt capitalistic methods in the productive process there is the difficulty that stems from the limited size of the domestic market in the early stages of a country's economic development.

The inducement to invest is limited by the size of the market. This proposition is, in effect, a modern variant of Adam Smith's famous thesis that ' the division of labour is limited by the extent of the market.'[1] The point is simple and has long been familiar to the business world. It is a matter of common observation that in the poorer countries the use of capital equipment in the production of goods and services for the domestic market is inhibited by the small size of that market, by the lack of domestic purchasing power, not in monetary but in real terms, in a sense to be presently defined. If it were merely a deficiency of monetary demand, it could easily be remedied through monetary expansion; but the trouble lies deeper. Monetary expansion alone does not remove it, but produces merely an inflation of prices.

This simple point, that the incentive to apply capital is limited by the size of the market, has a certain validity not only in the exchange economy of the real world, but even in the economy of an isolated individual like Robinson Crusoe, well known to our forefathers from elementary textbooks. Suppose that Robinson Crusoe had two or three hundred nails (which he got, let us say, from a wooden box washed ashore on his island) and wanted to drive them into some trees in order to hang up his fishing nets or personal effects. It would pay him first to sit down and make a simple hammer with which to drive these nails into his trees. His total effort would be reduced; he would do the job more quickly. But if he had only two or three nails it would not be worth his while to make a hammer. He would pick up and use a

---

[1] It was Allyn A. Young who suggested this re-interpretation in his well-known essay, ' Increasing Returns and Economic Progress,' *Economic Journal*, December 1928 (now reprinted in *Readings in Economic Analysis*, edited by R. V. Clemence, Cambridge, Mass., 1950, Vol. I). It is easy to see, and Adam Smith recognized it himself, that the division of labour is closely connected with the use of capital in production.

stone of suitable size. It would be a slow and inconvenient method; but it would be uneconomic to produce capital equipment in the shape of a hammer just for driving in two or three nails.

In the exchange economy of the real world, it is not difficult to find illustrations of the way in which the small size of a country's market can discourage, or even prohibit, the profitable application of modern capital equipment by any individual entrepreneur in any particular industry. In a country, for instance, where the great majority of people are too poor to wear leather shoes, setting up a modern shoe factory may be a doubtful business proposition; the market for shoes is too small. Many articles that are in common use in the United States can be sold in a low-income country in quantities so limited that a machine working only a few days or weeks can produce enough for a whole year's consumption, and would have to stand idle the rest of the time. In Chile, for example, it has been found that a modern rolling mill, which is standard equipment in any industrial country, can produce in three hours a sufficient supply of a certain type of iron shapes to last the country for a year. In these circumstances the inducement to install such equipment is lacking. In some cases foreign branch plants which had been established in certain Latin American countries were subsequently withdrawn because it was found that the local market was too small to make their operation profitable.[1]

These examples may exaggerate the difficulty, but I do believe that, to some extent, the difficulty is real. To produce with more capital per unit of output means generally, though not invariably, producing on a larger scale, in the sense of a larger output per plant. This is what matters in the present context, though it may be noted that in a given line of production any increase in output, even when it maintains the old degree of capital-intensity, will be discouraged by the smallness of the market.

The economic incentive to install capital equipment for the production of a certain commodity or service always depends in some measure on the amount of work to be done with this equip-

[1] For these and other examples, see G. Wythe, *Industry in Latin America* (New York, 1951).

ment. Naturally the individual business man must take the amount of work to be done—the size of the market for his commodity or service—more or less as he finds it. He may hope to be able to deflect some of the present volume of consumers' demand in his own favour; but where real income is close to the subsistence level, there is little or no scope for such deflection. The limited size of the domestic market in a low-income country can thus constitute an obstacle to the application of capital by any individual firm or industry working for that market. In this sense the small domestic market is an obstacle to development generally.

How can this obstacle be removed ? What is it that determines the size of the market ? Some people may think, in this connection, of monetary expansion as a remedy, others of high-powered methods of salesmanship and advertising. Some may think of the size of a country's population as determining the size of the market; others, again, may have in mind the physical extent of the country's territory. All these factors are of secondary importance, if not irrelevant. A popular prescription is that small adjacent countries should abolish restrictions on trade with each other. But the smallness of a country is not the basic difficulty. The difficulty can exist even in very large countries such as China and India.

The crucial determinant of the size of the market is productivity. In an all-inclusive view, the size of the market is not only determined, but actually defined, by the volume of production. In the economy as a whole, the flow of goods and services produced and consumed is not a fixed magnitude. With a given population, it is a variable depending on people's productive efficiency. It is sometimes said that, if only prices could be reduced (money incomes remaining the same), the market could be enlarged. That is true, but if this were to happen it would imply an increase in productivity and real income. The market would be similarly enlarged if people's money incomes could be increased while prices remained constant. Again, this would be possible only with an advance in productive efficiency, implying an increase in real income. We are here in the classical world of Say's Law. In underdeveloped areas there is generally no ' deflationary gap ' through excessive savings. Production creates its own demand, and the size of the market depends on the volume of production. In the last analysis, the market can be enlarged only through an all-round increase in productivity. Capacity to buy means capacity to produce.

Now productivity—or output per man-hour—depends largely, though by no means entirely, on the degree to which capital is employed in production. It is largely a matter of using machinery and other equipment. It is a function, in technical terms, of the capital-intensity of production. But, for any individual entrepreneur, the use of capital is inhibited, to start with, by the small size of the market.

Where is the way out of this circle ? How can the market be enlarged ? Even though in economically backward areas Say's Law may be valid in the sense that there is no deflationary gap, it never is valid in the sense that the output of any single industry, newly set up with capital equipment, can create its own demand. Human wants being diverse, the people engaged in the new industry will not wish to spend all their income on their own products.[1] Suppose it is a shoe industry. The shoe producers cannot live on shoes alone and must depend on the exchange of shoes for the other things they need. If in the rest of the economy nothing happens to increase productivity and hence buying power, the market for the new shoe output is likely to prove deficient. People outside the new industry will not give up other things in order to buy, say, a pair of shoes every year if they do not have enough food, clothing and shelter. They cannot let go the little they have of these elementary necessities. If they *were* willing to renounce some of their present consumption in exchange for an annual pair of new shoes, these things would become available for the shoe workers to make up the balance in their consumption needs. As it is, the new industry is likely to be a failure.

The trouble is due by no means solely to discontinuities in the technical forms of capital equipment, though these will accentuate it. It is due above all to the inevitable inelasticity of demands

[1] See Paul N. Rosenstein-Rodan, ' Problems of Industrialization of Eastern and South-Eastern Europe,' *Economic Journal*, June–September 1943, p. 205.

at low real-income levels. It is in this way that poverty cramps the inducement to invest and discourages the application of capital to any single line of production. The enlargement of the market through the rise in productivity that would result from increased capital-intensity of production is inhibited by the initial smallness of the market.

The problem of technical discontinuities, in turn, is due not merely to the fact that equipment produced in advanced countries is adapted to domestic mass markets there and is not, as a rule, best suited to conditions in the poorer countries. Even if equipment were devised particularly for the latter, discontinuities would still remain. Additions to capital equipment in any case are apt to come in relatively big units, and there is especially a character-istic lumpiness in the process of investment in overhead capital facilities such as railways, power plants and water works.

While thus the technical discontinuities may call for sizable forward 'jumps' in the rate of output, the small and inelastic demand in a low-income country tends to make such jumps risky if not altogether unpromising in any given branch of business considered by itself. If, in the past, attempts at jumping forward in particular branches have for these reasons come to grief, individual enterprise is likely to take a dim view of future investment prospects; the demand for capital will be de-pressed.[1]

We recognize, in one of its aspects, the vicious circle of poverty. We perceive a constellation of circumstances tending to preserve any backward economy in a stationary condition, in a state of 'underdevelopment equilibrium' somewhat analogous, perhaps, to the 'underemployment equilibrium,' the possibility of which, in advanced industrial countries, was impressed on us by Keynes. Economic progress is not a spontaneous or automatic affair. On the contrary, it is evident that there are automatic forces within the system tending to keep it moored to a given level.

[1] All this is superimposed on the fact that in communities afflicted with mass poverty the qualities of enterprise and initiative are usually in short supply to start with, and that the demand for capital tends to be sluggish for this reason alone. I am grateful to Mr. Robert G. Link for a detailed comment setting forth with more precision the possible ways in which the three factors—inelastic consumer demand, technical discontinuities and lack of enterprise—can keep down the demand for capital in low-income countries.

All this, however, is only part of the story. The circular constellation of the stationary system is real enough, but fortunately the circle is not unbreakable. And once it is broken at any point, the very fact that the relation is circular tends to make for cumulative advance. We should perhaps hesitate to call the circle vicious; it can become beneficent.

THE THEORY OF DEVELOPMENT AND THE IDEA OF BALANCED GROWTH

What is it that breaks the deadlock ? The nations concerned need not and will not accept the state of underdevelopment equilibrium as an inexorable decree of fate. Besides, we know that in some parts of the world economic development has actually occurred; something must have happened there to break the circle. So the theory of stagnation must be succeeded by a theory of development explaining the forces that are required, or that were observed in the past, to lift the economy out of the stationary state in which it would otherwise tend to settle. As we shall see, it is scarcely possible to consider this subject without finding one's mind turning to Schumpeter's great work.

For the moment, however, let us revert to the market problem which we have just examined. The difficulty caused by the small size of the market relates to individual investment incentives in any single line of production taken by itself. At least in principle, the difficulty vanishes in the case of a more or less synchronized application of capital to a wide range of different industries. Here is an escape from the deadlock; here the result is an over-all enlargement of the market. People working with more and better tools in a number of complementary projects become each others' customers. Most industries catering for mass consumption are complementary in the sense that they provide a market for, and thus support, each other. This basic complementarity stems, in the last analysis, from the diversity of human wants. The case for 'balanced growth' rests on the need for a 'balanced diet.'

The notion of balance is inherent in the classical Law of Markets which generally passes under the name of Say's Law. Take John Stuart Mill's formulation of it: 'Every increase of

production, if distributed without miscalculation among all kinds
of produce in the proportion which private interest would dictate,
creates, or rather constitutes, its own demand.'[1] Here, in a nut-
shell, is the case for balanced growth. An increase in the production of shoes alone does not create its own demand. An increase
in production over a wide range of consumables, so proportioned
as to correspond with the pattern of consumers' preferences, does
create its own demand. It goes without saying that, with a given
labour force and with given techniques and natural resources, it
is only through the use of more capital that such an increase in
production can be obtained.

Balanced growth may be a good thing for its own sake, but
here it interests us mainly for the sake of its effects on the demand
for capital. It appears in the present context as an essential means
of enlarging the size of the market and of creating inducements to
invest.

But how do we get balanced growth ? Ordinary price incentives may bring it about by small degrees, though here the
technical discontinuities can be a serious hindrance; besides, slow
growth is just not good enough where population pressure exists.
In the evolution of Western capitalism, according to Schumpeter's
well-known theory, rapid growth was achieved through the action
of individual entrepreneurs, producing recurrent waves of
industrial progress. Schumpeter's *Theory of Economic Development* has commonly been treated by economists in the advanced
industrial countries as a theory of business cycles. In the advanced
countries there has been a tendency to take economic development
for granted, as something like a natural process that takes care of
itself, and to concentrate on the short-run oscillations of the
economy. Schumpeter's work, properly understood, is just what
its title says it is : a theory of economic development. Business
cycles appear in it only as the form in which economic progress
takes place.

Schumpeter's theory seems to me to provide the mould which
we must use, although we may use it with slightly different
ingredients. As everyone knows, this theory assigns a central

[1] J. S. Mill, *Essays on Some Unsettled Questions of Political Economy* (London
School of Economics reprint, 1948), p. 73.

role to the creative entrepreneur, or rather to the action of considerable numbers of such entrepreneurs and their imitators, carrying out innovations, putting out new commodities, and devising new combinations of productive factors. Even if an innovation tends each time to originate in one particular industry, the monetary effects of the initial investment—and other circumstances as well—are such as to promote a wave of new applications of capital over a range of different industries. These waves result, in Schumpeter's own words, ' each time . . . in an avalanche of consumers ' goods that permanently deepens and widens the stream of real income although in the first instance they spell disturbance, losses and unemployment.'[1]

While the money-income effect of investment accounts, at least in part, for the bunching of investment activities in the course of the cycle, it is the effect of the investments on the general level of productivity that increases the flow of consumable goods and services. This real-income effect, although it may have depressive monetary repercussions in the short run, is indeed the sum and substance of long-run economic progress—provided of course that the composition of the increased consumable output corresponds, by and large, to the pattern of consumers' demands.

In our present context it seems to me that the main point is to recognize how a frontal attack of this sort—a wave of capital investments in a number of different industries—can economically succeed while any substantial application of capital by an individual entrepreneur in any particular industry may be blocked or discouraged by the limitations of the pre-existing market. Where any single enterprise might appear quite inauspicious and impracticable, a wide range of projects in different industries may succeed because they will all support each other, in the sense that the people engaged in each project, now working with more real capital per head and with greater efficiency in terms of output per man-hour, will provide an enlarged market for the products of the new enterprises in the other industries. In this way the market difficulty, and the drag it imposes on individual incentives to invest, is removed or at any rate alleviated by means of a dynamic expansion of the market through investment carried out

---

[1] *Capitalism, Socialism and Democracy* (3rd ed., New York, 1950), p. 68.

in a number of different industries. The rate at which any one industry can grow is inevitably conditioned by the rate at which other industries grow, although naturally some industries will grow faster than others since demand and supply elasticities will vary for different products. Through the application of capital over a wide range of activities, the general level of economic efficiency is raised and the size of the market enlarged.

The technical contribution which capital can bring about in backward countries is not in dispute. The possible increase in physical output with modern machinery, plus efficient management, may be tremendous. But this, after all, is merely the engineering side of the matter. The economic side is concerned, not simply with physical productivity, but with value productivity, and this is limited for any individual business by the poverty of potential consumers. When we think of the primitive methods of production that prevail in most countries and contrast them mentally with the physical productivity of a modern mechanized plant, we readily jump to the conclusion that the marginal productivity of capital in the economically backward areas must be enormous. The case is not so simple. The technical opportunities may be great; the physical increase in output may be spectacular compared with existing output, but value productivity is limited by the low purchasing power of the people. The technical physical productivity of capital can be realized in economic terms only through balanced growth, enlarging the aggregate size of the market and increasing individual investment incentives all round, while on any single investment project, if it were considered in isolation, the prospective return might be quite discouraging or at all events not sufficiently attractive to make the installation of more and better equipment worth while.

The notion of ' external economies ' seems applicable here, though not quite in the sense in which Marshall commonly used it. Each of a wide range of projects, by contributing to an enlargement of the total size of the market, can be said to create economies external to the individual firm. Indeed, it may be that the most important external economies leading to the phenomenon of increasing returns in the course of economic progress are those that take the form of increases in the size of the market, rather than those which economists, following Marshall, have usually had in mind (improvements in productive facilities such as transport, communications, trade journals, labour skills and techniques available to a certain industry and dependent on the size of that industry).

The external economies in the market sense, just like those of the more conventional type, can create a discrepancy between the private and the social marginal productivity of capital. The private inducement to invest in any single project may be quite inadequate because of the market difficulty, even where the marginal productivity of capital applied over a range of complementary industries, in the sense just indicated, is very considerable. This is why a wave of new investments in different branches of production can economically succeed, enlarge the total market and so break the bonds of the stationary equilibrium of underdevelopment. In the early dawn of industrial development, it takes the eye of faith to see the potential markets. Schumpeter's creative entrepreneurs seem to have what it takes, and as they move forward on a broad front, their act of faith is crowned with commercial success.

Schumpeter's theory of economic development was intended to apply primarily to the rise and growth of Western capitalism. It is not necessarily applicable in the same way to other types of society. It may be that in other types of society the forces that are to defeat the grip of economic stagnation have to be deliberately organized to some extent, at any rate initially. In the early industrial development of Japan, for instance, the state was the great innovator and the industrial pioneer on a wide front.[1] Japan's early industrial development seems to have been ' planned' and carried out in large measure by the state. Later, when the main obstacles—including the initial market difficulty—had been overcome, the state was able in many cases to turn over to private

[1] See Shigeto Tsuru, ' Economic Fluctuations in Japan 1868–93,' *Review of Economic Statistics*, 1941. The point has been made by a number of other writers. Japan's experience in this respect is well summarized by Joseph J. Spengler : ' The government . . . offset the lack of an adequate entrepreneurial class by performing many of the functions of this class and facilitating the accomplishment of others through the use of appropriate monetary, fiscal, and related policies.' (' Economic Factors in the Development of Densely Populated Areas,' *Proceedings of the American Philosophical Society*, February 1951, p. 44.)

hands the projects it had started. Incidentally, it appears that Japan's early industrial development, before 1914. was based predominantly on an over-all expansion of the domestic market, It was not until later that export markets became important for Japanese industry.

Whether the forces of economic progress are to be deliberately organized or left to the action of private enterprise—in short, whether balanced growth is enforced by planning boards or achieved spontaneously by creative entrepreneurs—is, of course, a weighty and much debated issue. But from our present viewpoint it is essentially a question of method. I feel no need to enter into it at length. We are here concerned with the economic nature of the solution, not with the administrative form of it. Whichever method is adopted, the nature of the solution aimed at may be the same. And the 'miscalculation' Mill warned against (in the passage quoted earlier) seems hard to avoid in either case. Experience has certainly shown that large-scale public investment plans, in their practical execution, if not in their conception, often have a tendency to develop a marked lack of balance. But disproportionalities of one kind or another have also been a feature of the cyclical booms through which economic progress was achieved by private enterprise.

The nature of the solution is what I have tried to indicate. The question of method must be decided on the ground of broader considerations; on the ground, especially, of the human qualities and motive forces existing in any particular society. The economist, as an economist, has no categorical imperatives to issue on this subject. One of the founding fathers of nineteenth-century liberalism, Jeremy Bentham himself, maintained an attitude of relativity in this regard. 'Whether government should intervene, says Bentham, should depend on the extent of the power, intelligence, and inclination, and therefore the spontaneous initiative, possessed by the public, and this will vary as between countries.'[1] For various reasons, some of which could probably be fairly clearly defined, the American economy has been abundantly

[1] Jacob Viner, 'Bentham and J. S. Mill: The Utilitarian Background,' *American Economic Review*, March 1949, p. 371. Bentham adds this illustration : ' In Russia, under Peter the Great, the list of *sponte acta* being a blank, that of *agenda* was proportionally abundant ' (Viner, ibid.).

supplied with the human qualities of enterprise and initiative; but we cannot take it for granted that they are present in the same degree elsewhere. In the industrial development of Western Europe the main source of these qualities was the middle class. In the United States this label, if applicable at all, might be said to cover the great bulk of the people, while in many of the backward countries to-day the middle class is virtually non-existent.[1]

DETERMINANTS OF THE SIZE OF THE MARKET

We have already observed that the deficiency of market demand that tends to keep down private investment incentives in the domestic economies of underdeveloped countries is a deficiency of real purchasing power, in terms of classical economics. It is not a deficiency of ' effective demand ', in terms of Keynesian economics. There is, as a rule, no deficiency of monetary demand; there is no deflationary gap. On the contrary, many of these countries suffer from a chronic inflationary pressure. Money demand, though low in absolute amount, is excessive in relation to the capacity to produce. Supply creates its own demand, yes; but supply is very small. There is a shortage of demand in the fundamental classical sense of supply to offer in exchange in the market. This supply is small because of low productivity, which in turn is largely due to the lack of real capital. There is little or nothing in this state of affairs that can be remedied by monetary expansion. Supply in poor agricultural countries being inelastic as well as small, monetary expansion leads merely to price inflation. The fundamental market deficiency as a deterrent to private capital investment remains completely unchanged. Monetary policy, though it may have other important functions, is not one of the main determinants of the size of the market in the sense in which we have discussed it.

[1] Joseph J. Spengler sums up these matters judiciously : ' Industrial progress is markedly dependent upon (a) the relative number of imaginative and energetic innovators and entrepreneurs present in the population, (b) the extent to which these qualified persons are empowered to make and execute relevant decisions, and (c) the degree to which these individuals are free of hampering legal and institutional arrangements. In the past this distribution has been most favourable in countries possessing a comparatively strong " middle class " that enjoyed sufficient support at the hands of the state; while countries lacking a sufficiently strong middle class have had to depend upon the state to provide entrepreneurial leadership in so far as possible ' (op. cit., p. 22).

Nor is the number of a country's inhabitants a basic determinant in this sense. A country with a large population will have only a small total capacity to produce if its people have a low productivity per head. Size of population can affect the average level of productivity only in so far as the notion of an ' optimum population ' is valid. And even if a country with a large population does produce a sizable aggregate output, this still does not mean that it constitutes a coherent market. There is the cost of transportation to be considered. But this factor, too, should not be considered alone. It has too often been picked out for almost exclusive attention (owing, no doubt, to its historical importance in a crucial period of economic expansion).

There is indeed a common misconception which tends to interpret the size of the market in the present context solely in terms of physical area, and which accordingly places a quite disproportionate emphasis on the cost of transporting goods. It is true that with given population density and productivity per head, improvements in transport will increase the physical extent as well as the economic size of the market. But physical extent and economic size are not identical. The latter depends on the efficiency, not only of transportation, but of production generally, even though it can readily be admitted that transport facilities do play a quite special role in economic development.[1]

Improvements in transport are important; so are reductions in tariff barriers and other artificial obstructions to the movement of goods. A recent United Nations report expresses the opinion that ' some underdeveloped countries are so small that their internal market is not large enough to support large-scale industries,' and proposes as a remedy the creation of preferential tariff

---

[1] Some confusion on this point may be due to Adam Smith, who, in expounding his great thesis that ' the division of labour is limited by the extent of the market', discussed, in the main, the market's geographical area and concentrated almost exclusively on the benefits of cheap transport (in particular, 'water carriage '). He realized that the division of labour was intimately bound up with the application of capital to the processes of production. When he said in effect, that the application of capital was limited by the size of the market, he pointed to a fundamental and important truth. But it was not quite the whole truth. Smith was not equally clear about the other side of the matter, namely, that the extent (i.e., size) of the market depends, in turn, largely on the division of labour (i.e., on the application of capital). Instead he emphasized transport facilities as the determinant. He shunned the circular relation and presented a straightforward linear sequence of causation.

systems, customs unions or even political federations among such countries.[1] If this were the real solution of the market problem, it would be relatively easy—a matter merely of legislation or government decree in a group of neighbouring countries; no great demands would be placed on the state.

The main trouble, however, is not that countries are too small but that they are too poor to provide markets for local industries. If Ecuador had the same level of productivity as Sweden or Switzerland, its domestic market would be sufficient to offer incentives for private investments of various kinds. As it is, it is not. Certainly, to remove trade restrictions with neighbouring countries would not be an entirely useless gesture. Something may be gained by combining Ecuador into a single customs area with Colombia, Peru and Venezuela, so as to remove the bad effect of the artificial transport cost which customs duties represent. But can this be the real answer to the problem of economic development ? Even with no trade restrictions, there would still remain the physical transport costs and, above all, the low general level of productivity.

Tariff barriers can be regarded as artificial transport costs. Reductions in transport costs, whether natural or artificial, do produce an increase in the size, as well as in the geographical extent of the market. But reductions in any cost of production, not only in that of transport, have that effect. Any increase in economic efficiency—not only in the efficiency of transportation —increases the size of the market in the way already indicated. Adam Smith had good historical reasons for his emphasis on transport facilities, and one can think of theoretical reasons as well. I would not deny for a moment the benefits of cheap transport and free trade. But to single out transport costs—natural or artificial—and to speak of the territorial extent of the market as the main or the sole determinant of its size, seems to me a case of misplaced emphasis (due, perhaps, to the common penchant for ‘ misplaced concreteness ’).

China, one of the poorest countries in the world, used to have

---

[1] *Measures for the Economic Development of Underdeveloped Countries*, Report by a Group of Experts appointed by the Secretary-General of the United Nations, May 1951, p. 23.

a system of internal customs duties, called 'Likin,' which had to be paid whenever goods were moved from one province to another. While their main purpose was revenue collection, there is no doubt that these duties acted effectively as interregional tariff barriers. In 1928 this system was abolished. China became, from the point of view of commercial policy, a 'single market'—one of the world's largest national markets in area as well as in numbers of people. Yet China remained one of the poorest countries in the world.

Those who point to the absence of internal trade barriers within the United States as an example for other parts of the world, stress what seems to me a secondary rather than a primary foundation of American prosperity. A primary foundation is the American level of productivity, due largely to the tremendous equipment of capital used in production. This is what constitutes the chief basis of the American mass market and of American mass production. Mass production, incidentally, would not be possible if it did not mean production for the masses. Economic development in the United States has made more and better goods and services available to the mass of people, including especially the lower income groups. Most of the things that are now generally regarded as characteristic of the American standard of living are to be found among the lower income groups in the United States. They are articles not only of mass production but also of mass consumption, thanks to the high productivity of the American worker; thanks largely to the fact that he is so well equipped with capital instruments, plant and machinery of all kinds. This is what seems to me the primary determinant of a mass market.

Balanced Growth and International Specialization

The limited size of the market in economically backward areas has important effects on the volume of international trade, on the pattern of foreign investment, and on the use of domestic savings. Each of these topics calls for some comment.

The size of the market is a basic determinant, not only of the incentives for the employment of capital, but also of the volume of international trade. Because of their low level of productivity and hence of real purchasing power, the backward agricultural countries play, as is well known, a minor part in world trade; by and large, the advanced industrial countries are each others' best customers.[1] The main influence of Keynesian economics on the theory of international trade was to stress the fact that the volume of trade among the industrial countries is closely dependent on the state of employment and effective demand in these countries, and that one cannot expect foreign trade to be active if the domestic economies are depressed. This was a good point to stress, but it is not the most fundamental. A more important determinant of the volume of international trade in the long run is the ' size of the market ' and the level of productivity. Balanced growth, as a means of enlarging the market and stimulating the incentives for higher productivity through capital investment, is an essential basis for expanding trade.

Yet the case which the poor countries advance in favour of the ' balanced growth ' and ' diversification ' of their domestic economies is not always well received. Does it not mean turning away from the principle of comparative advantage ? Why do these countries not push their exports of primary products according to the rules of international specialization, and import the goods they need for a ' balanced diet ' ? Very briefly, the answer is : because the notion of balance applies on the global scale as well. For fairly obvious reasons, expansion of primary production for export is apt to encounter adverse price conditions on the world market, unless the industrial countries' demand is steadily expanding, as it was in the nineteenth century when both population and productivity in Western Europe were growing rapidly, when synthetic substitutes for crude materials had not yet been discovered, and when Great Britain decided to abolish tariff protection and thus to surrender some of her own agriculture in the interests of international specialization. In the present century conditions have changed. There has been some sluggishness in the industrial countries' demand for primary products, and despite the recent raw-material boom there is no certainty that this sluggishness is gone for good.

[1] See Folke Hilgerdt's illuminating study, *Industrialization and Foreign Trade* (League of Nations, 1945).

To push exports of primary commodities in the face of an inelastic and more or less stationary demand would not be a promising line of long-run development. If it is plausible to assume a generally less than unitary price elasticity of demand for crude foodstuffs and materials, it seems reasonable also to conclude that, under the conditions indicated, economic growth in underdeveloped countries must largely take the form of increased production for domestic markets. (Whether these conditions will prevail in the future is a question of forecasting, into which we need not enter). Under these conditions, if there is to be any development at all, it must concentrate at least initially on production for local requirements; and so long as this development increases the level of productivity and hence of real purchasing power, it will tend in the long run to help rather than hinder the growth of international trade.

These are some of the considerations that explain the widespread desire for ' balanced growth ' and provide some economic justification for it. They do not constitute a case for autarky. The scale of comparative advantage is subject to change. Rash conclusions are sometimes drawn from static analysis. Undeveloped countries endeavouring to build up industries producing for their own market are often regarded as moving towards a state of self-sufficiency. But the size of the market is not fixed. When, for example, a country that consumes annually a certain number of shoes (our favourite commodity), all of which it imports, decides now to set up a domestic shoe industry producing just that number a year, it seems natural to conclude that it is making itself self-sufficient in shoes. But if the new shoe industry is part of an over-all process of growth, the market for shoes in that country may increase ten-fold, so that its shoe imports are increased instead of cut down to nothing. In Canada, for example, textile manufacturing was one of the first industries to develop, with the aid of tariff protection from 1879 on; yet Canada to-day is one of the world's biggest importers of textile manufactures.

As productivity increases and the domestic market expands, while the composition of imports and exports is naturally bound to change, the total volume of external trade is more likely to grow than to shrink. But even if it remains the same there is not necessarily any harm in 'balanced growth' on the domestic front. Take a country like Venezuela; petroleum accounts for 90 per cent of its exports, but employs only about 2 per cent of its labour force; the majority of the people work in the interior for a precarious subsistence in agriculture. If, through the introduction of capital and increased productivity, the domestic economy were to expand so that people working formerly on the land alone would now supply each other with clothing, footwear, houses and house-furnishings as well as food products, while all the time petroleum exports remained the same and imports likewise constant in total volume, nothing but gain would result to the inhabitants without any loss to the outside world. No doubt there would be a fall in the proportion of foreign trade to national income. But could it not be that this proportion, in the many 'peripheral' countries of this type, has been kept unduly high in the past, simply by the poverty of the domestic economy ?

The characteristically important role which international trade played in the world economy of the nineteenth century was partly due to the fact that there *was* a periphery—and a vacuum beyond. The trade pattern of the nineteenth century was not merely a device for the optimum allocation of a given volume of resources; it was, as D. H. Robertson put it, ' above all an engine of growth,'[1] but of growth originating in and radiating from the early industrial centres. Even in the United States we have been so accustomed to regard the early nineteenth-century pattern as normal that we seldom stop to notice that the economic development of the United States itself has been a spectacular departure from it.

With the spread of industrialization we have, however, noticed that the major currents of international trade pass by the economically backward areas and flow rather among the advanced industrial countries. ' Balanced growth ' is a good foundation for international trade, as well as a way of filling the vacuum at the periphery.

[1] ' The Future of International Trade,' *Economic Journal*, March 1938, p. 5 (now reprinted in *Readings in the Theory of International Trade*, edited by H. S. Ellis and L. A. Metzler, Philadelphia, 1949).

The Traditional Pattern of Foreign Investment

The inducement to invest is limited by the size of the market. Our general discussion of this theme is directly applicable to the field of international investment.

Why is it that private business investment abroad has tended in the past—in the last few years as well as in the nineteenth century—to shy away from industries working for the domestic market in underdeveloped areas and to concentrate instead on primary production for export to the advanced industrial centres ? There is little doubt that such a tendency has existed and still exists. Some illustrations of it will be given in Chapter IV. American direct investments abroad certainly conform to this pattern. In economically backward countries, they work mostly in extractive industries—oil fields, mines and plantations—producing for export markets; only in the more advanced areas (Canada and Western Europe) do they, significantly, show any great interest in manufacturing for local consumption. The fact that foreign investment often constitutes merely an outpost of the advanced creditor economy, to whose needs it caters, was noticed by J. S. Mill[1] and stressed more recently by J. H. Williams.[2]

Dr. H. W. Singer of the United Nations Secretariat takes it as the basis for his criticism of the ' traditional ' type of foreign investment.[3] According to him, foreign investment was foreign only in a geographic sense; it formed essentially a part of the creditor country's economy; it did little or nothing to promote—and, on occasion, may even have impeded—the economic development of the debtor countries.

Personally I find these generalizations a little too sweeping. In the first place, they seem to me to apply only to a part—and, as we shall find, a minor part—of international investment in the century before 1914. Private foreign loans to governmental authorities and public utility undertakings were very considerable; and the largest single form of British foreign investment in the

---

[1] *Principles of Political Economy*, Book III, chap. 25, sec. 5.

[2] ' The Theory of International Trade Reconsidered,' *Economic Journal*, June 1929 (reprinted in *Readings in the Theory of International Trade*, op. cit.)

[3] ' The Distribution of Gains between Investing and Borrowing Countries,' *American Economic Review, Papers and Proceedings*, May 1950.

years 1870–1914 was investment in railway securities, which un-questionably provided a useful foundation for the general develop-ment of the borrowing countries.

Secondly, I am inclined to believe that even in the case of the so-called ' colonial ' type of foreign investments—that is, foreign-owned extractive industries working for export to the industrial countries—various direct as well as indirect benefits were likely to develop, contributing gradually, even if only as a by-product, so to speak, to the growth of the local economy.

Be that as it may, it does seem true to say that, on the whole, foreign entrepreneurial investment in underdeveloped countries (that is, ' direct ' as distinct from ' portfolio ' investment) has shown a preference for activities connected with exports of primary products to advanced countries and an aversion from activities catering to the domestic markets of the debtor countries. But this, after all, is merely a statement of fact. What is the explanation of it ?

The general reluctance of private business capital to go to work for the domestic markets in the less developed countries, in contrast with its eagerness in the past to work there for export to the industrial creditor states, does not reflect any sinister conspiracy or deliberate policy, still less any concerted attempt of the rich countries to exploit the poor. Exploitation there may have been, but this pattern of foreign investment by itself does not constitute any proof of it. This pattern can be readily accounted for on obvious economic grounds. There is nothing sinister about it. The explanation lies, on the one hand, in the poverty of the local consumers in the underdeveloped countries, and on the other, in the large and, in the nineteenth century, vigorously expanding markets for primary products in the world's industrial centres.

In these circumstances it was natural for foreign business investment to serve merely as projections of the industrial creditor countries for the purpose of meeting the needs of these countries through cheap foodstuffs and raw materials. The incentive to invest was created by the investing countries' own demand for the primary commodities which they required. As a result a somewhat lop-sided pattern of development in the peripheral areas was inevitable. To the extent that the industrial countries' demand for primary products has in recent decades become less buoyant than it was in the nineteenth century, even this traditional type of foreign entrepreneurial investment may have lost some of its economic basis.[1]

There never was much inducement for foreign business capital to go to economically backward areas to work for the local markets there; these markets were too small to provide an incentive. Private investment generally is governed by the pull of market demand, and international investment on private business account is no exception to this.

The weakness of the market incentive for private investment in the domestic economy of low-income countries can affect domestic as well as foreign capital. It may help in some measure to account for a common observation about the use of domestic savings in such countries. The first difficulty is, of course, that the volume of domestic saving is small, because of the low level of income. But then there is the further trouble that such saving as does take place tends to be used unproductively : it tends to be put into real estate, gold, jewellery, commodity hoards and hoards of foreign or domestic currency.[2] This unfortunate tendency is usually explained by reference to inadequate financial organization or lack of education. While such institutional explanations undoubtedly have some validity, I suspect that this tendency may also reflect a more deep-seated economic condition : namely, the deficient inducement to invest, due to the poverty of the domestic market.

Private investment is attracted by markets. A particular instance of the relation between investment incentives and market demand appears in our old friend, the Acceleration Principle. The relation holds in space as well as in the time dimension. The conventional theory of factor proportions and capital movements is that in countries where there is little capital in relation to land

[1] Cf., Royal Institute of International Affairs, *The Problem of International Investment* (London, 1937), p. 14.

[2] Obviously it makes a great difference whether it is domestic or foreign currency that is hoarded. Hoarding of domestic currency represents saving that can be made available for domestic investment through a corresponding dose of credit expansion. Hoarding of foreign currency, by contrast, is saving exported, and represents a real drain on the country's economy.

and labour, the marginal productivity and hence the yield of capital will be high, and that, if it were not for risk and other extraneous impediments, capital would move to these countries from the areas where it is relatively abundant. This view is clearly subject to a qualification. It may be that the high potential yield of capital in capital-poor areas can be realized only through investment undertaken simultaneously in a number of complementary industries (or, what may be most important, in public overhead facilities that serve to raise productivity over a wide field). A balanced increase in production creates external economies in the form of enlarging the size of the market. As we have seen, there is on this account as well as for other reasons a possible discrepancy between the private and the social marginal productivity of capital. The marginal productivity of capital in the poor countries, as compared with the rich, may be high indeed, but not necessarily in private business terms.

Even if we abstract from political and other risk factors, there is no guarantee, therefore, that the motives that animate the individual businessman will automatically set in motion a flow of funds from the rich to the poor countries. They may, on occasion, induce 'perverse' flows from capital-poor to capital-rich countries, if private investment incentives are depressed in the former by the lack of consumer buying power and spurred in the latter by the existence of a prosperous mass market. Thus the high level of business profits in the United States in recent years is said to have been an important obstacle to the outflow of American business capital.[1]

---

[1] See Sir Arthur Salter, *Foreign Investment* (Essays in International Finance. Princeton, 1951), p. 36. All this fits in with the conclusion reached by John H. Williams : 'As regards American investment, it is quite unlikely that the main reliance can be on private foreign investment. A part of our puzzle has been that while the role we should play in the world is that of creditor country, the conditions are often more favourable for investment here, not only for Americans but for others. The history of the inter-war period is full of perverse capital movements of this kind, which disturbed rather than restored international equilibrium.' (' International Trade Theory and Policy : Some Current Issues,' *American Economic Review*, Papers and Proceedings, May 1951, p. 425). While I still feel that the disequilibrating capital movements of the inter-war period were due largely to political fears, speculation regarding exchange rates and other 'abnormal' factors described in *International Currency Experience* (League of Nations, (1944, it seems likely that they were based in part also on the perfectly ' normal ' play of private profit incentives.

On the other side, it is true that business profits sometimes appear to be high in underdeveloped countries, even in industries working for the home market. But this does not necessarily upset the hypothesis I have put forward. High business profits in these countries may reflect the high marginal productivity of capital that can be realized through an over-all expansion of the market, and some countries, though still backward, are in process of expanding their domestic economy. Even in the absence of development, however, profits may be high, partly because they may represent rewards of entrepreneurial and management services, which are very scarce factors in these countries and command a high price; and partly because they may include illusory inventory profits and profits due to failure to provide for fixed capital replacement, which are so common under inflationary conditions.

The doctrine of balanced growth leaves plenty of room for international investment, but it does reveal limits to the role of direct business investment. A private investor may not have the power, even if he had the will, to break the deadlock caused by low productivity, lack of real buying power and deficient investment incentives in the domestic economy of a backward area. It is the size of the local market that explains why American direct investments in manufacturing industries abroad have gone mostly to Western Europe and Canada, where industry has already been quite highly developed, and why they have tended to keep away from the industrially backward countries (see table, p. 84 below). It looks as if foreign business capital followed the rule that 'to those who have shall be given.' But this is not at all surprising. It is just another reflection of the general circular constellation of the forces affecting the accumulation of capital for economic development.

All this applies to direct entrepreneurial investment. Even in the heyday of private capital movements, however, this type of investment was only a part of the total international flow of funds. Private foreign loans for financing expenditures by public authorities were an important form of international investment. The greater part of British capital exports in the period 1870–1913 was in the form of fixed interest-bearing securities.[1] Overseas

[1] J. S. Pesmazoglu, 'Some International Aspects of British Cyclical Fluctuations, 1870–1913,' *Review of Economic Studies*, 1949–50, p. 120.

government bonds and railway securities together represented about two-thirds of total international investment in this period, and in addition there were other assets of a public-utility character (port facilities, gas and water works, electric power plants, etc.). This does not leave any major proportion for ventures of the ' colonial ' type—that is, foreign-owned mines and plantations producing for the creditor countries—which can therefore scarcely be regarded as typical of nineteenth-century foreign investment as a whole.

Capital outlay by public authorities financed from private, or for that matter public, foreign funds can be called ' autonomous ' investment, since it does not depend closely, if at all, on the state of market demand. By contrast, direct business investment must be classed predominantly as a form of ' induced ' investment, since it generally has to be induced by tangible market demand already existing or visibly coming into existence. Thus the general distinction between autonomous and induced investment, which has become familiar in business-cycle literature, seems to me to be applicable in a certain sense to the case of international investment as well, though here as in business-cycle theory the distinction is not absolute, but is essentially a matter of degree.

International investment on private business account is attracted by markets. In the poorer countries, which had no internal markets to speak of, only the markets for export to the great industrial centres could provide any strong investment incentives. Foreign business enterprise tended accordingly to concentrate on extractive industries working for export. In my opinion the trouble about foreign investment of this ' traditional ' sort is not that it is bad, or that it does not tend to promote development generally; it does, although unevenly and indirectly. The trouble is rather that it simply does not happen on any substantial scale, unless world demand for primary products is greatly and steadily expanding, as it was in the nineteenth century. We shall return to this problem once more.

The difficulty we have examined relates mainly to direct entrepreneurial investment, or ' induced ' investment, for which market demand is a prior causal condition. Clearly the market difficulty does not, or need not, affect the autonomous type of international investment. I must hasten to add that ' autonomous ' international investment, though it may be free from the handicap that cramps private business capital in poverty-stricken areas, is subject to certain difficulties and limitations of its own. But these have nothing to do with the topic we have been considering. They will come up for discussion in Chapter IV.

Let me sum up our present theme. In his criticism of the ' traditional ' type of foreign investment, H. W. Singer points out that, as a result of the past pattern of investment, ' the export industries in underdeveloped countries, whether they be metal mines or plantations, are often highly capital-intensive,' whereas ' by contrast, production for domestic use, especially of food and clothing, is often of a very primitive subsistence nature.'[1] In so far as this generalization is valid—and I do believe that it has some descriptive validity—there could be no better confirmation of the importance of the size of the market in relation to the induce-ment to invest. It strongly supports the thesis with which I started, namely, that there is a possible deficiency on the demand side of the problem of capital formation in under-developed areas.

It is clear, however, that this deficiency arises only on the private business level of individual investment incentives in low-income areas. For the economy as a whole there is of course no deficiency in the demand for capital in an underdeveloped country. In this respect the trouble on the demand side is different from that on the supply side of the problem of capital formation. Any failure of the demand for capital can be cured or offset by deliberate measures of organization, including measures designed to close the gap that may exist between the private and the social marginal yield of capital. Surely it must be possible either to make the social demand for capital effective in private business terms or else to exercise it directly through public investment. Once there is awareness of the problem, it should not be too difficult, in my opinion, to devise remedies suited to local conditions.

There is no suggestion here that, by taking care of the demand side alone, any country could, as it were, lift itself up by its boot-straps. We have been considering one particular facet of our

[1] Op. cit., pp. 473–44.

subject. The more fundamental difficulties that lie on the supply side have so far been kept off-stage merely for the sake of orderly discussion.

Capital formation requires an act of investment as well as a capacity to save. The two things can and should be distinguished, at least for purposes of analysis. Having examined the problem of investment incentives—which though troublesome is obviously not insuperable—I shall devote the following chapters to the more serious problem of the supply of capital required for economic development.

CHAPTER II

POPULATION AND CAPITAL SUPPLY

OUR discussion has been, and will continue to be, general in character, not related to any particular country or countries. However, as we turn to consider the potential domestic sources of capital formation in underdeveloped areas we find that it is impossible to go on without making at least a broad distinction between two types of countries, roughly described as ' overpopulated ' and ' underpopulated.' The problem of capital supply as it presents itself to the overpopulated countries, which will be taken up first, is in some respects significantly different from that in sparsely settled regions.

EXCESS POPULATION IN DENSELY SETTLED COUNTRIES

The problem of rural overpopulation is a characteristic feature of the densely populated peasant economies that stretch all the way from south-eastern Europe to south-eastern Asia. Chronic and large-scale underemployment in agriculture is what countries of this type have in common. There is a tremendous waste of labour—and labour, we are told, is the source of all wealth. What this implies in regard to capital formation is the question now to be discussed, and I should like to make use, in this connection, of the concept of ' disguised unemployment.'

These countries suffer from large-scale disguised unemployment in the sense that, even with unchanged techniques of agriculture, a large part of the population engaged in agriculture could be removed without reducing agricultural output. That is the definition of the concept of disguised unemployment as applied to the situation with which we are concerned. The same farm output could be got with a smaller labour force. The proviso that this is possible without any improvement in technical methods is important. With better techniques, one could always take some people off the land without reducing output. But here apparently we have a state of affairs where this can be done without any change in methods.

What do we mean by a change in methods ? The departure of the excess population would be a big change in itself and would inevitably involve some other changes. What are the changes that we exclude ? We exclude technological advance, more equipment, mechanization, better seeds, improvements in drainage, irrigation, and other such conditions. We exclude these things here only in order to isolate the possibilities that stem from the presence of large-scale disguised unemployment. There is, of course, no question of excluding them from any development programme in practice.

One thing, however, we need not and probably cannot exclude and that is better organization. If the surplus labour is withdrawn from the land the remaining people will not go on working in quite the same way. We may have to allow for changes in the manner and organization of work, including possibly a consolidation of scattered strips and plots of land.

The term disguised unemployment is not applied to wage labour. It denotes a condition of family employment in peasant communities. A number of people are working on farms or small peasant plots, contributing virtually nothing to output, but subsisting on a share of their family's real income. There is no possibility of personal identification here, as there is in open industrial unemployment. In industrial countries unemployment is a glaring waste of resources, visible to all, and has perhaps for this reason attracted more attention. In an overpopulated peasant economy, we cannot point to any person and say he is unemployed in disguise. The people may all be occupied, and no one may consider himself idle. Yet the fact remains that a certain number of the labour force on the land could be dispensed with, without making any difference to the volume of output.

In technical terms, the marginal productivity of labour, over a wide range, is zero. Some observers suggest that it may even be negative, which would imply that, by removing some people, farm output could actually be increased. The reason for this might be that under existing conditions people actually get into each other's way, so that if some go away those who remain are able to work more effectively. But this seems to me a doubtful and, in any case, unnecessary assumption, and I am not going to use it.

Changes in technical methods are excluded from the definition of disguised unemployment. Improvements in methods are extremely important. Experts seem to be agreed, however, that it is rather hopeless to try to introduce better farming methods unless the excess population is drained off first. There is little chance of any substantial advance in agricultural technique until some of the factors of production now engaged in that activity have been removed. This may sound paradoxical, but there is some basis for this view. And in this broad dynamic sense the marginal productivity of labour can perhaps be said to be negative.

The concept of disguised unemployment in the strict sense abstracts from technical changes. It denotes a state of affairs that exists, no doubt, even in the United States. But it is not characteristic of the United States; its extent in the United States is relatively limited. Nor is it, I believe, characteristic of Latin America, except for certain Caribbean regions such as Puerto Rico, and even in the Caribbean area it is by no means general.[1] It is typical of many countries in the area ranging from south-eastern Europe to south-eastern Asia. In these over-crowded peasant economies it is truly a mass phenomenon, due to social, economic and demographic causes. There are no alternative employment opportunities; two-thirds to four-fifths of the total labour force work on the land, and of this agricultural population, according to various estimates in the different coun-

---

[1] In an interesting book on *War Economics in Primary Producing Countries* (London, 1948), A. R. Prest cites the case of Trinidad where during World War II the armed forces of the United States employed much local labour for the construction of bases. As a result, the sugar plantations of Trinidad lost a part of their labour force. But their output of sugar could not be maintained; on the contrary, it was substantially reduced. In Trinidad apparently there was no disguised unemployment, though it is possible that the explanation can also be found in the high wages paid by the Americans, to which the native workers reacted—in a way that is not unusual—by working less than before. Besides, Trinidad is a plantation economy. In densely populated peasant economies such as Egypt and India, war-time experience tended to confirm the existence of a great deal of slack in the rural labour force. This experience was not anything like a scientifically controlled experiment. The war produced quite abnormal conditions and a great deal of disruption in trade, especially a drastic cut in imports. Egypt suffered acutely, for instance, from a lack of imported fertilizers, and India from a shortage of rice, which used to come from Burma and other areas then under Japanese occupation. Without these abnormal conditions the war-time experiment would probably have demonstrated more clearly the possibilities of making use of some of the disguised unemployment.

tries, 15 per cent, 20 per cent or as much as 30 per cent constitutes disguised unemployment in the sense in which we have defined the term.

In certain south-eastern European countries in the 1930's, estimates of the extent of concealed unemployment were made in some cases on the basis of detailed surveys and experiments in the field. They tended to show that disguised unemployment represented about 25 to 30 per cent of the agricultural labour force, and these estimates have been widely used in recent literature.[1] The highest estimates of the degree of disguised unemployment that I have seen—namely, 40 to 50 per cent—are for Egypt.[2] Naturally estimates of this sort are highly uncertain. We should not overrate the importance of this phenomenon, but it does appear to be quantitatively quite significant.

Some economists maintain that disguised unemployment on the land is only a seasonal phenomenon, and that at the peak of the harvest season all the available labour is needed and is actively at work. This is undoubtedly true in some countries, though in others even the peak harvest load might be managed by a smaller labour force if organizational changes, such as consolidation of plots, could be carried out. Seasonal underemployment is likely to be significant where an annual crop cycle, e.g. of cereal food crops, dominates farm activity and where this activity has not developed more advanced forms such as dairy farming. Even where disguised unemployment is mainly a seasonal matter, the question of making productive use of it still arises and still has

[1] See, e.g., Paul N. Rosenstein-Rodan, 'Problems of Industrialization of Eastern and South-Eastern Europe,' op. cit., and K. Mandelbaum, *The Industrialization of Backward Areas* (Oxford, 1945). According to Doreen Warriner's study, *The Economics of Peasant Farming* (London, 1939), it would seem ' reasonable to assume that over Eastern Europe as a whole one-quarter to one-third of the farm population is surplus, and that the proportion is higher in certain districts of which Galicia is the most important' (p. 68). All this relates, of course, to conditions before the Second World War.

[2] The data presented by W. W. Cleland in *The Population Problem in Egypt* (1936) make 40 per cent seem a reasonable estimate. In a later study by the same author, quoted in Doreen Warriner's *Land and Poverty in the Middle East* (London, 1948), p. 33, half the Egyptian farm population appears to be regarded as surplus. A similar estimate is given by Charles Issawi in his work, *Egypt : An Economic and Social Analysis* (London, 1947), p. 195 : 'An experiment carried out near Cairo by the American College seems to suggest that the present output, or something closely approaching it could be produced by abour half the present rural population of Egypt.'

important implications in regard to capital formation. I understand, however, that there are countries where it is more than seasonal and where a great deal of hidden unemployment exists throughout the year. In Egypt, for example, the various crops, some of which are harvested more than once a year, tend to overlap so that there is hardly any time of year when some crop is not being harvested. In such circumstances any underemployment that may exist must be more or less continuous.

Disguised rural unemployment differs in several ways from open industrial unemployment. It differs notably in that it cannot be absorbed by means of an expansion of monetary demand. The inelasticity of agricultural production makes this remedy quite ineffective. The supply of ' wage goods '—that is, mostly food—is rigid in the short run so that, when monetary expansion occurs, the result is merely an inflation of prices. There is the possibility, however, of taking the surplus people away from the land; anything they could produce elsewhere would be a clear addition to the real national income. But what can they produce without capital ? Very little. Then why not set them to work on producing real capital ? Here we get a first glimpse of what disguised unemployment can mean for capital formation. Even if the direct marginal yield of labour is zero, the indirect yield of labour when applied to roundabout methods of production—that is, to the accumulation of capital—is likely to be very high in countries where capital is scarce.

We should notice, incidentally, that this is a static view of the population resources in a country. We look at the population at a point of time and find, or think we find, that a certain proportion of it could be dispensed with in agriculture and shifted to other activities without reducing food output. I call this a static view in contrast to the dynamic view that concerns itself with population growth. I shall have something to say on the problem of population growth later on.

THE SAVING POTENTIAL CONCEALED IN RURAL UNDEREMPLOYMENT

Let us consider more closely the possibility of taking the surplus people off the land and setting them to work on capital projects—irrigation, drainage, roads, railways, houses, factories, training schemes and so on. The question arises at once : how are these various forms of capital formation to be financed ? In real terms, how are people to be fed when they are set to work on projects of this sort ?

First, it should be possible to feed them through the normal voluntary saving that may take place to some extent even in a poor, overpopulated peasant economy. The savers (mostly among the urban commercial classes, presumably) abstain from consuming the whole of their income and make some of it available for feeding the people now working on the new capital projects. This saving, however, is likely to be quite insufficient in relation to the labour resources to be mobilized and is likely, moreover, to be used for other purposes. It might be supplemented through compulsory saving by means of taxation aiming specially, perhaps, at the traditional as well as modern forms of ' conspicuous consumption ', but even this may turn out to be a mere drop in the bucket. The second possibility one can think of is an inflow of capital from abroad. But this again, besides being uncertain, is likely to be inadequate. There is a third possibility of feeding the people transferred from the land to the new investment projects, and this requires to be discussed at greater length.

On close examination we find that the state of disguised unemployment implies at least to some extent a disguised saving potential as well. This possible source of capital formation in underdeveloped areas has hitherto been neglected in economic literature. It can easily be illustrated in physical terms. As things are, the ' unproductive ' surplus labourers on the land are sustained by the 'productive' labourers. (It is convenient to use these terms even though, as I said before, personal identification and hence separation of the two groups is in the nature of the case impossible.) The productive labourers are performing ' virtual ' saving; they produce more than they consume. But the saving runs to waste, the saving is abortive; it is offset by the unproductive consumption of the people who could be dispensed with, who contribute nothing to output. If the productive peasants were to send their useless dependants—their cousins, brothers and nephews who now live with them—to work on capital projects and if they continued to feed them there, then their virtual saving would become effective saving. The unproductive consumption of the surplus farm population would become productive consumption.

Thus the use of disguised unemployment for the accumulation of capital could be financed from within the system itself. There is no question of asking the peasants who remain on the land to eat less than before, only of preventing them from eating more. What is wanted is that they go on feeding their dependants who leave the farms to go to work on capital projects and who, in effect, continue to be dependent for their subsistence on the ' productive ' peasants remaining on the farms. All that happens is a re-allocation of labour in favour of capital construction. There is in principle no necessity for either group of people to tighten their belts—always provided that the initial assumption is valid : that surplus labour does exist which can be withdrawn without a fall in total farm output.

Here we have a relationship between consumption and investment which stands midway between the classical and the Keynesian approach. In the usual classical model, an increase in the rate of capital formation requires a reduction in consumption. In the Keynesian world of industrial unemployment, consumption as well as investment can be expanded at the same time. In the case now before us, the situation differs from the Keynesian model in that it is impossible to expand both consumption and investment. On the other hand, it is possible to increase capital formation without having to cut down the level of consumption.

What has been said is probably enough to make clear the sense in which disguised unemployment in overpopulated peasant economies may be said to contain a hidden source of saving available for economic development. The point is really self-evident and needs, I think, no further demonstration. But even if we accept it as a general proposition, we are going to encounter all sorts of difficulties as soon as we begin to consider its practical application. I cannot enter into these complications in any detail; but I cannot entirely ignore them either.

Everything depends on the mobilization of the concealed saving potential in the shape of the food surplus that becomes available to the productive peasants when their unproductive dependants go away. This mobilization will be incomplete if the remaining peasants cannot be stopped from eating more than before. Even drastic measures may not succeed in preventing them from consuming a little more of their own produce which they gather from the land. A food deficit may also arise if the investment workers, our previous unemployed in disguise, have to eat a little more than before because they are now more actively at work or because they need to be given an inducement to leave the farms in the first place. How much inducement will be necessary is likely to depend on circumstances. One reason why the surplus people have not moved in the past is that there has been no place for them to move to, and so the mere provision of employment opportunities on construction projects may tend to make them move. Yet some increase in their means of livelihood is probably unavoidable.

In this way, through increased consumption by the remaining peasants or by the new investment workers, or both, leakages may develop in the subsistence fund available for capital formation. In itself it is no doubt a good thing for these people to eat more than before; still the increased consumption constitutes a leakage from the saving potential contained in the state of disguised unemployment. Moreover, a leakage arises through the cost of transporting the food from the farms to the places where the capital projects are established. This particular leakage can be reduced by scattering the projects in rural areas, but in practice it can probably never be entirely suppressed.

In these circumstances the formation of capital through the use of surplus labour is self-financing only if the mobilization of the concealed saving potential is 100 per cent successful. If it is less than completely successful, the scheme seems to break down; the amount of saving, or in real terms the subsistence fund available to support the workers engaged on real capital accumulation, proves insufficient. Let us suppose the leakage arises from the peasants who remain on the land consuming more of their own food crops. If their dependants, the investment workers, do not get enough to eat on their new jobs, they will run back to the farms to resume their previous existence and to absorb on the spot the food produced there. It seems to be a question of all or nothing. Either the whole of the food surplus that becomes available on the land through the withdrawal of the surplus labourers is mopped up to feed them in their new occupations, or nothing can be done at all.

On reflection, however, it will be seen that the surplus labour can still be employed for capital formation if some complementary saving can be secured from outside the system, to close the deficiency of saving that may arise within it. Some complementary saving might become available from domestic sources, and there is the possibility of capital imports. So it may not have to be all or nothing. Even if there is a leakage in the subsistence fund, provided only that it can be covered by means of resources obtained from outside the system, it will be possible to mobilize the whole or a part of the diguised unemployment for the purpose of capital formation. The degree of mobilization possible will depend on the amount of complementary saving available and on the relative size of the leakage.

Suppose, for example, that 20 million dollars is the annual value of the subsistence fund that should theoretically become available when the surplus workers leave the farms. Suppose further that the unavoidable leakages, due to somewhat higher consumption and also to the cost of transporting food from the farms to the capital projects, add up to 10 million dollars. In this case, if 10 million dollars of investible funds could be obtained from outside, the whole food surplus of 20 million dollars could be freed and used for investment. In other words, every dollar of outside resources would make it possible to realize two dollars' worth of the saving potential associated with disguised unemployment. In this way the funds from the outside can exercise a magnifying effect on the total rate of capital formation. Evidently a multiplier concept of a certain kind becomes applicable here, though we should hesitate to multiply the multipliers that have appeared in economic literature. We should only remember that the outside funds just mentioned can be, but do not have to be, of foreign origin; they can come, as already explained, from domestic saving, voluntary or involuntary. They are resources that originate outside the subsistence fund concealed in the state of disguised unemployment.

To illustrate this in a little more detail, let us imagine a country to which the following figures apply :

	Population	Annual Income : (in millions of dollars)
Total	1,000,000	120
Urban	200,000	40
Rural	800,000	80

Let the proportion of active to total population be the same throughout the country. The average income per head, 120 dollars a year, is not far out of line with actual estimates for countries of the type under consideration. The urban population has twice as high an income per head as the rural and saves, let us say, 5 million dollars a year. The rural population consumes all the income it produces, though it may send some of its food output to the towns in exchange for non-food consumables.

Suppose there is a farm labour surplus of 200,000 people, that is, 25 per cent of the farm population. The annual consumption of these people, at the average rural rate, amounts to a total of 20 million dollars. We will assume that they can be transferred to investment projects only if their consumption is increased to 22 million. If this were the only leakage, the provision of 2 million dollars from outside would make possible this transfer along with the release of the 20 million food surplus now available on the farms. (The multiplier is 10.)

But another leakage arises because the consumption of the remaining peasants increases from 60 to, say, 63 million. Now it takes 5 million dollars of outside resources to provide for the extra consumption and to release the 20 million food surplus for the investment workers. (The multiplier is reduced to 4.) If these are domestic resources coming from the urban sector, notice that they can only come from additional saving there, releasing food for the extra consumption of the peasants and investment workers.

The deficit due to the food transport cost—say, 5 million dollars (reducing the multiplier to 2)—is different in that it can be met by resources hitherto engaged on other types of investment and sustained by the pre-existing rate of urban saving without causing an increase in food requirements. In the present example, the previous urban saving of 5 million dollars would just suffice for this purpose.

All in all, an increase in urban saving from 5 to 10 million annually makes possible a total national rate of saving of 20 million dollars. The over-all saving ratio is increased from 4 per cent to 17 per cent of national income, despite the leakages.

In practice, however, it may be extremely difficult if not impossible to get the necessary complementary saving from domestic sources.[1] Although it appears that countries of the type we are considering do save at present about 3—5 per cent of their national income, much of this saving is directly invested in forms that make it useless for the present purpose. The leakage due to the cost of transporting the food might be financed partly or wholly out of the present flow of saving—if only the forms of this saving were sufficiently flexible. But any deficiency arising from higher consumption by the peasants and investment workers can be filled only by additional saving on the part of the urban population (that is, in the main, the commercial and the feudal upper classes). If the higher consumption is largely of food, while the additional saving, if forthcoming at all, releases mainly non-food items such as luxury manufactures or domestic services, then the food deficit may have to be met directly or indirectly by way of foreign trade. This shifts the problem abroad, but does not necessarily solve it, and can affect the terms of trade adversely.

Foreign grants or loans are a desirable means of meeting the deficiency in the subsistence fund. Even though used for imports of consumer goods, they can produce, as indicated, a multiple effect on the total flow of resources available for investment. But there is always the temptation—which, for reasons to be discussed, is nowadays stronger than ever—to use such external funds entirely for increased consumption without any increase resulting in the rate of accumulation. It is in order to forestall this possibility that external resources are now frequently tied to specific imports of equipment, a practice that tends to make them unserviceable for complementary uses in the mobilization of the disguised saving potential.

[1] I am indebted to Mr. Peter M. Gutmann for impressing this point upon me.

All this points to the need for preventing the leakages or holding them down to an absolute minimum.[1] A word must therefore be said at once on the all-important question concerning the methods by which the ' virtual ' saving inherent in disguised unemployment is to be realized for capital formation. There is no automatic release of the food supplies previously consumed by the unemployed in disguise. The main problem is to stop the peasant from consuming more of his produce when family members living off his output go away to work on capital construction projects. The peasants are not likely to save the surplus voluntarily since they live so close to subsistence level. And peasants are notoriously hard to tax. Something may be done through indirect taxation of the things they buy but they may not buy much, if anything. It may be possible to tax them through increasing their rents and taxing the landowners. Japan kept up a stiff land tax, which was highly effective and apparently very important in Japan's economic development in the late nineteenth century. Taxation in kind may be attempted, or some form of requisitioning and controlled deliveries.[2] This crucial problem of collecting the food seems to be solved in Soviet Russia by the system of collective farms. The word ' collective ' has here a double meaning. The collective farm is not only a form of collective organization; it is above all an instrument of collection.

Whatever the machinery employed may be, some form of collective saving enforced by the state may prove to be indispensable for the mobilization of the saving potential implicit in disguised unemployment. But even if the problem of saving is tackled in some such way, it is still quite possible to leave the investment function in private hands. The problem is that of getting hold of the food surplus with which to feed the workers in the various investment projects; these projects could very well be

[1] Another way out would be a widespread and radical improvement in farming techniques, accompanying the removal of the surplus farm labour, so that total farm output might be substantially increased and not merely held constant. This line of attack lies outside our present model, but is of course exceedingly important and will shortly be taken up for discussion.

[2] See A. R. Prest's account of what an efficient civil service achieved in the Sudan during the war of 1939–45 (op. cit., p. 172).

private undertakings. It is only the saving function that may need to be performed in part through the state.[1]

In the analytical scheme we have used so far in this chapter, there is theoretically no need for anyone to cut down his consumption below the original level. Yet it is a harsh and austere programme. It would be much nicer if the food required for the subsistence of the new investment workers could be got entirely from outside, through some form of foreign aid. Nevertheless, the theory discloses a subsistence fund within the condition of disguised unemployment, available for the accumulation of capital. It points to an important potential source of domestic financing.

The next point to notice is that the problem of financing this capital formation resolves itself into two distinct parts. First and foremost is the necessity of feeding the new investment workers, keeping them supplied with the consumption goods they need in order to work on the capital projects. This is the object of financing reduced to its elementary terms, financing in the sense of providing a fund of subsistence for workers who are not themselves producing anything consumable at present.[2] Here we have the fundamental classical rationale of saving.

Secondly, there is the financing which consists in giving the new investment workers tools to work with. It is helpful to have some capital goods co-operating with the current labour employed to produce more capital goods. This is a quite distinct problem of financing in real terms; and one that in my opinion is essentially secondary, although it usually receives the lion's share of attention in popular and sometimes even in economic discussion. The investment workers, before they start building a piece of fixed capital such as a road, could, after all, sit down and make the most necessary primitive tools with their own hands, starting if need be from scratch. They could make their own shovels, wheelbarrows, carts, hoists and other things to help them build the road. That is what they might have to do if the country were a closed economy, if no trade existed with any more advanced

---

[1] The possible role of public finance as an instrument of compulsory saving is discussed a little more fully in Chapter VII.

[2] Here, as in the classical wages-fund doctrine, the term 'fund' is to be interpreted as a flow rather than a stock.

region where capital goods were being produced more efficiently by means of capital goods, not with bare hands. In the real world, the underdeveloped countries of to-day have the advantage of being able to get capital goods through trade. Even without any foreign aid or foreign lending, capital goods can be acquired from abroad in exchange for current exports, but it is clear that an act of domestic saving is required in this case.

The densely populated countries in process of development do not need tools and machines of the same degree of capital intensity as those used in the advanced economies where labour is relatively scarce. Some of the equipment and hence also the techniques of production imported from more developed countries are likely to be highly capital-intensive and therefore not well adapted to countries where capital is scarce and labour abundant. American machinery in particular, being naturally designed with American labour costs in mind, is often much too elaborate, automatic and labour-saving to be economically suitable for operation in areas where labour is plentiful and cheap. Ideally, capital equipment imported into underdeveloped countries should be specially designed for the factor proportions prevailing in these countries, but in practice this consideration is frequently counterbalanced by the cheapness of equipment made by mass-production methods predominantly for the enormous domestic market in the United States.

In overpopulated agricultural countries, in building a road, for instance, it would be fantastically uneconomic to equip each worker with a bulldozer (besides having to invest in training him to operate a bulldozer). Much simpler tools and equipment may be appropriate to the relative factor endowment of countries of this type, in the early stages of industrial development. In such countries one can see river dams being built by men and women carrying earth in head-baskets. The same capital intensity as in economically advanced countries should be neither desired nor permitted. We should not expect the new investment workers at once to work on capital formation at a much higher level of efficiency. But at least they would be working, producing, contributing to the expansion of their country's productive capacity. They would no longer be unemployed in disguise.

It is well to bear in mind in this connection that by far the greater part of a country's real capital structure consists of objects that require local labour and local materials for their production or construction.[1] Things like buildings, roads, dams, water works and land improvements are in the aggregate far more important than the imported machinery and equipment which usually bulks so large in the imagination of the public. The question whether the physical capital is of domestic origin or imported bears no relation, in principle, to the question whether its construction or acquisition is financed from domestic or foreign savings. The purchase of an imported machine can be financed from domestic saving, just as road building by local labour can be financed by a foreign loan, though for purposes of over-all analysis there is little point in speaking of specific funds as being earmarked for specific pieces of investment. Our present discussion is concentrated on the potential sources of domestic saving, but in later chapters the external means of financing will also receive a certain amount of attention.

Under existing conditions, in some of the densely settled peasant economies, there is said to exist underemployment not only of labour but also of capital. The plots are small and widely scattered, and so there are more shovels, wheelbarrows, carts and draught animals than would be required if farms could be consolidated. This is a matter of organization rather than productive technique. A tremendous need for capital investment in agriculture, for drainage, flood control, irrigation and other improvements, exists and must sooner or later be met ; but this does not exclude the possibility of there being some immediate scope for organizational reforms that would release a certain quantity of simple tools which the investment workers could take with them and use on the capital projects.

What these projects are to be, I do not think we need discuss. They may be in agriculture as well as in manufacturing industry. They may well be ' community development projects ' specially designed to make use of local labour surpluses or of seasonal slack periods in the countryside. They are initially most likely

[1] This point was well stressed in Norman S. Buchanan's *International Investment and Domestic Welfare* (New York, 1945).

to be of the type now often called 'social overhead capital,' including public utilities, transport facilities, training schemes and various basic services. The importance of such over-all facilities can scarcely be exaggerated. They form an essential basis for small-scale private investments in miscellaneous industries. In an economically advanced country any individual businessman can take their existence for granted. In economically backward areas the individual entrepreneur might have to construct them himself if he wanted to establish any industrial plant; and he might be unable to earn a commercial yield on investments in such over-all public facilities unless he had some sort of monopoly position, which, however, would be undesirable on general grounds. These considerations apply also to the basic forms of capital investment in human skill, education and health.

Population Growth and Capital Requirements

The theory of capital formation under conditions of disguised unemployment rests, as already observed, on a static view of population resources. What about the dynamic problem of population growth? What about the danger of population explosion which might result from any increase in real income and which might soon nullify any improvement in the level of material welfare?

This is too vast a problem to tackle here, but there is one point I should like to insist upon. In the theoretical model which we have considered, the increase in real income, if the scheme is completely successful, is directed into capital formation. There is no increase in consumption. In so far as population growth depends on the consumption level, there is no reason to expect any growth in population since no increase in consumption takes place. The increase in real income is directed, or at least should be directed, exclusively into capital formation. That is the main point to remember, and it serves to emphasize once more the need for determined action to keep down the consumption leakages discussed.

It is widely recognized that emigration is not only an academic but actually an unreal solution to the population problem, because it does nothing to stop the population explosion at the source.

Exclusive reliance on foreign grants, loans or investments is like emigration in that it does not provide a check to the population growth which may occur in response to increased real income and consumption. The effective mobilization of domestic saving potentials is for this reason a basic initial prerequisite to increasing real income per head.

In the long run, we may perhaps hope that the dynamic population problem will solve itself through the widespread change in the scale of values which education and urbanization tend to bring about. In the short run, it may be possible to take active measures such as raising the legal minimum marriage age, or spreading the use of contraceptive methods, as is now being done apparently even in India, under a national ' fertility-control policy.'

Some increase in population may occur independently of consumption levels, through the spread of medical knowledge and facilities, and through the consequent reduction in disease and death rates. But this implies an increase in quality as well as size of the population. With greater physical health and vigour, there is likely to be an increase also in productive capacity. Surely this cannot be an entirely unfavourable factor economically, so long as the increased production potential of the population is fully utilized.

But the population increment has to be provided with capital. Population increase means, socially speaking, an increase in the demand for capital for extensive investment, as distinguished from intensive investment, in the familiar terminology used sometimes by demographers as well as by economists like Alvin Hansen. While intensive investment means an increase in capital per head and hence in productivity, extensive investment in the course of population growth serves merely to maintain the supply of capital per head of the labour force. The investments contemplated under the Colombo Plan may prove to be of the extensive kind, since it seems that they can be expected to do little or nothing beyond holding the existing per capita position in the face of the continued rapid growth of population in south-eastern Asia.[1]

---

[1] Cf. ' Colombo Plan's First Year,' *The Economist*, May 10, 1952, p. 355.

The theory of disguised unemployment is a static but none-theless legitimate and significant view of the population resources available for capital formation. It is a view that stresses a factor on the *supply* side of the problem of capital formation. ' Labour is the real source of wealth,'[1] and the supply of capital, we now see, can be increased by making use of unemployed labour. It can be increased, not only for extensive, but also for intensive investment for economic development.

In past discussions of disguised unemployment in relation to economic development, it has been customary to treat excess population, like population growth, as a factor determining the *need* for capital. A fashionable type of calculation has been to estimate the amount of capital ' required ' for the productive employment both of the annual increase in the labour force and of the existing surplus labour. It is assumed, for example, that 1000 dollars' worth of capital is required per worker, and although this is only a fraction of the capital per worker in the United States, it usually leads to a staggering total of capital requirements when multiplied by the number oi people. The domestic saving capacity is regarded as small or negligible in view of the low income level. Consequently this approach tends to be characterized by almost exclusive reliance on external resources.

The saving potential that is concealed in the existence of disguised unemployment has not been adequately recognized in economic discussion, at any rate in Western countries. It has certainly played a part, however, in the actual development, as well as the development plans, of some of the less advanced countries that have suffered from large-scale rural under-employment.

THE CASE OF SPARSELY POPULATED AREAS

I have just referred to the two possible views on the relation-ship between population and capital formation. One stresses the

---

[1] The words are Bentham's (quoted in F. A. von Hayek's ' Note on the Development of the Doctrine of Forced Saving,' *Quarterly Journal of Economics*, November 1932, p. 125), but the theme is frequent in the history of economic thought.

domestic resources that can be mobilized in a country where there is much surplus labour on the farms. Population is viewed as a possible source of supply of capital. An attitude of self-reliance may tend to be the consequence of this discovery of a concealed domestic saving potential. The other view stresses population size, as well as population growth, as a factor governing the total amount of capital required; a large population needs a large amount of capital and an increase in population calls for an increase in capital. This second view is apt to emphasize the need for foreign investment, to offset the adverse effect of population growth on living standards and also to make possible an increase in income per head (i.e., both extensive and intensive investment).

These two approaches do not exclude each other. Neither of them is likely to be universally valid. If the first approach applies to the densely populated peasant economies, it may be that the second is more applicable to sparsely populated areas including, for instance, South America.

It might seem paradoxical to suggest that such regions as South America, which, on the whole, have a higher per capita income level, are more dependent on foreign assistance than the overcrowded peasant countries. It is not a conclusion worth emphasizing for practical purposes. It is based only on the rapid rate of population growth in these regions coupled with the absence of disguised unemployment on any mass scale.

The rate of population increase in South America is, it seems, even greater than in south-eastern Asia. On the other hand, there is little or no evidence to show that South America has much disguised unemployment in the sense that, without any change in methods, large masses of manpower could be drawn away from food production without affecting the volume of output there, and used for real capital formation in industry, agriculture and public services. There may be disguised unemployment in a different, and to me rather dubious, sense. There are always some occupations that are relatively unproductive, while others are relatively productive. A transfer of labour from the former to the latter would increase total output and so the people in the relatively unproductive occupations might, in this sense, be considered underemployed.

A transfer of people from the unproductive to the productive occupations seems to be the solution, but it completely begs the question of capital supply. Why, after all, is one occupation unproductive and another productive ? The main reason may be that in one occupation little capital is used in production, while in the other, production is relatively capital-intensive. In particular, this may be one, though not the only, reason for the difference stressed so much in underdeveloped countries between the level of productivity in agriculture and in industry. It is not so much that agriculture is inherently less productive than industry, as is sometimes thought, although demand conditions, and other circumstances as well, do create important differences between the two types of productive activity. There exists apparently a statistical correlation between the degree of industrialization and the level of per capita income in different countries;[1] but from this it is not legitimate to conclude that the former causes the latter. The two things may both be due to a third factor : namely, the supply of capital. Modern industry is highly productive because it uses a lot of capital. In advanced industrial countries labour has the immense advantage of being supported by a great deal of capital, in agriculture as well as in manufacturing. For an underdeveloped country a transfer of labour from agriculture to industry is, by itself, no solution because it begs the question of capital formation; it does not by itself provide the capital necessary for industry. The problem of capital formation must be solved first.

In the densely populated countries which we considered earlier, the productive use of the rural excess population seemed

[1] Countries like Australia, Denmark and New Zealand are sometimes cited as highly prosperous agricultural countries, to disprove this correlation. It is true that their exports are predominantly agricultural. But when we look at their internal economies we find that agriculture employs only a minority —about one-fifth to one-third—of their working population. Their economic activity, considered as a whole, is more largely industrial than agricultural. A country's foreign trade does not always reflect the character of its national economy. The exports of Australia, for example, consist almost entirely of farm products, although only 20 per cent of the population is engaged in agriculture (see F. Hilgerdt, op. cit., p. 26). On the other hand, in a country like Bolivia the mining industry produces over 90 per cent of total exports but employs less than 3 per cent of the people; a large majority of the population is in agriculture, and yet the country has to import foodstuffs from abroad (see M. Ezekiel, ed., *Towards World Prosperity*, New York 1947, p. 431).

to provide at least a partial solution of this problem. It seemed to be possible to get more capital from domestic sources by drawing labour away from agriculture without a cut in consumption. Can we pull another rabbit out of the hat ? Is a solution of this sort conceivable for the underpopulated countries ? Perhaps; but not without a radical improvement in the techniques and methods of agricultural production. This is now a prerequisite; in the earlier case it could initially be excluded. However, conditions for an advance in farming techniques are favourable at least inasmuch as land, by definition, is relatively plentiful in these countries.

An increase in agricultural productivity must here have priority over everything else. Why this emphasis on improvements in agriculture ? First, because the great majority of the population even in the sparsely populated areas, such as South America, is in agriculture. If manpower is wanted for capital formation, agriculture is the place to look for it. Since food absorbs the greater part of a poor people's income and since consequently agriculture absorbs the bulk of a poor country's labour force, a given percentage increase in productivity here will have a far greater effect on the absolute amount of labour released for capital formation than a similar percentage improvement in, say, manufacturing or the service industries. Secondly, in agriculture some increases in productivity are possible that do not require much, if any, capital. There is the possiblity of applying improved knowledge in seed selection, soil conservation, crop rotation, the use of fertilizers, livestock feeding, fighting insect pests, etc. In a great many ways a great deal could be done, and is now being done, that does not require heavy capital investment.

Consider what happened in the original home of industrial development, in England in the eighteenth century. Everyone knows that the spectacular industrial revolution would not have been possible without the agricultural revolution that preceded it. And what was this agricultural revolution ? It was based mainly on the introduction of the turnip. The lowly turnip made possible a change in crop rotation which did not require much capital, but which brought about a tremendous rise in agricultural productivity. As a result, more food could be grown with much less manpower. Manpower was released for capital construction. The growth of industry would not have been possible without the turnip and other improvements in agriculture.

In densely populated countries, a substantial improvement of agricultural technique can come perhaps only as a result of industrial development. In sparsely settled countries, by contrast, an improvement in agriculture is the prerequisite for capital formation and industrial development. This conclusion is well stated in the United Nations report cited earlier : ' In a country where there is no surplus labour, industrialization waits upon agricultural improvement. The way to industrialization lies through the improvement of agriculture. . . The reverse is the case in a country where population is so large in relation to cultivable land, that the land is carrying more people than can be fully employed in agriculture. Substantial technical progress in agriculture is not possible without reducing the numbers engaged in agriculture.'[1]

Through an increase in agricultural productivity, a sparsely populated country, while maintaining or increasing its food output, can get a large supply of manpower released from agriculture and made available for real capital formation. There is hardly any need to stress the obvious point that it is not enough to get labour released from agriculture, that is, ' saved '. The labour must at once be employed for productive capital formation, that is, ' invested '. Otherwise the manpower released will be wasted and the advantages derived from the increase in productivity lost. As and when labour is set free from primary production, employment opportunities must be created in investment projects. The rise in agricultural productivity, though logically of prior urgency, is not necessarily prior in time.

Let me sum up the case of the sparsely populated areas. We can see what has to be done. Through technical improvements in farming, we must release manpower from agriculture and set it to work on projects of capital formation. How are we to feed the workers now engaged on capital projects ? Evidently an increase must occur in the rate of saving, so that the people transferred from farm production to capital construction can be pro-

---

[1] *Measures for the Economic Development of Underdeveloped Countries*, op. cit. p. 59.

vided with food and other necessities. The increase in farm productivity is not sufficient. It could easily be used by the agricultural producers for increased current consumption. If it is to be used for capital formation, a greater amount of saving must be forthcoming in one way or another; and it is clear that, given the improvement in farming, the saving *can* be forthcoming without any decrease in consumption below the original level.

The Two Cases Compared

The question of the methods by which the increased saving is to be achieved in the case just discussed is not essentially different from the question of how the concealed saving potential of disguised unemployment is to be mobilized. This question of method is a difficult practical problem, which differs widely in its technical aspects in different countries, but on which, nevertheless, I shall venture some general remarks in the final chapter. The present chapter has been concerned mainly with the potential sources of capital formation, rather than with the ways and means of tapping these sources. The existence of surplus farm labour constitutes, and the improvement of farming methods creates, an opportunity for increased domestic saving. The opportunity must be seized with both hands; it is only too easy to miss it.

I have thought it useful to consider the case of underpopulated countries for the sake of comparison with that of large-scale disguised unemployment. The two have one thing in common. In both cases, on the assumptions we have used, there is an increase in total output : in the one case it occurs through het use of previously unemployed labour, in the other through technical improvements in agriculture. Common to both is an increase in farm productivity in the sense of output per worker engaged in agriculture, even though in the first it comes about through a withdrawal of excess labour rather than an advance in farming technique. Where human energy is mostly occupied in food production (as is fairly generally true of both types of backward areas), greater efficiency in that activity is the basic source of accumulation. But the fruits of advance in farm productivity cannot be retained by the farmer; and here is one cause of conflict between town and country in the course of economic development.

Conservative critics are inclined to regard industry and public construction in these circumstances as a parasitic growth that has to be supported by levies on the rural economy—and we can see that there is some ground for this complaint.

In both cases the problem of saving is the problem of channelling as much as possible of the increment in total output into capital formation. It is not a matter of cutting down consumption. Ploughing back the increment is the normal way in which capital has been accumulated in the past. To keep a firm check on the rise in living standards should be easier than actually to reduce the level of living. Yet it is hard enough, in view of the forces pressing for higher immediate consumption.

A possible difference that appeared from the consideration of the two cases is that the argument for industrialization as a means of general economic development is, initially at any rate, stronger in the densely populated countries than in the sparsely settled regions. It would seem also that, as far as the prospects and potentialities of domestic capital formation are concerned, the countries with large-scale disguised unemployment might be better off, because of the very fact that they have large masses of unused labour that could be set to work on capital construction. The thinly settled countries do not have the surplus population that could be used for capital formation; they are faced with the prior problem of having to *create* the surplus manpower through improvements in agriculture.

In overpopulated peasant countries, agricultural improvements are not, in my view, a logically primary condition of economic advance. They should not be neglected; they are extremely important in practice. They may be the only way of breaking the deadlock that may result from leakages in the disguised saving potential and inability to procure complementary resources from outside. And yet it seems plausible to maintain that drastic improvements in farming methods are not the first crucial prerequisite in the initial stages of economic progress in a society endowed with large reserves of surplus labour on the land.

In other respects, however, the sparsely settled countries are better off. Many of them have a higher per capita income level to start with. The very fact that they have much land in relation to population should tend to provide more scope for increased productivity in agriculture. And in any case, the mere possession of a surplus labour force in the overpopulated countries is no guarantee of progress. It is an advantage only if, and in so far as, the surplus labour force can be effectively used for real capital accumulation. I have confined myself to a theoretical outline of the problem; I have no illusions about its practical difficulty.

CHAPTER III

THE STANDARD OF LIVING AND THE CAPACITY TO SAVE

ON the supply side of the problem of capital formation the vicious circle of poverty runs from (a) the low income level to (b) the small capacity to save, hence to (c) a lack of capital, leading to (d) low productivity and so back to a low real income per head. The preceding chapter, while not conflicting with this notion, appeared to give some ground for optimism by exploring possible ways and means by which even a poor subsistence-farm economy might achieve an increment in the flow of real income capable of being directed into capital formation. Now we shall have to face a set of circumstances whereby the self-perpetuating tendency for capital to be in short supply in low-income areas is aggravated rather than allayed.

It is natural to seek, at least in theory, an escape from the dead-lock by maintaining that outside help in one form or another—in the form, say, of foreign investment—is necessary to bring about the initial improvement in productivity and real income that is required for any substantial domestic saving to come about. Foreign investment, according to this widely held opinion, is the redeeming force that has to be invoked to break the circle on the supply side of capital formation in low-income countries. Foreign investment is regarded as necessary to bridge the transition period; once an increase in productivity has been achieved, a flow of saving will result, or can be extracted, from the increased real income.[1]

This theory begins to look somewhat dubious as soon as we realize that it is not only the absolute but also the relative level of real income that determines the capacity to save. Although the absolute level of even the poorest countries appears to have risen, it is doubtful whether saving has become any easier; on the

---

[1] See, e.g., Raul Prebisch, *The Economic Development of Latin America and its Principal Problems* (United Nations, 1950), p. 5, and Donald B. Marsh, *World Trade and Investment* (New York, 1951), p. 75.

contrary, it may have become more difficult for them, because there has occurred at the same time a decline in their relative income levels in comparison with those of the economically advanced countries. The hypothesis seems to me plausible and, at any rate, worth considering. The great and growing gaps between the income levels and therefore living standards of different countries, combined with increasing awareness of these gaps, may tend to push up the general propensity to consume of the poorer nations, reduce their capacity to save, and incidentally strain their balance of payments.

A New Theory of Consumption and Saving

The unequal income distribution in the world, which both theory and international economic policy have too often tended to ignore in the past, is our point of departure. From this crucial fact we shall proceed to develop a hypothesis that throws some light on the problems of economic development in their international setting. I should like here to draw upon a theory put forward in a recent book by James S. Duesenberry.[1] I believe that this theory, which in its original form relates to individual consumers, has some explanatory significance on the international plane also.

This view of consumer behaviour places great emphasis on the fact that individual consumption functions are interrelated, not independent. They are interrelated, first, through the desire for social emulation by means of conspicuous consumption. Over a hundred years ago, Nassau Senior called the desire for distinction ' the most powerful of human passions.' The point, made familiar especially by Thorsten Veblen, may be important in inter-personal relations and perhaps, as we shall see, of some use in the explanation of consumption and saving habits that prevail in economically backward countries. But it is not the point on which we are going to concentrate.

There is another way in which individual consumption functions are interrelated, and this will be our main concern. Duesenberry calls it the ' demonstration effect.'[2] When people

---

[1] *Income, Saving and the Theory of Consumer Behavior* (Cambridge, Mass., 1949).   [2] Ibid., p. 27.

come into contact with superior goods or superior patterns of consumption, with new articles or new ways of meeting old wants, they are apt to feel after a while a certain restlessness and dissatisfaction. Their knowledge is extended, their imagination stimulated; new desires are aroused, the propensity to consume is shifted upward.

In the United States we find from family budget studies what everybody would expect to find, namely, that higher income groups save a larger proportion of their income. In fact, the upper income groups comprising about 25 per cent of the population seem to account for all of the personal saving in the country; about 75 per cent of American families save virtually nothing.[1] Economists have long been puzzled by the fact that the positive correlation between income size and saving ratio, which family budget data so clearly bring out for any given point of time, fails to appear when we consider changes through time. It certainly does not appear in the national income as a whole. The Kuznets estimates by decades, starting from the 1880s, show a big increase in real national income but no increase in the percentage share that went into capital formation. On the contrary, from the 1890s to the 1920s, when real income expanded more than three-fold, there was actually a slight downward tendency in the national saving ratio. (In the 1930s the ratio dropped sharply as a result of the depression.)

Family budget data available for different periods also show certain puzzling features. The average urban family in the United States in 1917–19, earning 1500 dollars a year in terms of 1941 prices, saved 120 dollars or 8 per cent. An average family with the same real income in 1941 saved practically nothing.[2] How are we to explain this extraordinary change? The new theory of consumer behaviour explains it mainly by pointing to the fact that, although the absolute amount of the family's real income under consideration remained the same, there is no doubt that this amount in 1941 occupied a lower rank in the nation's income scale than it did in 1919. Average national income per head had increased. Therefore this family's friends and neighbours in 1941 were, on the whole, better off than in 1919; they were using

[1] Ibid., p. 39.   [2] Ibid, pp. 26 and 80.

many new goods and services and altogether keeping up more ample and complex patterns of consumption. Naturally our family's temptation to spend was greatly increased. Its contact with ' superior ' consumption goods and more 'advanced' ways of living had become more frequent. This wore down its resistance to new forms of spending, and accounts for the fact that its saving dropped to zero.[1]

We can construct a slightly different case, a hypothetical illustration which, though not based on actual statistics, is consistent with the facts. Suppose a man earned 1500 dollars in 1919, and his income increased to 2000 in 1941. (Let the income be valued at constant prices again so as to reflect a change in real volume.) He saved 120 dollars in 1919, or 8 per cent of his income. Because of the forces just discussed, his saving goes down to 100 dollars in 1941, or 5 per cent of his income. In spite of the increase in real income, there is a decline in the amount as well as the proportion saved. The man's friends and neighbours may have had their incomes increased even more; new goods consumed by others may have created new desires in him; or he may have simply become more familiar with superior forms of consumption.

Thus the interdependence of consumers' preferences, stressed by this theory, may significantly affect the choice between consumption and saving. The amount of saving performed by an individual depends not only, and perhaps not even mainly, on the absolute level of his real income, but also on the ratio of his income to the superior income level of other people with whom he may come in contact. (Whether it is the ratio or the absolute distance that matters is a question for further consideration. There is something to be said for treating the absolute gap rather

[1] The explanation concentrates on what is believed to be the principal factor : the decline in relative income rank. There is no denying that other factors may have played a part. For instance, the social security system may have reduced the propensity to save in 1941 as compared with 1917–19. One might object that the rate of saving may have been abnormally high in 1917–19 because of war-time restrictions, but this factor does not seem to have been important. The family budget data permit comparison over an even longer period, namely, from 1901 to 1941 ; and it is found, for example, that the average family with an income of 2,000 dollars a year, valued at 1941 prices, saved about 18 per cent in 1901 and only about 3 per cent in 1941 (see the diagram shown in Duesenberry's book, p. 80).

than the ratio between the consumption levels of different people as the factor that creates the tension and the change in the propensity to consume. In either case a statistical index problem presents itself, which has to be solved by some arbitrary convention, but this will be the same whether one chooses the ratio basis or the absolute distances in measuring inter-personal income discrepancies.)

When the interdependence of consumers' preferences is taken into consideration, we realize that a more unequal distribution of income may reduce the average saving ratio, instead of increasing it as is commonly supposed. The Kuznets data, mentioned earlier, appear no longer anomalous (though an adequate interpretation of these data would have to take many other factors into account). The reason why 75 per cent of American families save nothing is not so much that they are too poor to save. It is rather that the example of the consumption patterns kept up by people in the top 25 per cent income groups stimulates their wants to such an extent that virtually nothing is left over for saving. All this is only a hypothesis, but it seems to be consistent with the facts.

GROWING AWARENESS OF ADVANCED LIVING STANDARDS

The question I would like to raise is whether a hypothesis of this sort might not usefully be applied to international economic relations. Could it not be that the consumption functions of different countries are interrelated in a similar way? Human behaviour on the international as well as the inter-personal level may be affected by the forces just described. Here we can leave out Veblen's point that the propensity to spend is partly based on the desire for conspicuous consumption. I do not think that on the international plane the effect of unequal living standards depends on the idea of ' keeping up with the Joneses '. All it depends on is demonstration leading to imitation. Knowledge of or contact with new consumption patterns opens one's eyes to previously unrecognized possibilities. It widens the horizon of imagination and desires. It is not just a matter of social snobbishness.

New products constantly emerge from the course of technical

progress, which modify existing ways of life and frequently become necessities. In the poorer countries such goods are often imported goods, not produced at home; but that is not the only trouble. The basic trouble is that the presence or the mere knowledge of new goods and new methods of consumption tends to raise the general propensity to consume. New goods, whether home-made or imported, become part of the standard of living, become indispensable or at least desirable, and are actively desired as the standard of living rises. We should distinguish here between two senses of the term ' standard of living ' : first, standard simply in the sense of aspiration, the norm to which one aspires, or the measuring rod; secondly, standard in the sense of what a country or a community can afford on the basis of its own productive efforts. Some articles of luxury consumption may well be a part of a country's standard of living in the first but not in the second sense.

The outstanding example of this effect of disparities in consumption levels is at present the widespread imitation of American consumption patterns. It is partly perhaps a result of American methods of advertising. Advertising is the art of creating new wants, and Americans are supremely good at it; no wonder the rest of the world has a dollar shortage! It is much easier to adopt superior consumption habits than improved production methods. Hence fashions in consumption can spread more quickly than techniques of production. It is true that American production methods are also widely imitated; sometimes, indeed, too closely; the highly mechanized equipment that is suited to American conditions, where labour is the scarcest factor of production, need not be well suited to conditions elsewhere. But imitation of American production methods generally requires investible funds. The temptation to copy American consumption patterns tends to limit the supply of investible funds by inhibiting the willingness to save.

The goods that form part of American consumption patterns are ' superior ' not necessarily in any objective sense, but because they are regarded as such. There may be people of ascetic bent who have no use for American gadgets; most people seem to like them. Besides, it has come to be noticed that American consumption patterns include, not unnecessary luxuries alone, but also things that diminish suffering and prolong life. The American standard of living enjoys considerable prestige. This presents a serious problem for the poorer countries in the world to-day.

New wants, it is true, can be important as an incentive, making people work harder and produce more. But even so there is no assurance whatever that the extra output will be saved and invested, rather than immediately consumed.

The intensity of the attraction exercised by the consumption standards of the advanced countries—the demonstration effect on the international plane—is determined by two factors. One is the size of the disparities in real income and consumption levels. The other is the extent of people's awareness of them.

The disparities are greater than ever before. They are certainly greater in terms of absolute gaps, perhaps not when defined in terms of ratios. Probably all the poorer countries have made some headway in real income and consumption per head over the last hundred years or so; and yet over the same period the gaps have tended to widen.[1] The position we have now reached is reflected in the following table based on national income estimates for 70 countries, compiled by the United Nations Secretariat and expressed on the common basis of United States dollars of 1949 purchasing power :

World Income Distribution in 1949

	World Income	World Population	Income Per Head
High-income countries ...	67%	18%	$915
Middle-income countries ...	18%	15%	$310
Low-income countries ...	15%	67%	$ 54

Source: A calculation based on *National and Per Capita Incomes in 70 Countries, 1949*, Statistical Office of the United Nations, 1950.

It appears that two-thirds of the world's income goes to the top 18 per cent of the world's population. This group consists

[1] P. N. Rosenstein-Rodan, ' The International Development of Economically Backward Areas,' *International Affairs*, April 1944, p. 158. There is some evidence in Colin Clark's *Conditions of Economic Progress* to support this generalization.

of the United States, Canada, Western Europe, Australia and New Zealand. Then there is a small middle class, including Argentina, Uruguay, South Africa, Israel and some countries in Eastern Europe, especially Soviet Russia. In Russia's case it is particularly necessary to bear in mind that the underlying data are intended to measure the value, not of personal consumption alone, but of all goods and services produced, including those produced for investment and for military purposes.

The lowest income group represented in the table comprises two-thirds of the world's population and receives less than one-sixth of the world's income (that is, produces less than one-sixth of the world's output). It covers most of Asia, Africa, south-eastern Europe and Latin America. That the so-called backward countries of the world make up two-thirds of the human race is in itself a momentous fact that should never be forgotten.

Japan is included in the low-income group, but this is doubtless due to temporary post-war conditions. Normally Japan would now be classed probably as a middle-income country.

The last column of the table gives some idea of the average income levels in the three groups of countries. It will be seen that the per capita income of the first group is about seventeen times as high as that of the third. The figures have an air of precision which is, of course, illusory. The estimates on which they are based are in many cases extremely crude. They are subject to all kinds of doubts and reservations. Yet there is no reason to believe that the picture they give is grossly misleading. Let us remember that they do not take account of voluntary leisure, which is one way in which advanced nations have taken out their gains.

International discrepancies in levels of living are very great. But that is not all. Just as important is the fact that communication is so much closer than ever before, with the result that knowledge of these discrepancies has greatly increased. It is enough to mention such recent inventions as the American movies, the radio and aviation. There has also been an increase in education, which may tend at first to stimulate desires before it improves productivity. Anyway, contact in the modern world, in the free world at any rate, is very close. The attraction of consumption standards of the advanced countries may exert itself unevenly in different income groups in underdeveloped areas. It may be concentrated among the upper income groups in the cities; but it need not be confined to them by any means. It may be diffused, though faintly, even among the lower income groups, thanks to education and mass media of communication. It may affect the demand for social legislation and industrial labour standards as well as the demand for modern luxuries. I would therefore hesitate to make any class distinctions in this connection.

We can readily admit that the strength of the demonstration effect varies a great deal as between countries. I believe it is an important factor in most parts of Latin America. In India, on the other hand, it may be weak and relatively insignificant. I do think that practically all low-income countries to-day are to some degree affected by the attraction of the consumption patterns of economically advanced countries. And even within the group of high-income countries the demonstration factor may be operative : it probably affects Western Europe in relation to the United States.

Here we are dealing with the low-income nations. The factor we have discussed has undoubtedly contributed to produce what President Truman called 'the great awakening' among these nations. Their concern for economic development is itself, in an obvious sense, a demonstration effect; it would hardly be so pronounced if the high-income nations lived on a different planet. But let us try to keep away from the more nebulous regions on which our subject borders. Let us stick to the simple fact that in the world to-day the attraction of advanced consumption standards exerts itself fairly widely, though of course unevenly, among the poorer two-thirds of mankind.

EFFECTS ON THE PROPENSITY TO SAVE

This attraction is a handicap for the late-comers in economic development. It affects not only voluntary personal saving but also renders it politically more difficult to use taxation as a means of compulsory saving and to resist demands for government spending on current account. Some of the industrially backward countries have large masses of disguised unemployment on the land, which could be mobilized for real capital formation, but not without strict curbs on any immediate rise in consumption. Others may hope to introduce improvements in agricultural techniques so as to release labour from primitive subsistence farming and make it available for capital works, but again not without restraints to prevent the increment from being immediately consumed. The use of potential domestic sources of capital can be seriously hampered by the impatience and dissatisfaction which the demonstration effect tends to produce.

When we take into account that it is not only the absolute but also the relative level of real income that determines the capacity to save, we begin to realize that foreign aid or foreign investment may not be capable of removing this handicap. An increase in relative income in the industrially backward countries is not simply a matter of increasing productivity in these countries; it is a matter of diminishing the gap between their income level and that of the advanced countries. Foreign investment does not guarantee a reduction in this gap. The rate of saving and investment in an advanced industrial economy is not a fixed magnitude. If it were, then increased foreign investment would mean a reduction in domestic investment. But advanced countries have sometimes been subject to conditions of underemployment, in which an increase in foreign investment need not be at the expense of domestic investment at all, but may, on the contrary, increase the volume of domestic investment and saving. Even if we disregard the possible returns from foreign investment, we must conclude that foreign investment is no guarantee of diminishing the distance between the rich and the poor; it may increase it.

Moreover, there is the disturbing possibility that, even if the gap should remain unchanged, a rise in the living levels of the poorer countries, accompanied by an equal rise in those of the richer, may tend to increase the intensity of contact and communication between them and hence the strength of the demonstration factor. A country may be, in absolute terms, too poor to have much contact with the outside world. According to the United Nations statistics, Uruguay, one of the most prosperous countries in Latin America, has a per capita income eight times as high as Ecuador, one of the poorest in this area. From this it does not follow that the demonstration effect of United States living standards is stronger in Ecuador than in Uruguay. On the contrary, it may well be stronger in Uruguay. The people of Ecuador may be too poor to be affected by it to the same degree (too poor, for instance, to have radios and cinemas). In short, the strength of the demonstration factor may be partly a function of the absolute level of real income, since the degree of contact and communication depends to some extent on the absolute income level which a country has attained. It is for this reason that American consumption patterns may have a considerable effect on Western Europe.

The conflict between the desire to consume and the need to save is made more difficult in the underdeveloped countries by the international disparities in real income levels, though we must remember that a conflict of this sort is inherent in the accumulation of capital, and always exists in the minds of individuals weighing the attractions of current as against greater future consumption. Raul Prebisch in his stimulating essay places great emphasis on the familiar point that the level of productivity in Latin America is low because of lack of capital, and that capital is scarce because of the small margin of saving, which is due, in turn, to low income and low productivity. He also recognizes the importance of the attraction exercised in the poorer countries by the consumption patterns of the more advanced.[1] This second point, however, substantially modifies the first. The small rate of saving is due not only to the low absolute level of real income but also to the high propensity to consume, caused by the allurement of superior forms of consumption. Remember : the reason why even in the United States 75 per cent of the people save nothing is not that they cannot afford to save, or do not want to, but that they live in an environment which makes them want new consumption goods even more.

In spite of the absolute increase in levels of real income per head in most, if not all, of the poorer nations over the past century, it may have become harder rather than easier for these nations

[1] *The Economic Development of Latin America and its Principal Problems*, Op. cit., pp. 5, 6, 37.

to do any saving out of their increased incomes, as a result of the decline in the relative position of their income levels. (While their ability to save should have increased, their willingness to save has been adversely affected. The old distinction between ability and willingness to save becomes, however, somewhat blurred when relative as well as absolute income levels are recognized as an important governing factor.) There has been an increase in the tension, impatience and restlessness which causes an upward shift in the consumption function, and which acts as an impediment to saving.

Here we have the problem of economic development in its international setting. It is perhaps not a problem of ' pure ' economics—not, at any rate, until the pure theory of international economics has taken notice of elements hitherto neglected. The fact that the elements which I am introducing into the discussion might be classed as matters of international *political* economy, or even international sociology, does not make them any less relevant to our theme. No good purpose is served by keeping these matters under a shroud of silence. They must be brought out into the light of day and considered dispassionately in relation to the economic problem that concerns us.

The conventional view of international economic relations generally implies that a high level of productivity and real income in one country cannot possibly hurt other countries and that, on the contrary, prosperity tends to spread. Of course there are many ways in which one country's prosperity will help its neighbours. The late-comers can benefit, for instance, from scientific advances made by the leaders. But the particular effect now discussed is unfavourable. A high income and consumption level in an advanced country can do harm in that it tends to reduce the domestic means of capital formation in the underdeveloped countries; it puts extra pressure on countries with a relatively low income to spend a high proportion of it.

This is quite apart from the possibility that some countries— for instance, in the Middle East—may suffer from a cultural aversion to saving, due to the presence of traditional domestic forms of conspicuous consumption. The demonstration factor creates an added difficulty. Only when it leads to a switch from native to imported forms of consumption does it impose no additional strain on saving capacity. (Whether the imported forms of consumption directly involve imported goods as well is a separate question, which will be touched upon later.) The traditional and modern forms of consumption can interact in a variety of ways. In some countries land ownership is a means to superior social status and prestige, and so the savings of traders and industrialists are habitually devoted to a considerable extent to the purchase of landed estates. The sellers of the land, in turn, often use the funds for urban forms of consumption or need the money to pay off debts because they have already succumbed to the temptations of modern ways of living.

In the most general terms the possible significance of the demonstration factor can be considered in conjunction with a well-known classical model. In Ricardo's famous illustration of the comparative cost principle, it takes Portugal 80 hours of labour to produce a gallon of wine and 90 hours to produce a yard of cloth, whereas in England the labour cost of wine and cloth is 120 and 100 hours respectively. Thus England has a somewhat lower absolute level of productivity and must be content with a lower real income than Portugal. Yet trade will take place in accordance with comparative costs (Portugal exporting wine, England cloth), and there seems no reason why trade should not balance. With a moderate difference in productivity and income levels, the possible interdependence of national consumption functions can be ignored. The trade model—that is, the pattern of comparative advantage—would still be the same if productivity, while remaining unchanged in England, increased in Portugal to a point where only 8 hours of labour were needed for wine and 9 hours for cloth. But as a result of so great a discrepancy in levels of productivity and hence real income, it may be that, while Portugal has a large margin of saving available for capital formation, the English—faced with the attractions of the Portuguese living standard—find themselves unable to save any part of their income. Incidentally, as will be explained in a moment, England would probably suffer in these circumstances from persistent difficulties in balancing her external accounts.

The interdependence of consumption functions can significantly affect the choice between consumption and saving. The hypothesis seems applicable to some extent on the international as well as on the inter-personal plane. As already indicated, the international disparities can inhibit not only voluntary private saving but also the use of public finance as an instrument of capital formation. I do not wish to exaggerate the effect of the international disparities. A very poor country might find it extremely hard to produce any saving for its economic development even if it knew nothing about higher living standards in the outside world. The vicious circle that keeps down the domestic supply of capital in low-income areas is bad enough by itself. My point is that it tends to be made even worse by the stresses that arise from relative as distinct from absolute poverty. How much worse is a question that cannot be precisely determined; it is a matter of judgment and one that presumably varies from country to country.

Effects on the Balance of Payments

The poorer nations, in contact with the richer, feel continually impelled to keep their money incomes and outlays above what is warranted by their own capacity to produce. The result is an inflationary pressure at home and a persistent tendency towards disequilibrium in the balance of payments.

A popular theory of the postwar ' dollar shortage ' ran in terms of differences in the general level of productivity between countries. It seemed a common-sense approach. The explanation was that the United States had acquired such a commanding superiority in all lines of production, especially in manufacturing industry, that it could out-sell all other countries in the world market and so develop an export surplus, which of course was an inport surplus, a balance-of-payments deficit, for the other countries. This theory, which was held by some professional economists, gained a wide circulation since most laymen found it an easy and obvious explanation.

The classical school of international economics has a devastating answer to this theory: the doctrine of comparative costs. International trade is governed not by absolute, but by comparative differences in productivity, in conjunction with the rate of exchange. With a proper exchange rate a country can always balance its external accounts, even if in relation to other countries it has a much lower over-all level of productivity. At a certain rate of exchange, it should be able to export articles in which it has the least absolute disadvantage, while importing those in which it has the greatest disadvantage in terms of productivity.[1]

I myself find the classical answer convincing, except for special cases where the elasticities of demand and supply are such that no change in the exchange rate, either upward or downward, can bring the balance of payments into equilibrium. Although theoretically conceivable, it seems in practice unlikely that the elasticities over the whole relevant range should happen to be precisely at or near the critical point at which the price system is incapable of restoring balance. To build the explanation of a persistent, or persistently recurrent, international disequilibrium on such special cases does not seem plausible. There must be, one would think, a wider explanation of such a disequilibrium if, in fact, it should persist or recur.

The classical view was that a lack of balance in international trade can continue only because some countries insist on trying to live beyond their means, and are constantly tending to expand money income above their level of productivity. We may accept this proposition; but we must note that it is only a statement of fact. What is the explanation of it?

We have found a simple general hypothesis to account for the tendency of some countries to 'live beyond their means.' We reject the simpler forms of the productivity theory of the dollar shortage; yet we seem to reach—by the back door, as it were— a theory of balance-of-payments disequilibrium based similarly upon differences in general levels of productivity. But here the comparative cost principle is fully respected. Discrepancies in productivity as such are no explanation of balance-of-payments disequilibria. However, productivity determines real income. International discrepancies in levels of productivity are reflected

---

[1] For recent applications of this principle to the problem of the dollar shortage, see, for example, Gottfried Haberler's essay in *Foreign Economic Policy for the United States* (edited by Seymour E. Harris, New York, 1948) and Howard S. Ellis, *Economics of Freedom* (published under the auspices of the Council on Foreign Relations, New York, 1950), pp. 69–71.

in discrepancies in real income levels of different countries and hence in their consumption levels as well. Disequilibrium in the balance of payments does tend to result indirectly from differences in general levels of productivity, not because productivity determines a country's export costs and competitive power in the world market, not because the most productive country necessarily out-sells all others in all lines, but because a country's productivity determines its real income and consumption levels, and because differences in levels of living, when they are very large and widely known, exercise an upward pressure on the consumption propensity of the poorer countries.

I have been impressed for some time with the importance of unequal wealth and income distribution in the operation of the international monetary mechanism. The gold standard was never universal. Many countries were too poor to hold reserves adequate to tide them over cyclical and other short-term fluctuations in their balances of payments, and hence found it peculiarly difficult to adhere to a system of stable and unrestricted exchanges. The poorer countries are naturally impatient to spend their foreign earnings on badly needed imports, and tend to place a low priority on the maintenance or accumulation of a foreign exchange reserve. To some extent again we find on the international plane what we find among individuals. The holding of a cash balance of a size that would be considered normal by a rich man might be felt by a poor man as a wasteful luxury.[1]

The persistent tendency of the poorer countries to overspend on international account is only another aspect of the low priority they place on international cash reserves and, indeed, of their relative poverty. There seems to me to be some basis for the idea, therefore, that there is something like a natural tendency towards disequilibrium in the balance of payments between a rich and a poor country.[2] I would only add once more that this is so, not because of the rich country's high productivity making for low

[1] See my essay, 'Conditions of International Monetary Equilibrium,' Essays in International Finance, Princeton University, 1945, pp. 15–17 (reprinted in Readings in the Theory of International Trade, op. cit.), The point is also made, in more than one place, in International Currency Experience (League of Nations, 1944).

[2] Cf. Paul A. Samuelson, ' Disparity in Postwar Exchange Rates,' in Foreign Economic Policy for the United States, op. cit., p. 408.

export prices and great competitive strength, but because of the poor country's propensity to spend, which, for the reasons described, tends to be excessive in relation to its own capacity to produce.

In these circumstances the classical prescription—'stop inflation and adjust the exchange rate'[1]—does not seem to work. Many countries seem to find it peculiarly difficult to apply. When tried, it may help for a while, but then the inflationary pressures continue, the balance-of-payments disequilibrium re-appears, or at least tends to re-appear, being possibly held in check by import restrictions and exchange controls. International income disparities can affect the balance of payments by causing a direct increase in the demand for imported goods. The imitation effect can, however, operate equally well on the demand for leisure, services or goods that cannot enter into international trade, and can indirectly affect the balance of payments in much the same way as where imports are directly involved. The theory does not depend on demand for imports from advanced countries, though in reality this is undoubtedly an important factor. The demonstration factor on the international plane operates in part directly on the demand for American products.[2]

One might ask why a persistent disequilibrium of this sort did

---

[1] This is how Charles P. Kindleberger in his book on *The Dollar Shortage* (New York, 1950) characterizes the classical prescription. In reality most adherents of the classical view have been ready to make allowance for various qualifications and complications in practice. Thus Haberler writes : ' It would be a serious misunderstanding to believe that the problem is simple or easy to solve, because we have reduced it to a short formula ' (op. cit., p. 444).

[2] This has nothing in common with Kindleberger's thesis (op. cit., p. 14) that American exports encounter a high income elasticity of demand in the rest of the world so that any increase in income abroad creates a more than proportionate increase in the demand for American exports. In the theory here presented, what induces the increased demand for American exports is not a rise in the level of income in the poorer countries but rather a widening (or an increased awareness) of the real income gap between them and the United States. Kindleberger's book is full of ideas, but I have found no systematic exposition of this point in it. There is, however, a passage at the end of his earlier essay on ' International Monetary Stabilization ', in *Postwar Economic Problems* (edited by Seymour E. Harris, New York, 1943), which comes fairly close to the theme with which I am dealing here. Thomas Balogh in *The Dollar Crisis* (Oxford, 1949) occasionally speaks of the dollar problem as being caused by the widening discrepancy between the standard of life, as well as productivity, of the United States and of other countries (e.g., p. 149). He may have had the ' demonstration effect ' in mind, but I cannot find any clear statement of this in his book.

not arise in the nineteenth century when, similarly, one country was far ahead in productivity and real income, namely, Great Britain. One could point to certain episodes of 'sterling shortage' in the nineteenth century, but there was no persistent disequilibrium, and the term 'sterling shortage' was not known. Why not? First, the absolute discrepancies in real income levels must have been smaller, and the discrepancies in consumption standards were probably still smaller, in view of England's high propensity to save, which was favoured by the puritan mentality of the new industrial middle class. Secondly, contact and communication among nations was not nearly as close as at present; the cinema, the radio and aviation did not exist. Thirdly, Britain practised a commercial policy that culminated in the unilateral abolition of all tariff protection and was not bound by the principle of reciprocity in tariff bargaining. Fourthly, Britain exported capital almost continuously and on a relatively very large scale.

A hundred years ago, for all these reasons, the acceptance of equilibrium as the normal state towards which the international balance of payments always tended to move was not wildly unrealistic. Thus J. S. Mill spoke about 'foreign commerce in its natural state of equilibrium.'[1] More recently, Barrett Whale[2] expressed the classical view as follows: 'The idea that there exists a natural tendency to equilibrium in international trade is the central principle of the whole theory of our subject.' He added a note of scepticism: 'Just for that reason, however, its truth must not be taken for granted too readily.' Even the income approach to the adjustment mechanism of the balance of payments, although it discloses a possibility of persistent imbalance due to saving leakages in the multiplier process, still confirms the idea that there is at all events a tendency towards equilibrium. In the world we live in to-day, it may be that this idea had better be consigned to a subsidiary position. Is it not at least equally plausible to say that, in such a world, disequilibrium is the normal state and the natural tendency in international trade?

The inflationary pressures and balance-of-payments difficulties, which nowadays tend to result from the discrepancies in

---

[1] See the passage quoted on p. 122, below.
[2] *International Trade* London, 1934), p. 86.

income and consumption levels, are not as such the basic trouble. They are a symptom. They could conceivably come from increased domestic capital outlays and not from consumer spending. The real trouble, from the view-point of capital supply, is that the growing disparity between the real income levels of different countries tends to lead in the poorer countries to increased consumption or attempts at increasing consumption, rather than to increased investment. At any rate it puts a brake on any increase in saving, as and when incomes and investment increase.

It is for this reason that international income disparities may have to be treated, not merely as a source of strain in the balance of international payments, but actually as an impediment to domestic saving and capital formation in the poorer countries.

THE DEFEATIST SOLUTION : ECONOMIC ISOLATION

The attraction of advanced consumption standards represents a handicap for the late-comers in economic development. What can be done about this handicap ? We must face the fact that isolation is one possible remedy, and that it has played a part in the development of two important countries. It is well known that Japan, in the early course of her industrialization, imitated the Western world in everything except consumption patterns.[1] She had kept herself in a state of complete isolation for centuries, and it was comparatively easy for her to maintain this isolation in regard to consumption patterns. There is no doubt that this was part of the secret of her success in domestic capital formation and industrial development. According to such estimates as are available,[2] Japan managed to save between 12 and 17 per cent of her national income at the beginning of the present century. Government borrowing from abroad was comparatively unimportant, and hardly any foreign business investments came in until the 1920's. Japan did all her capital formation virtually unaided.

[1] E. P. Reubens, 'Foreign Capital in Economic Development : a Case Study of Japan,' in *Modernization Programs in Relation to Human Resources and Population Problems* (Milbank Memorial Fund, New York, 1950), p. 118.

[2] See, e.g., E. Staley, *World Economic Development* (International Labour Office, 1945), p. 72.

The other instance of radical isolation is Soviet Russia's iron curtain (which of course is not merely a result of the present tension but was well established before World War II). While it certainly has other reasons for its existence, I am inclined to attach significance also to its economic function; that is, to the possible ' materialist interpretation ' of the iron curtain. Needless to say, it is only the economic aspect of the iron curtain that concerns us here, purely from the point of view of the theory we have considered. It may be that the iron curtain is necessary for the maintenance of a high rate of saving and investment in the Soviet Union. From the estimates that have been made, however doubtful they may be, it seems that something like 25 per cent of the Soviet Union's national income has in recent years been directed into capital formation, apart from purely military expenditure.[1] To maintain such a high rate of investment may not be possible without isolating the country from the Western world. A free and open view of the consumption standards in the West might mean a psychologically intolerable and politically ignominious contrast. (While an important function of the iron curtain is to prevent the insiders from looking out, a useful subsidiary function may be to prevent outsiders from looking in, so as to preserve the legend of the workers' paradise.)

Isolation alone is incapable of promoting development; Japan was isolated for centuries without experiencing any significant economic advance. Isolation by itself rather promotes stagnation. And yet the two cases illustrate the possibility that isolation might help to solve the economic problem of capital formation, in a world of great discrepancies in national living standards, by severing contact and communication among nations. Without communication, the discrepancies in living standards, however great, may become of little or no consequence. They do not affect people's desires, aspirations and activities; they do not constantly enter into the consciousness and the imagination of consumers. In this way the demonstration effect may lose at least some of its potency.

That this should be a possible, and perhaps a necessary, solution is a disquieting thought. The cost of isolation may be tremendous, not only in political relations, but in purely economic

[1] See, e.g., Howard S. Ellis, *The Economics of Freedom*, op. cit., p. 18.

terms also. The economic cost alone would be prohibitive for any small country. Isolation is a defeatist solution. One naturally turns in search of an alternative.

INTERNATIONAL AND INTERREGIONAL INCOME TRANSFERS

Could the alternative be for the richer countries to provide, to some extent, for the needs of the poorer? So far we have discussed international income disparities and their effects, on the one side. On the other side, there may exist certain deep-seated forces making for unilateral income transfers—in plain English, gifts—from rich to poor countries. The desirability of such transfers need not be questioned, at least so long as they are compatible with the maintenance or, better still, expansion of world income. Besides, we need not entertain any exaggerated notions about the size of such transfers. Let us remember, for example, that 2 per cent of the United States national income would be equal to about 7 per cent of the combined national income of all low-income countries outside the Soviet orbit and would probably be as much as or more than these countries could at present effectively absorb from abroad for investment purposes.

The foreign aid programmes of the United States have certainly departed from traditional practices. It is possible that we have seen the beginnings of a system of international income transfers. The pressures for such a system come from both sides, not only from that of the low-income countries. As a result of closer contact and communication, some of which has been a by-product of the war, people in the United States have become increasingly conscious of the discrepancies in living standards; the humanitarian aspects of Point Four make no little appeal to a nation with an early tradition of giving protection to the economic underdog as well as the political and religious outcast. There has been an emotional tone in the reports and official pronouncements concerning these problems, with frequent reference to the hunger, poverty, disease and illiteracy that prevail in two-thirds of the world. Both the Gray Report of November 1950[1] and the

---

[1] *Report to the President on Foreign Economic Policies*, U.S. Government Printing Office, 1950.

Rockefeller Report of March 1951[1] came out in favour of a sizable flow of governmental grants from the United States to the low-income areas of the world.

In the United States, however, as elsewhere, isolation also has its advocates and is indeed, as we have noticed, a conceivable alternative in a world of wide discrepancies in income levels.

There exists a mechanism that tends automatically to produce transfers of resources from the richer to the poorer regions within a given country. Suppose that government expenditure on public works and welfare is approximately the same per head of the population in all regions, but that taxation is proportional to income. The point comes out even more strongly if taxation is progressive, but all we have to assume is that taxation per head varies with income per head. The result is a tendency towards automatic transfers of public funds from the richer to the poorer regions. The point is hard to verify, though often brought up in countries with a federal structure. In the United States we observe a persistent tendency for funds to be transferred through the Federal Treasury from the northern and eastern to the southern and western parts of the country. In Brazil there is a marked tendency for such transfers to take place from the fairly prosperous southern states to the primitive tropical northern regions. Another federal country where the interregional aspects of the fiscal system have received a good deal of attention is Canada.

I introduce this fiscal mechanism not simply for the sake of analogy, but because it is a significant way in which economic development may be financed in the poorer regions of a given country. It depends on the fact that taxation is not a constant sum per head, but varies with income.[2] The principle of ability to pay, or equal sacrifice, is not satisfied with a constant sum of taxation per head or even with a constant proportion of income; according to what has long since become orthodox doctrine, it requires progressive taxation. The resulting interregional income transfers are admitted by people living in the rich as well as in the

[1] *Partners in Progress*, Report of the International Development Advisory Board, U.S. Government Printing Office, 1951.

[2] This refers not simply to an income tax, but to the combined effect of all forms of government taxation.

poorer regions. They are acknowledged as a natural consequence of the principle of ability to pay and as part of the fiscal system in which this principle is embodied. They are accepted in the last resort because people live in fairly close contact culturally and politically; because they recognize a common interest and are, more or less, agreed on the need for a fair allocation of the costs of governmental investment and welfare activities.

Could it be that what we have had in international relations by way of unilateral income transfers is nothing but a groping and imperfect approximation to what happens within a country quite automatically, and would happen similarly between different countries if they were under a world government ? Is the principle of ability to pay, carrying with it this fiscal mechanism of inter-regional transfers, waiting to be extended beyond national boundaries ? The pressures that lead to interregional transfers through proportional or progressive taxation within a country also exist in some degree on the international plane. They have to do with the co-existence and increasingly close association of people on widely divergent levels of living.

In the past, international unilateral transfers may have occurred to some extent under the guise of foreign investment. It has been argued that foreign investments have, in part, turned out to be haphazardly distributed gifts, because of subsequent default.[1] But this is a very awkward solution since default interferes with the continuity of the flow. Default is therefore considered unwise as well as immoral.

We encounter the basic pressures that make for income transfers from rich to poor when relatively advanced countries are associated with economically backward areas in the form of colonies. In Western European countries in the last two or three decades it has been a fashionable question to ask : do colonies pay ? The answer of the experts has usually been in the negative. Recent colonial history seems, on the whole, to support this view. For example, M. M. Knight, the American economic historian,

[1] A. E. Kahn, ' Investment Criteria in Development Programs,' in *Quarterly Journal of Economics*, February, 1951, p. 61. For an outspoken complaint that many of Britain's foreign investments in the nineteenth century were undesigned gifts, see A. M. Samuel, ' Has Foreign Investment Paid ? ' in *Economic Journal*, 1930. Cf. also T. Balogh, op. cit., p. 166.

who has worked on this question in North Africa, finds that in Algeria the local government's budget deficits were covered directly by the French Treasury and that ' the framework of a system of railways, roads and ports was laid down . . . as an outright gift from the French taxpayer.'[1] The tendency for the metropolitan country to subsidize its colonies appeared in the 1920's even in Portugal.[2] While in earlier centuries there is no doubt about the fact of colonial exploitation, in recent times we find that colonies probably do not pay. But why should they pay ? A transfer of current resources from the relatively wealthy metropolitan countries to their dependent territories is a natural application of principles long accepted and practised within any civilized country. The grants which Puerto Rico receives from the United States Treasury are an instance of such a relationship established on a steady and regular basis.

Generally, whenever nations enter into an increasingly intimate association and recognize a vital community of interests, the problem of pooling and allocating economic resources tends to arise, just as it does between different areas of the same country.[3] If we lived under a world government, automatic transfers from the richer to the poorer parts of the globe would occur as a matter of course through the fiscal mechanism. We have no world government. On the other hand, if we depart from the automatic market mechanism of private capital movements, or if this mechanism fails to function, there are no objective, non-political criteria for guiding the flow of funds. The problem of devising a system of international grants is a political problem and, in the nature of the case, political considerations cannot be kept out of it. A system of international grants-in-aid does not stem from the economic mechanism of the market; nor does the principle of progressive taxation. Both are based of necessity on political value judgments.

Inter-governmental grants are inevitably matters of inter-

---

[1] M. M. Knight, *Morocco as a French Economic Venture* (New York, 1937), p. 16.

[2] *The Course and Control of Inflation : A Review of Monetary Experience in Europe after World War I* (League of Nations, 1946), p. 41

[3] H. Mendershausen, ' Foreign Aid With and Without Dollar Shortage ', *Review of Economics and Statistics*, February 1951, pp. 41–2.

national political economy; if not deliberate instruments of foreign policy, they are at any rate shaped by the totality of a country's relations with other nations. If we are realists, we can hardly expect a pure, automatic and non-political mechanism of international income transfers to come into existence. Such transfers as may occur will inevitably be based in part on the shifting grounds of political expediency. It seems to me therefore that there is little or no foundation for the belief, which some economists express as a matter of course, that inter-governmental capital transfers are inherently more stable and reliable than the private capital movements of the era that ended in 1929.

Quite apart, however, from the inconvenient but inevitable political aspects of international gifts and grants, do such transfers provide a sufficient and satisfactory solution to the problem of capital accumulation in underdeveloped countries ? Even if they fill the gaps in the balances of payments of low-income countries, do they offset the handicap which the demonstration factor imposes on the domestic saving capacity of these countries ? Such transfers may be desirable on general grounds. They spring in part from the tensions produced by the disparities in living levels and serve to mitigate these disparities. But do they meet the needs of capital development ? That is one of the questions to be considered in the next chapter.

Chapter IV

EXTERNAL SOURCES OF CAPITAL

Direct Business Investments

THE Point Four Programme of the United States originally laid great emphasis on direct foreign investment by American business firms as a source of capital for underdeveloped countries. Undoubtedly, this type of investment has some special advantages. Being subject to private profit motives and business calculations, it is likely to be productively employed. It helps to promote the spread of modern technology and efficient management methods. It is free from the rigid interest and amortization requirements that affect international loans.

Recent American documents concerned with Point Four (especially the Gray and Rockefeller reports) seem to make a partial withdrawal from the almost exclusive reliance placed on direct business investment in earlier pronouncements. Thus the Gray Report, after examining the possibilities of American direct investment abroad, says : ' it must be frankly recognized that private investment cannot be expected to solve the problem of financing development alone ' (p. 63). Indeed, anyone who tries to study closely the possible role of direct business investment in the development of the economically backward countries must become impressed with certain difficulties. I leave aside the various obstacles due to restrictive laws and regulations in the underdeveloped countries, and those due to exchange control, double taxation, or the risk of nationalization. I want to concentrate on a basic economic difficulty that appears clearly from the facts.

If we consider the figures for private American foreign investment in the three years 1947 to 1949, as shown in the Gray Report (pp. 61 and 121), we see, first, that 92 per cent of it took the form of direct business investment and, secondly, that 78 per cent of this direct investment went to underdeveloped countries. This seems very good, but we must notice, thirdly, that over 90 per cent of the direct investment in underdeveloped countries went into petroleum production. Perhaps the most important fact is that American private foreign investment was—and still is —very small, but I am drawing attention here to the nature rather than the size of the capital flow.

Foreign capital in underdeveloped countries went into extractive industries working mainly for export to the advanced industrial centres. It may be thought that this was so because of the risk of exchange control and the fear that transfer difficulties might be more serious in the case of investments working for the domestic market in underdeveloped countries. But the tendency of direct business investment to go into export industries in these countries has been equally marked in earlier periods. It can, I believe, be observed in the case of British investments in the nineteenth century. It was an outstanding feature of American capital exports in the 1920's, at a time when exchange control was non-existent and no one paid much attention to the risk of transfer troubles on private foreign investments. Such capital as flowed to low-income countries in the 1920's in the form of direct investments went mainly into production for export. Very little of it went into manufacturing for the home market.[1]

Looking at the total amount of American direct investments outstanding abroad at the end of 1948, we find it about evenly divided between underdeveloped countries and developed countries, with just over five billion dollars in each group. (The 'developed' group includes Western Europe and Canada.) From the table below, a striking contrast is apparent between the occupational distribution of American business capital in the two groups of countries. In the underdeveloped countries, most of it (59 per cent) works in extractive industries (petroleum, mining, agriculture), producing mostly for export. In the developed countries, the major part (it happens to be 59 per cent again) is engaged in manufacturing and distribution, in activities catering largely for the domestic market in these countries.[2]

[1] See United Nations, *International Capital Movements in the Interwar Period* (1949), p. 32.
[2] See H. J. Dernburg, 'Prospects for Long-Term Foreign Investment,' *Harvard Business Review*, July 1950, p. 42.

Percentage Distribution of U.S. Direct Investments in 1948

	Under-developed countries	Developed countries
Extractive industries	59	23
Manufacturing and distribution ...	22	59
Public utilities	16	7
Miscellaneous	3	11
	100	100

Source : U.S. Department of Commerce, *The Balance of International Payments of the United States, 1946–1948* (Washington, D.C., 1950), pp. 162–165.

Direct business investment is the type of foreign investment to which Singer's thesis applies with special force : that private foreign enterprise in the past has not done much to spread industrial development to the backward agricultural countries, but has concentrated rather on primary production for export to the advanced countries. Foreign capital, instead of developing the domestic economies of low-income countries, has served to harden and strengthen the system under which these countries specialized on the production of raw materials and foodstuffs for export. Foreign investment, according to this view, tended to promote a pattern of specialization based on a static scheme of comparative advantage in international trade. Even if this concentration on extractive export industries did not necessarily mean exploitation for foreign profit, or still less exploitation in any popular political sense, it meant all the same that foreign investment served primarily the interests of the industrial creditor countries, and that the economic growth resulting from it was inevitably somewhat unbalanced in character.

This pattern was not, however, a result of deliberate planning, concerted action or political pressure by the industrial creditor states. It was a perfectly natural result of the free play of private profit motives. The direction of private investment is naturally swayed by the pull of the market. The big markets in the past were in the industrial countries. Foreign capital in the underdeveloped areas found it profitable to work for these markets, rather than for the domestic consumers whose purchasing power in real terms was usually miserably low. The market difficulty, which we considered in Chapter I, accounts for it quite easily. In the domestic economy of a low-income country the inducement to invest is weak because the size of the domestic market is small. The individual foreign entrepreneur has not the incentive or even the means to defeat this vicious circle.

Lack of public overhead capital is also sometimes mentioned as an obstacle to private foreign investment for domestic production. In underdeveloped areas general facilities such as roads, railways, waterworks and power plants are inadequate or non-existent. Any one starting a business may find it necessary to provide some of these things from his own funds. The lack of such public services may have had something to do with the lack of incentive of foreign capital to work for the domestic market.

Yet it can hardly be a valid reason for the extraordinary difference which we find between export industries and home market industries. Surely the lack of public works and utilities is a difficulty that must affect foreign investment in the two fields more or less equally. But apparently it has not prevented investments in export industries when such investments have been sufficiently profitable, as they frequently seem to have been. Here the necessary public facilities were often created by the foreign investor as part of his project; here it paid him to do so. In home market industries, as a general rule, it did not—for a very obvious reason.

And so we find that in underdeveloped countries there is relatively little foreign business investment in industrial production for the domestic market, whereas in a country like Canada, which accounts for more than half of the investments in the group of developed countries shown in the table above, American direct investment is largely concentrated in manufacturing and distribution activities catering for the domestic market—because the domestic market enjoys a high level of productivity and purchasing power. A country like Brazil occupies perhaps an intermediate position. Certainly in the southern part of Brazil the local market is big enough to support a sizable industry financed in part by foreigners. But in underdeveloped countries proper, domestic purchasing power is so small that foreign business capital does not find it worth while to come in to work for the home market. If it comes in at all, it comes in to work for the export market, and there is nothing surprising about it.

The extent to which a foreign business enterprise helps to promote a country's development does not depend in any simple fashion, if at all, on whether it works for export or for domestic consumption. Much depends on how far it increases the demand for labour and other local resources, on how much of its profits it reinvests in the country, and on a variety of other factors. Foreign capital is not to be despised just because it works for the export market. Not only does it increase the country's export and import capacity, but also it contributes to the growth, though perhaps only a slow growth, of various external economies—such as labour skills and public works—which cannot fail, sooner or later, to benefit the domestic economy.

True, the nature and usefulness of these external economies may vary a great deal, depending often on technical and accidental features of a particular project or industry. For instance, the pipeline laid down at great expense to pump the oil of Saudi-Arabia to the Mediterranean cannot, as it happens, serve any wider purpose; whereas a railway built to carry copper from the interior of, say, Peru to the sea coast will be suitable for carrying other things as well and will thus directly benefit the country's general development. Undoubtedly Britain's investments for railway building overseas, in the sixty years before 1914, were stimulated by Britain's high and rising demand for wheat, wool, meat and other such products. The railways were often built in the first instance to serve the export trade of the primary producing countries; they radiated from the ports and did not do much to develop communications between different regions in the interior. Still, these railways furnished an essential and very expensive prerequisite to over-all economic development in the ' vast open spaces ' of countries like Canada, the United States, Argentina and Australia.[1] The following contemporary testimonial from an Argentine source is characteristic : ' In the

[1] A. J. Brown, ' Economic Development and World Trade,' *Columbia Journal of International Affairs*, Spring 1950, p. 41.

Argentine the railway is like a magic talisman, for wherever it goes it entirely transforms the economic and productive conditions of the country.'[1]

Foreign investment of the traditional type, extracting primary products for export, is not to be despised. Why is not even this type of investment moving into underdeveloped countries in greater volume ? There is only a small trickle of it now. That foreign business investment does not show much interest in home market production in the truly backward economies we can understand. Why does it not flow then into production for export markets ?

Aside from the obvious political impediments—which alone may be sufficient at present to account for the virtual absence of private investment abroad—perhaps a part of the answer is that the export markets for raw materials and foodstuffs have not been enjoying the same rate of secular expansion as that which came about in the nineteenth century from the extraordinary growth of population as well as productivity in the Western industrial countries, and also from Britain's willingness to sacrifice her own agriculture to the requirements of the international division of labour. The import propensity and import policy of the United States are different from those of Great Britain in the nineteenth century. In the twentieth century, two destructive wars have weakened Western Europe's power to purchase raw materials and foodstuffs from overseas. In recent decades, synthetic substitutes have affected unfavourably the demand for a number of staple products (such as nitrates, raw silk and natural rubber), and this development is continuing. The great raw-material boom which began after the Korean invasion, but which has already lost most of its force, is widely regarded as being due to special and possibly temporary circumstances, and has not, in fact, been accompanied by any appreciable increase in American direct investment in backward countries. It may take more than a boom—it may take something like a secular expansion of demand—to induce private foreign investment in underdeveloped areas for the production of primary commodities for export.

[1] A. B. Martinez and M. Lewandowski, *The Argentine in the Twentieth Century* (London, 1911), Chapter II, p. 108.

These are some of the economic conditions that may explain why even the ' traditional ' type of foreign investment is virtually non-existent to-day.   Our preoccupation with the economic side of the picture should not make us forget, however, that there are other obstacles: legal, cultural, political, as well as economic.

In short, the hopes that have been placed on direct business investment for the financing of economic development abroad are exposed to disappointment for two reasons of a general economic character. First, there is little or no incentive for private business capital to go to work for the expansion of the domestic economies of low-income countries. Secondly, even for the expansion of raw-material supplies for export, private business funds will not want to move out in any steady or sizable flow unless there is confident expectation of a steady and sizable expansion of demand for such commodities. In these circumstances the theory of international investment on private business account is reduced to an attempt to explain, not why capital moves, but why it does not move.

It is worth emphasizing once more that direct business invest-ment has at all events this to be said in its favour that it goes directly into capital formation, even if not into capital formation directly for domestic development. Normally and almost inevit-ably, foreign entrepreneurial investment creates a real addition to the productive capacity of a primary producing country. I stress this because it is not true of all the possible external sources of capital.

The other advantage which is commonly stressed, namely, that direct investment carries with it modern technology and know-how, leaves perhaps some room for debate. It could be argued that improved techniques are likely to be of lasting value only when the people themselves learn how to use them and adapt them to their own needs and conditions. That foreign business establishments have not been eager to impart technical and managerial knowledge to the local population, unless compelled to do so by government regulation, has been a perennial complaint against them in underdeveloped countries. Naturally it does not always pay a foreign-owned business enterprise to invest in the education and technical training of local labour, especially if any labour so trained is not tied to that firm and can at any time go to another employer. When we consider Japan's experience we see that there was practically no direct foreign investment in the early stages. Japan, nevertheless, got the technology and the know-how by hiring foreign technicians and by sending her own people abroad to learn and to observe. Capital and technology are closely related, but this does not mean that they must be jointly supplied. Thus a great deal of technical assistance, under national and international auspices, is now flowing to underdeveloped countries without being connected with movements of capital.

INTERNATIONAL LOANS AND GRANTS

Foreign loans for capital expenditure by public authorities have the advantage that they can be used for domestic economic development in accordance with a coherent over-all programme. Foreign investment of this type is not exposed in the same degree, if at all, to the criticism that it serves primarily the needs of the creditor economy and tends to neglect the domestic economy of the debtor country. We should remember that even in the golden age of private international investment a large proportion took this form.[1] Loans to governmental authorities (central, state and municipal) accounted for over half of French and German foreign investments outstanding in 1914. In the case of Britain, 30 per cent of the total outstanding at that time consisted of government bonds. This does not include private railway securities, which occupied the first place with 40 per cent of the British total, nor does it include investments in other public utilities, which formed an additional 5 per cent. The total is somewhat incomplete and does not take full account of British business investments abroad, but even if allowance were made for this[2] the percentages given would not be significantly lowered. The position in 1930 is similar. British investments in primary producing countries in that year are said to have been ' overwhelmingly the result of the borrowing of public authorities and public utility undertakings,'

[1] See Herbert Feis, *Europe, the World's Banker*, 1870–1914 (New Haven, 1930).
[2] See Eugene Staley, *War and the Private Investor* (New York, 1935), p. 525.

about 70 per cent of long-term British capital employed in such countries being in securities of this type.[1] Evidently not very much remains for the strictly ' colonial ' kind of foreign investment to which the above criticism is mainly intended to apply. Even in Africa, where mining has played a great role in attracting foreign venture capital, 'the large preponderance of investment which has taken place under the aegis of Government ' is one of the outstanding features brought out in Frankel's authoritative study.[2]

In comparing direct foreign investment with foreign loans, it is instructive to consider the contrast between China and Japan. Let us take the position in 1930, the year in which the world total of private international investments outstanding reached its peak. Nearly 80 per cent of foreign capital in China was then in the form of direct business investments.[3] These investments were mostly in the coastal regions, in places like Shanghai, employed more or less directly in the export industries.[4] They played a rather peripheral part in the Chinese economy. In Japan the percentage of direct business investment in total foreign capital was as low as 26 per cent; practically three-quarters of the foreign capital employed in Japan in 1930 was in the form of loans to the government. These loans had come in mainly during the early phases of industrial development, in the years 1895–1914 and even earlier. Thus the Japanese got their foreign capital mostly through government borrowing abroad, and their government was free to use the funds in accordance with the dominant ideas of national economic development.[5] Yet we should note that foreign loans were a relatively minor, not a major, source of capital for the Japanese economy as a whole. Thanks to various domestic measures Japan was able to direct 12 to 17 per cent of her national income into capital formation in that period. For a country whose per capita real income was then certainly lower than, say, the Latin-American average to-day, that was a high saving ratio.

It was not until the 1920's that Japan began to receive any

[1] Royal Institute of International Affairs, *The Problem of International Investment* (London, 1937), p. 19.
[2] S. Herbert Frankel, *Capital Investment in Africa* (London, 1938), pp. 169 and 214.
[3] C. F. Remer, *Foreign Investment in China* (New York, 1933), pp. 68, 86.
[4] *The Problem of International Investment*, op. cit., p. 264–65.
[5] E. P. Reubens, op. cit., p.112.

considerable direct investments from abroad, while government borrowing from abroad virtually ceased. This sequence is interesting. First in the country's development came government investments financed in part by foreign loans; much later, in the 1920's, came direct foreign investments. By that time the market had grown, the public overhead facilities were established, and so the inducement for private entrepreneurial investments had become substantial.

The same sequence can be observed in certain other countries that have attained a substantial degree of development. In Australia, ' all the primary industries (with the exception of the pastoral industry) were developed partly as a result of State action and organized support of some kind. . . The State came in to encourage settlement by building railways, providing irrigation and supplying capital to the settlers.'[1] Foreign borrowing by public authorities, which had been very large and fairly continuous, stopped abruptly in 1930. In that year, external public indebtedness constituted about three-quarters of the total foreign capital employed in Australia.[2] Since then there have been two great waves of direct business investments of private foreign capital in Australia, first in the period 1935-1938, and subsequently in the years after 1945.

Past experience suggests that governmental investment financed by foreign loans can be a suitable method of laying the foundations of a country's economic development in the form of public services and social overhead capital. Nor should we forget investment in agriculture, which in the nature of the case must often be financed by public authorities. Foreign loans may leave the borrowing country free to use these resources in accordance with an over-all development programme, as seems to have been the case with Japan.

But it is nearly always possible to some extent to substitute foreign funds for domestic saving so that the country's con-

---

[1] Douglas B. Copland, as quoted by S. Herbert Frankel, *Capital Investment in Africa* (London, 1938), p. 14.
[2] C. P. Haddon-Cave, ' Some Aspects of Private International Investments with Special Reference to Australia ' (Australian and New Zealand Association for the Advancement of Science. Perth Conference, 1947, mimeographed), p. 9.

sumption is increased and little or no addition is made to the rate of accumulation. This can happen even if each foreign loan is earmarked for a specific productive project. If the inflow of capital is accompanied by a relaxation of domestic saving efforts, there may be no change in the total rate of capital formation. Strong and persistent pressures in this direction are set up nowadays by the disparities in real income and consumption levels. In short, while direct investments run into the market difficulty which formed the subject of our first chapter, it is conceivable that the use of international loans may be subject to the difficulty discussed in the third chapter, namely, the high and rising propensity to consume which is induced in the poorer countries by the great and growing discrepancies in per capita income and consumption levels. Direct business investment, though it may lead to lop-sided development, has at least a solid merit in that it almost inevitably results in a net increase in the amount of real capital situated within the country's boundaries. In the case of 'autonomous' international investment, there is nothing inevitable about it; the increase may be nullified through direct or indirect substitution. The effectiveness of autonomous foreign investment depends essentially on complementary domestic action in the receiving country.

This applies to inter-governmental grants even more than to loans made by either private investors or governments to public authorities in underdeveloped countries. International grants can of course be used for capital formation in the same way as loans. In the case of loans, there is generally some pressure to use them at least for specific productive purposes so that interest and amortization requirements can be met later on. In the case of grants, even this pressure does not exist. Grants can be used directly or indirectly for consumption without any subsequent inconvenience.

This brings us back to the questions with which the last chapter ended. It was the spectre of economic isolation that made us turn to a discussion of international income transfers as a possible alternative. In effect, we seemed to be dealing with a model in which, on the one side, international income disparities open up gaps in the balance of payments and, on the other side, international income transfers come in to fill these gaps.

The first part of this supposition, representing the hypothesis that the attraction of advanced living standards tends to breed international payments disequilibria, is less uncertain than the second; it seems to me quite plausible. The second may turn out to be a mirage. There are forces tending to bring about such transfers, but nothing like an automatic mechanism exists. It is inevitably a matter of international political economy.

Assuming that they are forthcoming, such income transfers fulfil an equilibrating function as far as the balance of payments is concerned. If governmental transfers do not fill the gaps in balances of payments that tend to arise from international income disparities, we can hardly expect private capital movements to fill them. The chronic or recurrent balance-of-payments difficulties are likely, on the contrary, to frighten private funds away or even to make them move in the wrong direction. Although the transfer risks that result from exchange control could perhaps be mitigated through government guarantees, the fact remains that balance-of-payments disequilibria are, under present conditions, an obstacle rather than an inducement to private foreign investment.

But even if we assume that both parts of our hypothetical model are true to life, we must ask what is to happen to capital formation for economic development. International income disparities make for gaps in balances of payments; international income transfers fill them. Foreign aid will undoubtedly help to relieve the ' dollar shortage ', but will it relieve the shortage of capital ? The problem of capital formation may remain completely unsolved. If nature is left to take its course, the gifts received will be used in the poorer countries for the satisfaction of the higher propensity to consume that is brought about by the disparity in real income levels. No permanent basis will be created within these countries for higher living standards in the future.

I am not saying that it is a bad thing in itself. A transfer of consumable resources from the rich to the poor may increase the world total of human happiness. It may be desirable on grounds of welfare economics, though even on this level the system might not be without its drawbacks.[1] All I am saying is that it does not provide an automatic solution to the problem of capital formation in underdeveloped areas.

While a country's capacity to absorb foreign aid for current consumption is presumably unlimited, there exist fairly definite bounds to absorptive capacity if the aid is to be applied to capital formation. They arise from a country's backwardness itself and from the lack of various overhead facilities in the early stages of development. Capital development schemes usually require large movements of people as well as of material goods. In undeveloped countries, mobility is impeded by lack of transport, housing and public facilities of all kinds. For instance, a river valley development may mean that many people have to leave their accustomed occupations and places of residence, that roads have to be built on which to move the people and goods needed in the valley, and that houses must be built for the workers there before work can even begin on the development project itself. All this takes time and presents a real limit, especially in the early stages, to the rate at which foreign aid can be effectively utilized for capital formation.[2] Conditions are not as fluid now as they were in the sparsely settled areas to which the bulk of foreign investment moved in the nineteenth century along with a great migration of people.

Without deliberate efforts to extend the local bottlenecks, any added provision of external resources, even if directed into the investment sector in the first instance, will indirectly spill over into consumption. Again, the point is not that this is bad,

[1] See Jacob Viner's strictures against inter-governmental grants as a permanent institution, in his *International Economics* (Glencoe, Illinois, 1951), pp. 371–72. It is not difficult to see that such an institution might engender unattractive benefactor or mendicant attitudes, and hence possibly embitterment, in international relations.

[2] These points are well stated in a paper by J. J. Polak, ' Projections of the International Sector of Gross National Product,' prepared for the Conference on Research in Income and Wealth, May 1951, to be published in the series of *Studies in Income and Wealth*, National Bureau of Economic Research, New York. It is from considerations such as these that one might guess that 2 per cent of the national income of the United States, which is equal to about 7 per cent of the present total national income of the low-income countries outside the Soviet orbit, would certainly strain and probably exceed their present capacity to absorb outside aid for productive investment.

but that it may fail to contribute to laying the local foundations of durable economic development. America's post-war aid to the Philippines (which in six years absorbed $760 million, apart from a roughly equal sum of U.S. government payments on current account) is sometimes cited in the United States, and I believe with some justification, as an example of such failure.

The bottlenecks that limit a country's absorptive capacity for investment purposes tend to accentuate the general difficulty of ensuring the productive use of external contributions, though conceptually the two points are distinct. The general difficulty arising from the demonstration effect of international income disparities is largely a matter of judgment, and we must leave room here for differences in emphasis. In my own opinion the attraction of advanced living standards can seriously interfere not only with the harnessing of domestic saving potentials but also with the use of external resources for economic development. This attraction, though natural and understandable, makes it more than ever necessary for a low-income country to keep a tight rein on the national propensity to consume. The strength of the demonstration effect in the contemporary world is such that domestic action to this end assumes a basic importance if foreign aid is to be channelled into capital construction. In our theoretical model, at all events, it would seem only too easy for a low-income country to fall into the pattern in which gaps tend to appear in the balance of payments and international loans or grants come in to fill them. In this model the needs of capital development can easily be altogether overlooked.

The earmarking of particular foreign loans or grants to specific investment projects may do something to ensure the productive use of funds, but is not by any means a basic remedy. Only where there is no domestic saving at all to start with can such earmarking be fully effective. It is not otherwise an infallible method of increasing the rate of investment, for it cannot prevent a substitution of external for domestic sources of finance. Under the European Recovery Programme the specific project approach was followed to some extent in the release of counterpart funds for reconstruction and new investment projects. I have heard the following story which, though doubtless quite apocryphal, may serve to illustrate the futility of the specific project method of control. The Austrian government, so the story goes, asked for the release of counterpart funds to reconstruct the Vienna opera. The E.C.A. is said to have replied that this would not be a productive investment and that the release could not be granted for this purpose. Then the Austrian government remembered that it was itself financing the construction of an electric power plant in the mountains. It went back to the E.C.A. and asked for a release of counterpart funds to pay for this piece of construction, to which the E.C.A. agreed. So all that happened was a switch : the wily Austrians, having got the E.C.A. to take over the financing of the power plant, now financed the reconstruction of the opera from their own resources.

The desire of the lending or giving country to tie its aid to specific investment projects is understandable, but this procedure by itself cannot assure the desired effect. There is no substitute for comprehensive planning and budgeting of national resources, as was practised indeed under the European Recovery Programme with the general encouragement of the E.C.A. itself. The planning preferred by the United States was through over-all fiscal and monetary policies rather than physical controls, but planning it was none the less. ' It is one of the ironies of our time that "capitalist" America, the country which supposedly stands for free enterprise, strongly encouraged the European countries in their central planning.'[1] It seemed paradoxical, but was really in accord with the needs of the situation. The European Recovery Programme was first and foremost an investment campaign. Much can be learned from it in regard to the international financing of capital formation, but its main lesson is the vital need for plans and policies designed to make sure that top priority is given for capital formation in the over-all allocation of available resources, domestic as well as external. The American E.C.A. was insistent from the start that American aid should be matched by the greatest possible mobilization of domestic resources in the receiving countries. In fact, under this programme the domestic resources used for capital formation in Western Europe as a

[1] Gottfried Haberler, ' Some Economic Problems of the European Recovery Program,' *American Economic Review*, September 1948, pp. 517–18.

whole were several times greater than the amount of American aid.[1]

THE SIGNIFICANCE OF THE TERMS OF TRADE

The invasion of South Korea in June 1950 caused the question of American aid for economic development to recede somewhat into the background. The defence effort became the primary need. But in place of deliberate aid to the low-income countries, another external source of capital formation came rapidly to the fore : a great improvement in the terms of trade of these countries. A large part of this improvement was lost in the course of 1951 but some of it still remains. It has been estimated that on the basis of raw-material prices ruling at the end of 1950, the primary producing countries would earn in 1951 an extra three or four billion dollars for the same volume of exports as in 1950. In view of the recession of prices in 1951, the extra income realized—account being taken also of the increased prices of industrial goods—was reduced to, say, two billion dollars (i.e., $2,000 million); but this was still a good deal. (If it had meant merely an accumulation of unspendable dollars, it would not have been of much use. But the United States was still able to export a great variety of capital goods, and additional imports of equipment could be obtained from Western Europe where some pockets of unemployed capacity continued to exist in the engineering industries of Western Germany, Belgium and Italy.)

This shift in the terms of trade was equivalent to an international income transfer from the industrial to the primary producing countries. Recent United Nations reports have drawn the world's attention to this method of financing economic development and have placed great emphasis on the resources which better terms of trade can make available for capital formation in the poorer countries of the world. A rise in export prices of these countries increases their export proceeds and makes it possible for them to import larger quantities of capital goods needed for their economic advance. The U.N. study on *Relative Prices of Exports and Imports of Underdeveloped Countries* (1949) estimates that putting the 1947 terms of trade back to the

[1] See Howard S. Ellis, *The Economics of Freedom*, op. cit., pp. 22, 34.

1913 level 'would yield the underdeveloped countries $2,500 million to $3,000 million for economic development through international trade' (p. 17) and goes on to say that 'the sums involved would be in a form which would be readily at hand to import goods for economic development as needed and desired' (p. 18). If, as Colin Clark predicts, the terms of trade of primary producers continue to become better in the future, this will give added resources to the needy countries and might indeed solve the whole problem that concerns us in this book.

The great advantage of this potential source of capital formation is that it gives rise neither to a foreign debt burden nor to the various frictions that may arise from inter-governmental loans and grants. That it is very uneven and haphazard in its incidence must be counted among its disadvantages. From the raw-material boom of 1950–51, India, for instance, derived no net improvement for her terms of trade, whereas Malaya benefited a great deal. The distribution of this possible source of capital is in accordance not with needs, but rather with ability to supply goods in special demand on the world market.

This unevenness in the incidence of better price relations for primary commodities is generally recognized. What is not so generally recognized is that an improvement in the terms of trade does not by any means automatically contribute to an increase in capital formation, either in the field of domestic construction or even in the specific form of increased imports of capital goods from abroad. There is a widespread tendency to assume that if only the terms of trade could be moved in favour of the low-income countries this would take care of financing economic development. This assumption is questionable.

The increase in a country's export proceeds due to higher export prices enters into and expands the flow of money income in the country. Although part of the extra income may be saved, some of it, and probably the great bulk of it, will lead to increased consumer spending on both domestic and imported goods. Since we are considering an agricultural country with supply conditions generally inelastic in the short run, the increased consumer expenditure on domestic goods is likely to push prices upward, which will accentuate the tendency for imports to rise.

There is nothing in this process to guarantee that the whole or even a sizable part of the additional imports will consist of capital goods. An improvement in the terms of trade makes more foreign exchange available, but if nothing is done it affects the domestic income flow and leads to increased consumer spending on both home produced and imported goods. It is not an automatic source of capital formation.

If the additional import capacity is to be reserved in full for capital goods, then the whole of the increase in income that results from the rise in export prices must be channelled into new saving. If the increase in saving does not come voluntarily—and the forces discussed make it very unlikely that it will—this requires very definite and deliberate action by the fiscal and monetary authorities. It is odd that this little matter of extracting the saving out of the enlarged income stream should so often have been overlooked by those who stress the importance of improved terms of trade for the financing of capital development. If the increase in export proceeds is to bring about a corresponding growth in the volume of imports of capital goods, the increment in income resulting from the greater value of exports must be saved. This saving, if it does not come voluntarily, may have to be extracted through taxation.

Taxation for this purpose may be of two kinds, special or general. By ' special ' I mean a system whereby export products are bought by a government agency from the producers at a fixed price and sold abroad at a profit. New Zealand started a system of this sort in 1936; at the present time a more notable example is Argentina. This amounts to a tax falling on the producers of export commodities. It can indeed openly take the form of a variable export tax designed to leave the price actually realized by the domestic producer more or less constant. It is a very effective method but, in my opinion, rather unfair. Why penalize particularly the producers of export commodities ? The supply of these commodities may remain unchanged in the short run, but before very long the producers are likely to turn away to other lines of production. Serious damage may thus be inflicted upon a country's most efficient source of foreign exchange.

The alternative is general taxation. In this case the increment in export proceeds is matched immediately, or as soon as practicable, by an increase in government taxes and in government tax revenue. The additional taxation can be imposed according to the principle of ability to pay. As a result some people's disposable income may be cut down while that of others, including perhaps the producers of the export crops, may increase. It would depend on general standards of fiscal fairness. In any event the increase in foreign-exchange receipts is thus offset by compulsory saving. Only in this way can two things be prevented : inflation in the domestic economy and dissipation of the increased export proceeds on imports of goods for current consumption. Only in this way does the increase in export proceeds become fully available for imports of capital goods, or alternatively for increasing the country's gold or foreign exchange reserve as a precautionary counter-cyclical measure.

We are not here concerned with this policy as a counter-cyclical device, but rather as a device for mobilizing a potential source of capital formation. In either case the distinction between money of direct action and money of indirect action, which Eugenio Gudin stresses in his *Principles of Monetary Economics*,[1] is relevant here. With private movements of short-term funds, neutralization as practised by the exchange equalization funds in the 1930's—essentially a form of open-market policy—is appropriate and sufficient, involving merely a transfer of idle cash balances (money of indirect action). But with an increase in export proceeds neutralization of this type is not enough. Here we have to act not simply on the quantity of money or credit, but directly on the domestic income flow in the way just indicated.

Questions of commercial policy are reserved for separate treatment. I should at once, however, state my view that in this situation the imposition of new import restrictions designed to prevent the increase in imports for personal consumption, is not in general a true and effective solution. It is the domestic income circulation that must be acted upon. An increase in imports of capital goods constitutes an act of investment, which calls for a corresponding act of saving out of the income currently received.

[1] *Principios de Economia Monetaria*, Vol. II (Rio de Janeiro, 1952), pp. 42 ff.

Now let us assume that the increase in saving is all extracted through taxation. The increase in tax revenue then represents the new act of saving required.[1] This additional taxation has the effect of making the increment in export proceeds available for imports of investment goods (or alternatively for increasing the country's reserve of gold or foreign exchange). We may note that this compulsory saving does not release any domestic factors for domestic investment expenditure. All it ' releases ' is the increment in export proceeds due to the rise in export prices. If even a part of the additional tax revenue were to be spent on domestic factors for investment at home, inflation would result, leading to an increase in imports of consumption goods and draining off the foreign exchange that comes in from the additional export proceeds. With a given labour force and unchanged productivity an increase in domestic capital outlay is possible without inflationary effects only if other domestic expenditures are correspondingly reduced; that is, if consumer spending on domestic goods and services is reduced below the level that existed prior to the rise in export prices. One way of securing such a reduction in consumer spending is a lowering of import restrictions, leading to a diversion of expenditure from domestic to imported goods, thus making room for an increase in domestic investment expenditure. It is conceivable that an increased flow of imported consumer goods can in this way release domestic factors for domestic capital production.

Along these lines the analysis could be pursued in further detail. The general conclusion, however, is clear. An improvement in the terms of trade will make no significant contribution to capital formation unless the increment in export proceeds, and hence in people's income, is directed into saving, voluntary or involuntary. If this is not done, what will happen ? Little was done in this direction in the great raw material boom of 1950-51, and we saw what happened. The increase in export prices leads

---

[1] Again it should be noticed that compulsory saving through government taxation does not imply that the government must take charge of the investment side as well. The investment activity can be left entirely in private hands. It can be financed apparently by the banking system, but in the last analysis what permits it to be thus financed without inflationary effects is the compulsory saving imposed through taxation. In the present case investment takes the form of imports of capital goods, but the general principle remains the same.

to higher domestic money incomes and expenditures. With full employment to start with, and domestic supply in an agricultural economy being inelastic in any case, the result is inflation of the general level of prices. A great increase occurs in the demand for imports, partly as a direct result of the increased money income and partly because of the rise in domestic as compared with import prices. The resulting increase in imports of consumption goods constitutes a leakage of purchasing power and relieves to some extent the domestic inflationary pressure. At the same time it swallows up the additional exchange receipts. I can see no significant contribution to capital formation in this process. It may be that the accompanying inflation is of such a character as to produce a certain amount of forced saving through shifts in income distribution. But inflation can always be had, even without an improvement in the terms of trade.

Suppose this process gets under way, and no attempt is made to make use of the better terms of trade as a source of capital. But now suppose that the government becomes inflation-conscious and wants to curb the inflation which has started as an automatic by-product of the rise in export prices. There are two ways in which it can try to curb the inflation : increased taxation or reduced government expenditure. Some governments tried the first while others stressed the second in the commodity boom of 1950–51. From the point of view of inflation control, both methods seem equally good. They both work at least in the same direction. In their effects on capital formation, however, they are widely different.

The first method, increased taxation, leads belatedly to the right path which we have outlined for the purpose of capital formation. It tends to assure, or can be made to assure, that a higher proportion of the extra resources made available by the change in the terms of trade is withheld from consumption and directed into investment.

The other method of curbing inflation is a drastic reduction in government expenditure. Now if this affects public works and other developmental projects, it means that the government is making room for more consumer spending by cutting down its own spending on investment and basic services. As an anti-inflation policy it is just as good as increased taxation; but on the development front it signifies retreat.

This chain of events could be illustrated from recent experience, but the conclusion is all that matters. We see that an improvement in the terms of trade, instead of leading to an increase in capital formation, can actually lead to a reduction in the country's investment activity. This is not as strange as it may look. It is obvious that in an inflationary situation a reduction in governmental investment expenditure, just as in private investment expenditure, is an effective way of reducing the inflationary pressure. But if capital accumulation is regarded as important for the nation's progress, a better way is to check consumption expenditure through increased saving, enforced if necessary by fiscal policy.

In taking advantage of an improvement in the terms of trade, just as in mobilizing disguised unemployment or using labour released through advances in farming methods, there is, by and large, no need to cut down private consumption. It is essentially a matter of directing an increment in the country's income into capital investment, and of preventing consumption from rising at once. No hardship is involved except that of forgoing an immediate rise in the level of living in favour of a greater permanent increase in the future. But this, of course, is a hardship inherent in the very nature of capital formation.

Chapter V

COMMERCIAL POLICY AND CAPITAL FORMATION

WHAT can commercial policy do to promote the accumulation of capital in underdeveloped countries ? Can import restrictions help by increasing the incentive to invest ? How, if at all, can the supply of capital be enlarged through foreign trade ? Can capital formation be increased by restricting imports of consumer goods ? These are the questions to be taken up in the following pages.

In pure theory the two subjects—commercial policy and capital formation—may not seem to have anything in common, In the world of practical affairs we often find them linked together, although the exact nature of the connection sometimes remains obscure. The one form in which the connection has been extensively discussed in the past is the 'infant industry' argument for tariff protection. I would like to begin by confronting, very briefly, this argument with the problem of capital formation in underdeveloped areas.

Infant Protection and Infant Creation

The theory of tariff protection for infant industries has been associated with nationalist movements and aspirations. Alexander Hamilton and Friedrich List can certainly be called economic nationalists. The situation is somewhat paradoxical in view of the fact that this is the only argument for import restrictions that can be held even from a cosmopolitan point of view, on the grounds of world benefit. If it is true that a temporary interference with the freedom of trade can develop new skills and aptitudes, and bring dormant resources into active use so that production of goods and services is greatly expanded, there is a distinct possibility of ultimate gain for all countries.

If protection, however, were all that is needed for economic development the problem would be very simple. Indeed, one would have to be surprised that the problem is not much nearer to its solution, since there has been no lack of tariff protection in underdeveloped countries. This does not prove that the argument is wrong, but it does suggest that tariff protection alone is an ineffective means of promoting economic growth.

Why is it ineffective ? Because infant industry protection overlooks the problem of capital supply. This is the task of creation, of finding the sources, open or concealed, available for accumulation, and of devising the ways and means of moulding them into productive forms. Infant creation must take precedence over infant protection. In industrial as in human life the most perfect arrangements for the protection of infants will not guarantee that infants actually come into existence. For this certain steps of prior importance are required. Tariff protection of infant industries has failed because it has done little or nothing to create the capital needed for industrial development.

How could infant protection be expected to contribute to capital formation at all ? One might think that even if it could do nothing directly to increase the supply of capital, it could at least make a contribution on the demand side by increasing the incentive to invest in domestic industry. Undoubtedly an important underlying motive for tariff protection has been the desire to preserve the domestic market, small as it may be, for domestic investment and so at least partly to overcome the weakness of investment incentives. It is highly questionable, however, whether this alone can release a process of ' balanced growth ' in the domestic economy. Without such over-all growth, the inducement to invest in a certain protected industry is not likely to endure beyond the point at which imports have been replaced. At that point the expansion of that industry may come to a stop, so that little, if anything, will have been achieved. This limitation of tariff protection has been observed, for example, in India in some particular industries (such as cotton cloth and sugar).

But even if we accept any contribution that infant protection can make on the demand side of the capital problem, an increase in the rate of accumulation is nevertheless not certain. Who is to supply the capital required ? The increase in profit prospects, by itself, may not increase the flow of domestic voluntary saving in an underdeveloped country. The domestic capital supply may remain unaffected by the rise in the inducement to invest caused by tariff protection. It has been customary in economic theory to treat the rate of personal saving as independent of, and irrespon- sive to, the rate of return from capital. An increase in the rate of return, while it may induce some people to save more, will lead others, those who save for a given future income from capital, to save less.

It is more likely that the rise in the inducement to invest in the protected industries will lead to credit expansion for the establishment of these industries and hence perhaps to a flow of forced saving resulting from inflation. This possibility is doubtless important in practice. But forced saving through inflation, if it can be had at all, can be had even without tariff protection. It can be brought about, for instance, by government outlays financed by monetary expansion.

Another possible effect of the restriction of imports is that foreign capital will respond to the increased inducement and will come in to set up ' tariff factories ' producing for the domestic market. In fact, however, private business capital in the past has not moved in large volume to low-income countries for the purpose of producing for the domestic market. This may have been due to many reasons but the underlying obstacle has generally been the limited size of the existing market in these countries. As a means of giving foreign capital a greater inducement to come in, tariff protection does not help much because there is not much of a market to protect. It is of little or no use as an incentive for foreign business investment unless a substantial domestic market is already in existence. To put it bluntly : tariff protection, if it can help at all, can only help the strong—it cannot help the weak.

Here is an example to illustrate this proposition. Of the total American business investments outstanding abroad, Canada has about 30 per cent. More than half of the investment in Canada is in manufacturing and distribution. Apparently American capital finds it profitable to work in Canada for the local market. That is because the country is highly productive and prosperous. It may be to some extent because of the Canadian tariff; it is probably impossible to find out exactly to what extent. But this much I think we can say : the Canadian tariff alone would have made very little difference as an inducement to foreign capital if the Canadian people had been miserably poor.

It is sometimes said that the imperial preference system set up in 1932 gave American business firms an incentive to establish factories in Canada, to produce for the United Kingdom and British Commonwealth markets. If this were an important factor, it would show up in the composition of Canadian exports; actually it does not do so in any significant measure: Canadian exports have continued to be mainly foodstuffs and raw materials.

American business investments in manufacturing industries in Canada seem to work largely for the Canadian market. In low-income countries they concentrate on production for export, in spite of the tariff protection enjoyed by domestic markets. Abstracting from all political difficulties, it seems doubtful whether even a super-tariff would be capable of attracting much foreign business capital to work for the domestic market in a country like China. A country like Brazil is probably in an intermediate position and may well be able to induce some capital imports through restrictions on commodity imports. For underdeveloped countries as a whole, however, the figures shown in the last chapter do not suggest that import restrictions have so far had much effect in this respect.

So we see that, even on the demand side of the problem of capital formation, the contribution which import restriction can make, by stimulating the incentive to invest, is of doubtful efficiency in attracting an increased supply of capital. It is conceivable that domestic saving is increased in response to the rise in the prospective rate of return, but it is not likely on general grounds, and particularly unlikely in poor countries that live fairly close to the subsistence level. It can happen that tariff protection sets into motion the inflationary process of forced saving, but this is a particularly painful and objectionable method of infant creation. It is possible that foreign business capital comes in because the tariff protection may at least reduce the discouraging effect of the small size of the local market, but it appears that the inducement has been relatively ineffective. Foreign capital has gone to underdeveloped countries to work for export rather than for domestic markets.

Some people take the view that tariff protection could bring about an increase in the real national income directly, in the case where surplus agricultural labour is absorbed in a new industry protected by a tariff. The productivity of the labour transferred to that industry was very low before, and is now much higher. The result of tariff protection, according to this reasoning, is a clear increase in national product.

This argument is subject to three reservations. First, from the apparent increase in national product we have to deduct the loss in real income which is suffered by the consumers of the product because of the higher price they have to pay. (If, as is possible, this deduction is even greater than the gain in productivity of the labour transferred, then the industry is clearly uneconomic and results in a net loss in real national income.)

Secondly, the deduction on this account, representing both a subsidy to the protected industry and a tax on the people who happen to be consumers of the product, is greater than it needs to be. Financing the subsidy in this way creates an excess burden compared with financing it from general taxation in accordance with ability to pay, which would eliminate the need for tariff protection and replace it by a direct subsidy.

The third point is the most important and also the most obvious. Even if the net change after applying the deduction turns out to be positive, we cannot credit this increment in national product to tariff protection. It must be credited to the capital embodied in the new protected industry. It is the application of capital, not tariff protection, that increases real national income. Protection as such tends rather to reduce real income and must be counted as a negative offset to the output increment that results from the use of capital. The infant industry argument rests on the hope that the initial comparative disadvantage from which the industry suffers, and because of which it needs protection, can be overcome in the course of time so that this negative offset eventually disappears.

But where has the capital come from, the capital now embodied in the protected industry ? That is what we have to ask when we look back, draw up the accounts, so to speak, and try to explain what has happened. Looking forward, if we should contemplate adopting such a policy, again the question is, where is the capital to come from ? Protection by itself does not provide it. In nearly all statements of the infant industry case it seems to be tacitly assumed that capital is available for setting up the new protected industry. In the low-income countries at the present time the availability of capital cannot be so taken for granted. Perhaps it could be taken for granted in some of the countries which, in the past, practised infant industry protection in a big way and with success : countries like the United States and Australia, which received a great inflow of both capital and labour from Europe. In these countries, and under these conditions, infant industry protection was probably a quite effective policy. Under the entirely different conditions that face the economically backward areas to-day, tariff protection alone is probably of little or no use. From the point of view of capital formation, it seems a completely secondary matter.

I hope I will not be misunderstood. I am not opposed to infant protection. I am only directing attention to the prior need for infant creation.

Effects of Import Restrictions on Money Income and Saving

The major point now to be examined is of a different order. We shall abstract completely from international capital movements and assume that there is no foreign aid or foreign investment. We want to consider how, if at all, a country's stock of capital equipment can be increased by way of foreign trade and what, if anything, commercial policy can do for this purpose. The infant protection argument is mainly concerned with incentives to invest, that is, with the demand side of the capital problem. Here we revert, in the main, to the supply side.

Foreign trade is a means of obtaining capital goods from the advanced countries, and it is tempting to suppose that by restricting imports of consumption goods a country can increase its imports of investment goods. For an undeveloped country the possibility of acquiring machinery and equipment by means of international exchange is one of the great benefits of trade. It was a great advantage for Russia in the early stages of her industrialization, especially in the 1930's when she imported much modern equipment in exchange for her exports of primary products. Great Britain, when she was the first in the field of industrial development, did not have this advantage. She had to start by developing her own capital-goods production almost from scratch. Russia was able to import capital goods in exchange for her exports, but not without an act of saving.

The importation of capital equipment into any country necessarily presupposes an act of saving in that country. It may be merely ' retained ' saving, in the form of depreciation and obsolescence allowances, if the equipment is imported for replacement purposes. It requires new saving if the equipment is imported as an addition to existing plant and machinery.

In an all-inclusive view, a country that is importing capital equipment is *ipso facto* saving, in that it is abstaining from the enjoyment of the consumer goods it could have imported in place of the capital goods brought in, or else abstaining from the consumption of the goods that it now exports in order to pay for the imported equipment.

In a completely planned economy there is perhaps nothing more to say. The state decides to impose more saving on the people, the state invests this saving in imports of capital goods. Saving and investment can become indistinguishable, merged in a single act of state.

In an individual exchange economy at least partly based on price, profit and income incentives operating in a monetary system, there is more to be said on the matter. This is the case that applies to underdeveloped countries outside the Soviet orbit (and perhaps even to some within). For these countries it may not be proper to suppose that it is a simple matter for the state to change the composition of imports, increasing imports of investment goods and slashing those of consumption goods, as if that were all there is to it.

Even in countries still largely based on price and income incentives, it is true that the state has tended to assume a greater degree of conscious direction of the process of capital formation and is beginning to take a more active interest in the share of national income going into investment. It is possible that even in an economy mostly run by private business the choice between national consumption and national saving may become more and more a state decision.

Is a decision of this sort being taken when the government decrees a restriction of imports for current consumption and allows more imports of investment goods to enter instead ? There is certainly a widespread notion that, by cutting down imports of consumption goods through direct controls or prohibitive duties, a country can make more real capital available for its economic development in the form of imports of capital goods. Governments seem to be firmly convinced that they are promoting the accumulation of capital whenever, in their commercial policy, they banish consumable imports in favour of imports of machinery and equipment. And so this type of commercial policy—the policy of what we may call ' luxury import restrictions '—is very common in underdeveloped countries to-day.

In order to isolate as clearly as possible the effect of import restrictions of this sort, it is best to use as our starting-point a position of equilibrium in which imports are equal to exports and national income is at a level corresponding to full employment without inflation. Restrictions are imposed on imports of consumption goods, especially goods of a so-called luxury or semi-luxury character, with the object of making room for a greater volume of imports of capital goods. Unessential complications concerning, for instance, customs revenues or quota profits can be left aside by assuming that these restrictions consist of absolute import prohibitions imposed on certain specified commodities not produced at home. The country's export proceeds are assumed to remain unchanged, or at any rate are taken to be outside the country's control.

Imports of consumption goods are reduced and imports of investment goods can now be increased. This is only the beginning of the story. What happens to the domestic flow of money income and to the balance between saving and investment ? It all depends on what people do with that part of their income which they previously spent on imported consumption goods. Let us make two different assumptions and watch the consequences.

In the first place, suppose that people save all this part of their income. They cannot get the foreign commodities, nor think of anything else on which to spend money, so they save all of it. Call it forced saving if you like, but the saving is real enough. Though this may be an unlikely case, it is none the less a possible assumption. The increase in the flow of investment goods imported will be matched by an increase in the flow of domestic income saved. Domestic monetary equilibrium remains undisturbed. (If we think of ' leakages ' in terms of the multiplier analysis, an artificial reduction in the leakage of income spent on imports is exactly offset by an increase in the leakage of income into domestic saving.) The increased imports of investment goods will represent a genuine addition to the rate of capital formation.

In the second place, however, it is equally possible to assume that what can no longer be spent on imported consumer goods is spent entirely on domestic consumer goods and services. We now suppose, in other words, that import restrictions lead, not to any change in the volume of consumers' expenditure, but to a complete switch in the flow of spending from imports to domestic commodities. It is true that imports of investment goods can here again be increased, since export proceeds remain the same and less is spent on imports of consumer goods. The country's foreign-exchange account, considered by itself, seems to leave room now for more capital formation in the shape of imported equipment. But in terms of local currency the purchase of this equipment is likely to require financing through domestic credit expansion.

The crucial point about this case is that the people of the country have not voluntarily consented to any reduction in their consumption. They will seek to make up for the reduction in their imports by an increase in their expenditure on domestic goods and services. The result is a disruption of monetary equilibrium—an inflationary pressure on money costs and prices. When the escape valve of consumable imports is shut off, the pressure of the steam in the system increases; demand becomes excessive in relation to domestic supply and tends to push up the level of prices.

So much for the monetary aspect. What happens to the real volume of capital formation ? Imports of investment goods have been increased, but that is not all. It is likely that domestic investment activities will suffer from the increased consumer expenditure in the home market. Even in a poor country some factors of production are always engaged on capital production if not for new investment, at any rate for replacement and maintenance. Imports of capital goods represent usually the lesser part—something like one third perhaps, or even less—of the accumulation of capital in an underdeveloped country. The greater part consists of things that cannot enter into international trade, such as roads, buildings, public works and land improvements. The increase in consumer expenditure will tend to bid factors of production away from domestic investment and maintenance and will draw them into activities catering for current consumption. Domestic capital production will have to make room for the increased domestic consumer spending. Consumers have not agreed to any cut in their total consumption, and their expenditure forces instead a cut in the resources devoted to the maintenance or expansion of domestic real capital. In this way the increase in imports of investment goods tends to be offset by reduced domestic investment activities, or actually by domestic disinvestment caused by failure to maintain and replace capital as it wears out. So long as there is no increase in saving, there can be no increase in total net capital formation.

An increase in saving can come about in the present case only in the form of forced saving resulting from inflation. The effect of inflation is unpredictable *a priori*, depending as it does on the speed and other characteristics of the rise of prices, and on the psychological attitude of the public. We can merely point to some general possibilities. If the pace of inflation is moderate, there is a fair chance of some forced saving being imposed on the community through the lag of wages and salaries and through the shift of income distribution in favour of the wealthy (if the marginal saving ratio of the wealthy is higher than that of the poor). Here we do have a possible new source of real saving to finance the increase in real investment that occurs in the form of larger imports of capital goods as a result of import restrictions on consumption goods. Unfortunately, it is not only a socially painful but also an unstable and unreliable source. A general rise in prices may, after a while, lead to a reduced willingness to save in monetary form. No one will want to hold money as a store of value or to direct his saving into assets expressed in monetary terms. Saving, if it occurs at all, may immediately seek real forms such as residential construction, and will to this extent not be available for the financing of the additional imports of equipment. Inflation is apt to lead to misdirection of resources; not formally, perhaps, to a decline in total investment, but probably to malinvestment. Moreover, inflation can have a bad effect on capital formation when it leads to failure to replace inventories and fixed equipment through insufficient provision being made for actual replacement costs.

We have so far discussed each of the two extreme assumptions in turn. In actual fact the result is more likely to be a mixture of the two cases, where the money income previously spent on imports will partly be saved and partly spent on domestic goods and services. The inflation in this mixed case may be quite mild. The nature of the result will depend largely on the proportion in which the money flow hit by the new import barriers is divided between the two uses, saving and domestic spending. What can be said about the forces that influence this proportion?

The first point is that import restrictions on luxury goods are not unlikely, on the whole, to induce some new saving. The alternative to luxury expenditure is often just leaving the money unused.

Secondly, much depends on the composition of a country's imports. If practically all the non-essential consumer goods that enter into a country's consumption are imported, then the government, by imposing restrictions on a wide range of such imports, can perhaps enforce a substantially increased rate of saving.

In the third place, if import restrictions are announced as a temporary measure, or if it is widely believed that they will sooner or later come to an end, then consumers may be willing to accumulate their pent-up demand in the form of temporary saving. They will postpone their expenditure on imports. Spending will be deferred, but not permanently forgone. This is a temporary kind of saving which cannot be relied upon for the financing of capital development. It represents 'saving up' for future expenditure. It is apt to be followed by dissaving. If hope for a lifting of the import restrictions fades away, it may come to seek an outlet in domestic objects of consumer expenditure.

This leads to a general point. The proportion of saving is likely to decline in the course of time. Consumers will gradually readjust their spending pattern, which is never fixed, except possibly in the short run. In the longer run, the pattern will change, and domestic spending will increase to take the place of the spending previously directed to imports. Thus the proportion that is saved out of the income previously spent on imports is likely to fall as time goes on and people adjust their consumption habits.

The conclusion from all this is not entirely certain; it depends on varying circumstances. In any event some points of principle now stand out clearly. For the government to impose its decision in regard to investment and consumption in the composition of imports alone is of little or no use. Any such decision to increase the share of capital goods in this sector may be offset by opposite shifts in the domestic sector. The simple idea that more capital can be got for the country merely by pinching and twisting the foreign trade sector of the economy is, in my opinion, an instance of the fallacy of misplaced concreteness.

When we realize how the foreign trade sector enters into the circular flow of income, it becomes immediately evident that every piece of capital equipment imported represents an act of investment which, in the absence of external financing, calls for a corresponding act of saving at home. If this act of saving is not forthcoming, we have seen that the capital equipment imported may be offset by reduced investment or by disinvestment in the domestic economy, if the expenditure of money previously spent on consumable imports now draws away domestic factors from capital construction or maintenance. Only if this money is left unspent is the necessary saving generated quasi-automatically; this is in some degree possible, but is not likely to create anything like the whole amount of the necessary saving.

The real problem is not just to extract more capital goods from foreign trade, but to extract more saving out of the national income. It is only with a complementary domestic policy of voluntary or compulsory saving, in which public finance must probably play a vital part, that luxury import restrictions can make a fully effective net contribution to the supply of capital in the form of imported equipment. And even then the contribution will be attributable more properly to the increased saving than to the import restrictions as such.

In the absence of such a policy, any net investment that may result from the increased imports of capital goods is likely to be financed mostly through the forced and haphazard levy imposed by inflation, as long as inflation has not yet passed the point where it ceases to be effective as an instrument of forced saving. We cannot therefore deny the possibility that, even without a deliberate complementary policy of domestic saving, luxury import restrictions can lead, through the channels outlined, to some increase in the rate of capital formation in an underdeveloped country.

EFFECTS ON THE PATTERN OF INVESTMENT

Besides the quantity of investment, however, there is also a question of quality. In order to isolate some of the effects of import restrictions on money income and saving, we have ignored up to now their protective effect. This we must now take into account.[1]

The restrictions we have discussed affect the luxury or semi-luxury type of goods. They are often justified on the ground that the country's export earnings should not be wasted on goods of this kind, but should rather be used for the purchase of machines and equipment. But unless these restrictions are accompanied by corresponding restrictions—duties, licences or prohibitions—on the domestic production of these goods, there will be nothing to prevent domestic resources from being ' wasted ' on luxury consumption.

Import restrictions unaccompanied, as they generally are, by domestic restrictions will set up a special inducement to invest in domestic industries producing the goods—or substitutes for the goods—that can no longer be imported. If the domestic market is considered at all sufficient to warrant the establishment of such industries, the inducement will prove effective. We must note,

---

[1] Discussions with Professor Alexander Kafka have been very helpful to me in this context.

however, that the inducement will not operate fully, if at all, unless the restrictions are expected to be permanent. The factor that maximizes the incentive to invest is therefore precisely the one that tends, as we saw, to minimize people's propensity to save that part of their income which they previously spent on imports. This makes it all the more likely that the investment will call for credit expansion.

Thus again the engine of inflation goes to work trying to grind out the forced saving required, not merely to finance the investment in increased imports of capital goods, but now also to release the domestic resources needed for the construction of the new protected industries. The type of industry to be constructed is here determined by the type of imports against which the restrictions are directed. Since these are goods of a luxury or semi-luxury character, the result will be that the country's capital supplies, scarce as they are, and painfully brought into existence, will be sucked into relatively unessential uses. At the same time, the basic overhead capital facilities may not be able to attract or hold the productive factors they need and may actually suffer decay, for reasons indicated earlier.

Latin America is one of the areas to which this picture seems to apply. In a number of Latin American republics the rate of internal capital formation is far from negligible.[1] But some notice should be taken of the content as well as the size of the total volume of investment. Under the influence of inflation and luxury import restrictions, both of which are very common in Latin America, investment has tended in recent years to concentrate on residential construction, largely for the upper income groups, and on luxury industries, while essential public installations such as railways and ports have in some cases tended to fall into disrepair. It cannot be denied that economic development is going on, but it is taking a needlessly painful and contorted form.

THE RATIONALE OF LUXURY IMPORT RESTRICTIONS

A general interpretation of the ' luxury import restrictionism ' so prevalent to-day suggests itself in the light of the hypothesis

[1] A table on p. 76 of the United Nations report on *Measures for the Economic Development of Under-Developed Countries* (op. cit.) suggests that in Latin America as a whole the average saving ratio was about 8 per cent of national income in 1949.

set up in Chapter III, concerning the international income disparities and their effects on the balance of payments and on the domestic saving capacity of low-income countries. The bars to the entry of ' advanced ' consumer goods can be viewed as a defence measure against these unfavourable effects, intended both to suppress the disequilibrium in the balance of payments and, what is more important, to offset the deleterious effect of foreign consumption patterns upon domestic capital formation. The luxury import restrictions of the underdeveloped countries in the world to-day seem to represent, in the last analysis, a desperate effort to offset the handicap which the ' demonstration effect ' imposes on the poorer nations; an effort to isolate the local consumption pattern from that of the advanced countries and so to make possible more domestic saving and capital formation.

This effort deserves our sympathy. The attraction of advanced living standards is an obstacle to the late-comers in economic development. No attempt to overcome this obstacle should be lightly condemned.

The method of import restriction, however, attacks only the surface of the problem. It attacks only that part of the propensity to consume which directly involves expenditure on imported goods. The demonstration effect tends, however, to operate through an upward shift in the general consumption function and not in the import consumption function alone. Luxury import restrictionism does not stop this pervasive indirect influence of international discrepancies in consumption levels.

A more basic attack, in my opinion, would be compulsory saving through public finance. But this is precisely one of the things that is made politically more difficult in the poorer countries by the enormous disparities in living standards. Commercial policy is easier. Commercial policy always appears as the easy way of doing things. When it is a matter of stimulating employment in an industrial economy, shutting off imports is a very simple method. When the problem is to collect taxes for the government, revenue tariffs are not difficult to establish, and have been very popular in the less developed countries in the past. When protection is wanted for infant industries, restricting imports is again easier than raising funds with which to pay direct subsidies to the protected industries. Commercial policy is the line of least resistance in all these cases, not the most effective or equitable line.

Similarly, commercial policy is easier than keeping domestic consumer demand in check by measures of, say, fiscal policy, but it does not go to the root of the problem. It is perhaps the best that can be done; the root of the problem may be insoluble.

To summarize: luxury import restrictionism can be interpreted as a way in which the authorities in underdeveloped countries try to put spikes in the way of the great attraction which advanced consumption patterns exercise upon their nationals. The spikes are at least partly effective in keeping consumption goods out and allowing more investment goods to come in. But let us not be dazzled by the sight of more machines being landed in the ports. The crucial question to ask is whether the spikes erected against luxury imports result in a net increase in saving. If the answer is in the negative, an increase in capital formation is not possible. And even should the answer be in the affirmative, it would still be necessary to keep in mind the possible misdirection of the country's supply of capital.

CHAPTER VI

RECENT TRENDS IN THE THEORY OF INTERNATIONAL CAPITAL MOVEMENTS

IT might reasonably be supposed that the problems of capital formation in undeveloped areas could best be approached through the theory of international investment. Although we find that this theory, in its conventional forms, does not throw much light on the particular matters that have concerned us so far, a brief review of it will none the less be useful for rounding off some of the preceding discussion.

CLASSICAL AND NEO-CLASSICAL THEORY

Economic theory tends inevitably to lag behind the actual course of events. But in the field of international capital movements this lag has been unusually great. The theory of capital movements received its fullest treatment after the long era of large-scale private foreign investment came to an end in the late 1920's. Since then, there has been little or no migration of private capital for productive investment across national frontiers. Yet the theory has been and continues to be quite a live subject of discussion. ' John Brown's body lies a-moulding in the grave, but his soul goes marching on.'

In the case of international capital movements, the lag between fact and theory has a special reason. The international immobility of the factors of production (labour and capital) was one of the central assumptions upon which the classical theory of international trade, especially in Ricardo's version of the comparative cost doctrine, was built up. Why this assumption was regarded as necessary is a question that need not detain us. At all events it formed an essential basis for the position which Ricardo took : that the rule which regulates the value of commodities in international trade is not the same as in domestic trade. It was from this position that he was led to enunciate the principle of *comparative* costs for the case of international trade.

In the century during which international capital movements were extremely active there developed, therefore, no capital-movement theory worthy of the name, except in regard to the transfer mechanism. In the theory of the transfer mechanism, capital movements were treated as merely one of many possible disturbing factors in the balance of payments, entirely on a par with such fortuitous events as crop failures or changes in the direction of consumers' demand. Even so, capital movements did not lead a very conspicuous existence. For instance, when John Stuart Mill discusses the transfer mechanism, he does not discuss a transfer of productive capital; he takes as his example the payment of a tribute from one country to another. Evidently he feels that it would be awkward to talk openly about international movements of investment capital, since with him, and with even later writers, the theory of international values is still based on the assumption that factors of production, including capital, do not and cannot move from one country to another. This is an extraordinary situation in a century during which capital as well as people moved from Europe to other continents on a large scale.[1]

It was Bertil Ohlin who, virtually for the first time, attempted systematically to incorporate the movement of labour and capital into the theory of international economics. Quite apart from his treatment of transfer theory, he investigated the relations between international trade and movements of factors of production, and between the movements of different kinds of factors. But by the time his work came out,[2] the classical assumption of international immobility of productive factors had become almost perfectly valid in fact. The theory which at last emerged was appropriate to a world that had just disappeared.

In his transfer theory Ohlin revived and reinforced earlier approaches by emphasizing the direct equilibrating effect of the shift in buying power from the lending to the borrowing country, which appeared to make both gold movements and price changes

---

[1] John H. Williams's comment in his well-known article of 1929 is worth recalling: 'Even to-day, in most treatments of international trade theory. capital movements are discussed mainly in connection with the balancing of payments, being limited to their currency ('purchasing power' or 'substitutes for gold flow ') functions in connection with trade adjustment mechanism, and are not discussed as transfers of productive power; and international movements of labour are scarcely discussed at all.' (' The Theory of International Trade Reconsidered,' *Readings in the Theory of International Trade*, op. cit., p. 255).
[2] *Interregional and International Trade* (Cambridge, Mass., 1933)

unnecessary in the process of capital transfer. If the lenders relinquished precisely the commodities or groups of commodities for which the borrowers' demand increased as a result of the loan, then there was clearly no need for prices or price relationships to change, and no need for gold to flow from one country to the other. In this view, the terms of trade, if they changed at all, were just as likely to turn in favour of the lending country as in favour of the borrowing country. Correspondingly, gold, if it flowed at all, was just as likely to flow into the lending country as out of it. The direction of the gold movement could serve, in effect, as an index of the direction of the change in the terms of trade.

What is now commonly regarded as the ' classical ' doctrine in the form in which especially John Stuart Mill presented it, emphasized by contrast the necessity for the terms of trade to turn against the capital exporting country in the process of transfer.[1] It can be shown that if the 'neo-classical' shift-of-buying-power analysis is pushed to its rigorous conclusion and account is taken of the existence of domestic commodity groups—commodities which, because of transport costs or trade restrictions, do not enter into international trade—then an adverse movement in the barter terms of trade of the lending country appears as the gener-ally probable outcome, though not an inevitable necessity. In the case of domestic commodities, by definition, a decrease of demand in one country cannot be offset by an increase of demand in the other; only for internationally traded commodities is this at all possible. In so far as the transfer of buying power affects domestic goods, internal shifts of factors become necessary, tending to lower the export supply schedule in the lending and to raise it in the borrowing country. As a result of the imperfect mobility of goods, therefore, a change in the terms of trade in

[1] ' If, before the country became liable to the annual payment, foreign commerce was in its natural state of equilibrium, it will now be necessary for the purpose of effecting the remittance, that foreign countries should be induced to take a greater quantity of exports than before : which can only be done by offering those exports on cheaper terms, or, in other words, by paying dearer for foreign commodities. . . . The result is that a country which makes regular payments to foreign countries, besides losing what it pays, loses also something more, by the less advantageous terms on which it is forced to exchange its productions for foreign commodities.' J. S. Mill, *Principles of Political Economy* (Ashley edition, London, 1929), p. 627.

favour of the borrowing and against the lending country is generally more likely than a change in the opposite direction. A presumption is thus established, after all, in favour of the ' classical ' conclusion.[1]

But the whole debate over the terms of trade in the transfer process, besides being concerned with incidental and subsidiary matters, was practically incapable of conclusive verification. If it was true that a capital movement was likely to turn the terms of trade in favour of the borrowing country and against the lending country, it was also true that an improvement in a country's terms of trade—due, say, to an increased world demand for its products—was exactly the sort of thing that would stimulate foreign capital to move to that country. A favourable change in the terms of trade could therefore be the cause of a capital movement, just as well as an effect. The relation between capital movements and the terms of trade was evidently a reciprocal one, and unless observation revealed significant time lags, this made it very difficult, not to say impossible, to ascertain precisely what effect on the terms of trade was produced by a transfer of capital.

In Haberler's as well as Ohlin's works, both of which appeared in 1933, the doctrine of comparative advantage was re-shaped into new forms in which the assumption of international immobility of factors was no longer required. The way was opened for a comprehensive consideration of capital movements in relation to international trade and development problems, in place of the almost exclusive preoccupation with the transfer mechanism. Ohlin himself, as mentioned before, made a good beginning in placing capital movements in a broader frame of reference.[2]

CAPITAL EXPORTS AND THE INCOME APPROACH

Only a few years later, however, the Keynesian revolution broke out; and its impact on the theory of foreign investment was to divert attention from fundamental long-run matters relating to capital as a factor of production, and to turn it once again in favour of incidental matters important only in the short run,

[1] I showed this in some detail in my *Internationale Kapitalbewegungen* (Vienna, 1935), Chapter III.
[2] I made some further attempts along those lines in Chapters I and IV, ibid.

namely, the effect of foreign investment on the degree of employment in the advanced creditor economies. Under the impact of Keynesian economics, capital exports came to be associated with an increase of effective demand and employment in the capital-exporting country, and indeed, in the universe as a whole.

Even Ohlin's neo-classical version of the transfer theory had still been influenced by the notion that the aggregate volume of demand in the universe was a constant magnitude, so that a capital transfer meant a loss of buying power in one country and a gain in the other. This survival of the classical view of conservation of purchasing power tended to imply, even in Ohlin's presentation, that the typical effect of a movement of capital was a depression in the lending country and a boom in the borrowing country, a kind of see-saw effect quite alien to the real world. In the real world Taussig, for instance, found when he studied the facts that periods of active lending were generally associated with rising rather than falling prices in the lending country, and with business prosperity rather than depression. The facts which puzzled Taussig appeared perfectly natural in the light of the Keynesian income approach.

This new approach also gave some attention to the possibility, which Keynes had stressed earlier, that capital movements might take place in response to changes in the trade balance, instead of being always the independent causal factor which the traditional theory usually assumed them to be. And so the distinction between autonomous and accommodating capital movements finds a prominent place in Machlup's book on the multiplier theory. This distinction, though it tends to fade away in a long-run view, is useful for short-term process analysis. But it omitted a third and very important possibility: the case where trade and capital movements, instead of being caused one by the other, were both of them caused by a third force having to do, say, with business fluctuations in one country or another. For instance, an investment boom that develops in one country will tend to induce both commodity imports and capital imports into that country simultaneously. The increased commodity imports cannot properly be regarded either as the cause or the effect of the capital imports. Both commodity and capital imports are effects of a common cause, the investment boom, which produces a rise in interest rates, money income and demand for imports all at the same time.[1]

Whether a capital movement is regarded as autonomous, accommodating or, in this third case, co-variant, it is associated in any event with an increase in effective demand and employment. The word 'associated' is used so as to leave room for any one of the three possible causal relationships. Actually, the classical viewpoint has persisted in that the capital transfer is usually treated as the autonomous factor, leading to a change in income and employment as well as in the trade balance. There is good reason for this treatment. A change in trade balances cannot be long maintained unless it is matched by a corresponding movement of capital. Even if, in the first instance, it is an increment in exports that causes an expansion in money income and employment, it may well be that this higher level of exports and hence of income and employment cannot be kept up unless the export surplus that is likely to remain is covered by an export of capital. In the longer view, therefore, it is this capital export to which the higher level of income and employment has to be attributed. The multiplicand is then the export surplus, not simply the increment in exports as it appears in the short-run analysis in which gold and exchange reserves can be relied upon to take care of any temporary discrepancies in the trade balance. This shift of emphasis appears in several recent writings[2] and tends on the whole to justify the picture in which the capital movement stands out as the factor of prior causal significance. Without it, a lasting change in the trade balance cannot be sustained.

[1] J. Knapp, 'The Theory of International Capital Movements and its Verifications,' *Review of Economic Studies*, 1943. From the point of view of a capital exporting country, this possibility is illustrated in the fluctuations of the U.S. export surplus and foreign bond issues in the United States during the 1920's. Both can be related to the domestic business fluctuations in the United States during that period. See Arthur I. Bloomfield, 'The Mechanism of Adjustment of the American Balance of Payments,' *Quarterly Journal of Economics*, May 1943, and Ilse Mintz, *Deterioration in the Quality of Foreign Bonds Issued in the United States, 1920–1930* (National Bureau of Economic Research, New York, 1951), Chapter I.

[2] Roy F. Harrod, *Towards a Dynamic Economics* (London, 1949), pp. 101–15; Erich Preiser, 'Kapitalexport und Vollbeschäftigung,' *Economia Internazionale*, May 1950; Paul A. Samuelson, 'The Simple Mathematics of Income Determination,' in *Income, Employment and Public Policy* (Essays in Honor of Alvin H. Hansen, New York, 1948), pp. 148–9.

The general income-generating effect of foreign investment can come from one or both of two sources. First, the foreign loan can be financed out of idle balances or newly created money, in which case the expenditure of the loan, whether it takes place in the lending or in the borrowing country, will give rise to a process of expansion all round, even if the marginal propensities to spend are the same in the two countries. New or reactivated money is clearly one possible source of the expansion effect. The second source is one that has been demonstrated especially by Lloyd A. Metzler.[1] It stems from the possibility that the marginal propensities to spend—on consumption, investment and imports—are higher in the borrowing than in the lending country. In this case (which, for obvious reasons, is likely to be met in fact) a transfer of capital will result in an expansion of money income and expenditure all round, even if the loan is financed in the first place not from new or inactive money, but at the expense of domestic capital outlay or consumer spending in the lending country.

FOREIGN INVESTMENT AS AN ECONOMIC STIMULANT

The recognition of these income-generating and employment-stimulating effects gave rise to a discussion concerning the possibility of using foreign investment as a counter-cyclical device in business cycle policy in advanced industrial economies. The conclusion was, on the whole, negative.[2] First, the practical difficulties of a counter-cyclical timing of foreign investment were seen to be enormous. The practical difficulties even of a domestic public works scheme as a counter-cyclical policy are very great ; and we have observed from recent experience how long it can take for international loan applications to be investigated and processed.

Secondly, it came to be realized that a counter-cyclical foreign

[1] 'The Transfer Problem Reconsidered,' *Journal of Political Economy*, June 1942, reprinted in *Readings in the Theory of International Trade* (Philadelphia, 1949). For an illuminating commentary on this theory, see Roberto de Oliveira Campos, ' Lord Keynes e a Teoria de Transferencia de Capitais,' *Revista Brasileira de Economia*, June 1950.

[2] See, e.g., Kenneth K. Kurihara, ' Foreign Investment and Full Employment,' *Journal of Political Economy*. October 1947, and Erich Preiser, op. cit.

investment policy might lead to disturbing fluctuations in capital formation in the underdeveloped countries, if foreign investment was to be made inversely dependent on the cyclical degree of employment in the advanced industrial centres. True, the export proceeds of primary producing countries usually fluctuate in a pronounced cyclical manner, and one might conclude that if their capital imports were made counter-cyclical the effect of the two things together would be to stabilize their total import capacity. A country's import capacity, however, is not the same thing as its means of capital formation, including its imports of capital goods. If the rate of capital formation in a primary producing country subject to counter-cyclical foreign investment were to be kept stable, the domestic income effects of the fluctuations in export proceeds would have to be eliminated, which is a big assumption to make and not an easy prescription to follow.[1]

The use of capital exports as a counter-cyclical device has, for these and other reasons, dropped into the background. But the difficulties in the short-term use of foreign investment as an instrument of business cycle policy do not preclude its use as a long-run offset to a domestic propensity to save that might be excessive in relation to domestic investment opportunities. Foreign investment may appear as a desirable stimulant to a mature industrial economy. In any event, there is here an obvious affinity between Keynesian and Marxian doctrine, except that the Marxian did not stem from Marx himself, but from J. A. Hobson, who wrote on this subject at the very beginning of the present century, and from whom Rosa Luxemburg and Lenin took it over ten to twelve years later. Hobson and his theory of underconsumption anticipated some features of Keynes's general theory, and this explains the affinity in the foreign investment field.

According to this Marxian or rather neo-Marxian doctrine of economic imperialism, advanced capitalist economies are under a compulsion to export capital, and in this way to dump their surplus produce abroad, in order to keep the internal economy operating at a prosperous and profitable level of activity.

My own reaction to this doctrine is that if such a compulsion

[1] See Chapter IV, pp. 99 ff., above.

existed—and it may have existed to some extent in the past—there would be nothing sinister about it. On the contrary, it would be a highly beneficent compulsion. It would be extremely fortunate if the rich countries felt themselves continually induced, for their own salvation, to export capital to the poorer countries, and thus to contribute to the economic advance of the backward areas. It would truly be a case of pre-ordained harmony.

I realize that this propensity to export capital is not all there is to the Marxian doctrine of economic imperialism. Another thesis contained in it relates to the exploitation of backward areas by monopoly capitalism. The first comment to be made on this thesis is that the biggest capital exporter before 1914—England—was a country without trusts or cartels, in contrast to Germany or the United States.[1] Another comment that seems to me pertinent is that even where foreign investment has been associated with exclusive concessions in the debtor countries, there may have been occasionally some economic basis for it. Economically backward areas are deficient in public utilities and improvements, which the private investor often has to set up with a part of his capital if he wants to initiate a specific productive activity. In order to reap an appropriate return from investment in facilities which incidentally benefit the economy generally, he may need an exclusive concession. This is not the whole story, but it does furnish a plausible argument in defence of the monopoly element in past foreign investment. The argument would fall to the ground if the overhead capital facilities were set up by public authorities, financed if necessary by foreign loans.

To go back to the first-mentioned thesis of the Marxian doctrine, concerning the deep-seated urge for mature capitalist economies to export capital abroad. Keynesian economics tended to confirm this thesis and lent some prestige to it. For some time after the war of 1939–45, there seemed to be a widespread belief in underdeveloped countries that sooner or later the United States would simply have to start exporting large amounts of capital to them in order to keep its own economy happy and

[1] Cf. E. Preiser, op. cit. This did not, of course, prevent British companies from attaining monopoly positions occasionally, and there was also a curious revival of the system of specially privileged chartered companies towards the end of the nineteenth century in Africa (see S. H. Frankel, op. cit., pp. 21 ff.).

prosperous. This attitude became evident, for instance, at the Havana trade conference in 1948. It has been said that the measures regulating the conditions under which the less developed countries were prepared to admit foreign capital have sometimes been based on the assumption that the United States would find itself compelled to embark on foreign investment in order to maintain full employment at home. Whether or not this is true I do not know. What I do want to stress is that it is unsafe to make this assumption, and that to act upon it might lead to unfortunate consequences.

It is true that the Keynesian analysis brought out the favourable income and employment effects of foreign investment upon the economy of the lending nation. But it is important to realize that Keynesian economics itself devised a system of fiscal and monetary policies for the maintenance of a steady level of good employment in any advanced industrial country, without the aid of foreign investment. In theory at any rate, but probably to some extent in practice also, the income and employment effect of foreign investment, which never was more than an incidental effect of the capital transfer, has become quite unimportant as a means of domestic economic stabilization in the wealthier countries of the world. The compulsion to export capital has been removed by the very doctrine that furnished an improved explanation of it.

THE REAL CASE FOR FOREIGN INVESTMENT

Unfortunately, therefore, the wealthier countries are no longer under a necessity to transfer their surplus output to the world's poorer regions. If such a transfer is to occur, it will have to be on grounds other than its temporary income and employment effect on the lenders' economy. And perhaps it is not so unfortunate either. After all, there would be something rather perverse about it if the movement of capital to the less developed countries were to be dependent on, and to change inversely with, the state of employment in the advanced industrial economies. The economic case for international investment stands on its own merits and does not depend on its incidental and transient effects on monetary expansion. These effects, whenever they are needed to combat depressive tendencies, can equally well be achieved by domestic policies.

When we look at the world as a whole, lack of monetary demand appears as a local, temporary and exceptional disease. Far deeper are the troubles that arise from lack of capital in underdeveloped countries and from the great discrepancies in living standards. Foreign investment is fundamentally a means of improving the distribution and use of the world's productive resources. Keynesian economics, by substituting an armoury of domestic policies of economic stabilization for the income and employment effects of foreign investment, clears the approach to the developmental aspects of the international movement of capital, which ought to have been in the centre of the stage from the start. Capital movements can at last be thought of primarily as movements of a basic factor of production.

What is usually meant by a movement of capital is a change in the location of new investment, so that new saving performed in one country serves to build up real capital elsewhere. It can, and perhaps should, mean more than that. In the world as we know it, there exist tremendous discrepancies in the supply of capital in relation to other factors of production. If the world were run on purely economic lines it is conceivable that a highly developed country like the United States would not only export all its current new saving, but also, for a time anyway, some of its replacement and amortization funds. In other words, the principle of real income maximization, applied on a world scale, might call for a geographical redistribution not only of the current new investment, but also of the previously accumulated stock of real capital in the world. This should be the literal meaning of the term ' movement of capital '. So long as a capital movement merely comes out of current new saving all it involves is the geographical location of new investment activity in the world, not a shift in the existing stock of capital.

The nineteenth-century experience of foreign investment was unique in the way it was associated with the migration of people from Europe to the great ' empty ' plains in other temperate regions. Both capital and labour moved out in quest of the higher earnings offered by new lands rich in natural resources.

Barriers to the movement of one would have reduced the flow of the other. The two were complementary; but this relationship is by no means one of universal validity. The capital exports from the United States in the twentieth century may perhaps be viewed in part as a *substitute* for the movement of people to the United States, which has been restricted by law. Cheap labour, instead of being allowed to come to the United States to work with American capital, is supplied with American capital abroad; supplied by the American government (as in the period 1945–52) if not by private investors seeking higher returns (as in the 1920s).

A theory of capital movements that is concerned with capital as a factor of production would direct attention to the unequal proportions in which capital co-operates with labour and land in the different parts of the world; to the technical forms which capital should assume in response to different relative factor endowments; to the relations between capital movements, population growth and migration; and to other such fundamental matters. Only fragments of this type of capital-movement theory exist to-day, but the great awakening is forcing the attention of economists all over the world to these basic questions—with some benefit, one may hope, not only to the theory of capital formation and development, but to international economics generally.

The Problems of the Return Flow

I should like to think that Keynesian economics, by emphasizing the domestic methods of economic stabilization in the advanced industrial countries, has opened the way to a better appreciation of the basic developmental aspects of international investment. In reality, it may turn out to be over-optimistic to assume that the malady of business depression is gone, never to return. It is too early to be absolutely confident that in the absence of war or defence requirements there would be no trouble about keeping up employment without the stimulus of an export surplus financed, if necessary, by foreign investment.

Foreign investment may come in handy. But then the next problem to face is this : if foreign investment is good for business activity and employment, the return flow of income and amortization, to which sooner or later it is supposed to give rise, must be bad for employment in the creditor economy. This problem arises, of course, equally if the outward flow of foreign investment takes place without regard to its possible use as an economic stimulant.

In the last six or seven years a number of American economists have devoted their attention to the problem of the return flow arising from private foreign investment. Their main worry has not been that, if Americans were to invest abroad, foreigners might not repay. Their concern has been with the prospect that, if foreigners did repay, the American economy might suffer from depressive effects due to the import surplus required for the inward transfer of interest, dividends and amortization. Norman S. Buchanan, in his well-known book, raised the question of ' how and at what sacrifice the United States can accept payment.'[1] Hal B. Lary, in his paper on the domestic effects of foreign investment, called the adjustment of the American economy to the return flow ' probably the most disturbing problem connected with the investment of American capital abroad.'[2] Evsey D. Domar, in his recent analysis of the effect of foreign investment on the balance of payments, says that ' to many, it [the need for an import balance] appears as the main obstacle to a successful foreign investment programme.'[3] The import surplus with which these and other writers have been concerned as the ultimate, and not very distant, outcome of American foreign investment could easily be avoided if the creditor country were to forgo the return payments. On the face of it, the discussion would seem to suggest unilateral transfers as a form of capital export more appropriate to the underlying situation. But this is not a practicable form of private capital export.

Domar's study provides comfort to those who fear an import surplus. He finds that the ratio of the annual inflow on foreign investment account (amortization plus income payments) to the annual outflow (gross foreign lending) reaches, as a limit, the expression $\dfrac{a+i}{a+g}$, where a is the rate of amortization, i the rate of

---

[1] *International Investment and Domestic Welfare* (New York, 1945), p. 179.
[2] *American Economic Review, Papers and Proceedings*, May 1946, p. 678.
[3] *American Economic Review*, December 1950, p. 808.

interest on the foreign loans and g the percentage rate of growth in new foreign lending from year to year. There is no need to report how this formula is derived. The obvious conclusion from it is that so long as the rate of growth is greater than the rate of interest, the above expression will be less than one, and an import surplus need not arise. For instance, if America were to devote a fixed percentage (say, 2 per cent) of her national income to foreign investment each year, and if American national income were to increase by 3 per cent per annum, then an import balance would not develop so long as the rate of interest on this foreign investment is less than 3 per cent. In Domar's words, ' as far as the required rate of growth is concerned, foreign investment does not give rise to any problems intrinsically different from those created by domestic investment, public or private. In all of them, the presence of certain conditions regarding the relative magnitude of the investment and its productivity or yield leads to a compound interest solution, and in all of them the absolute magnitudes involved, unless the assumed conditions change, become " fantastically " high with time.'[1]

While earlier writers had come to the rather pessimistic conclusion that the rate of foreign lending would have to be tremendously accelerated in the future in order to prevent an import surplus from arising, Domar reassures us by demonstrating that, as long as the rate of new lending is geared to the rate at which the American national income advances, and as long as the average rate of return on the loans can be kept below this annual rate of advance, all will be well : no import surplus will be necessary.

This is accepting for the sake of argument the common view that an import surplus is a depressive influence to be avoided at all costs. Needless to say any depressive effect of an import surplus can be offset by appropriate domestic fiscal and monetary policies.

Domar's theoretical formula, though it certainly illuminates the problem of the return flow, lumps together income payments and capital payments. In actual fact, people are apt to treat receipts on income account differently from receipts on capital

[1] Ibid, p. 807.

account. A man who receives a repayment of principal may not feel at liberty to spend any of it; a man who receives a dividend or interest cheque usually feels free to spend all of it. I prefer therefore to separate the two elements of the return-flow problem.

As far as the capital account is concerned, I am inclined to agree with those who argue that net repayment is not necessary and should not be expected before the creditor and debtor countries have changed their place in the relative scale of economic development. Individual loans will be repaid, but new ones will be granted; net repayment should be neither required nor desired by the creditor economy as long as the investment yields a good return. Just as net repayment of internal government debt must be geared to the state of the whole economy and not to the provisions of a particular loan contract, so the return of capital invested abroad must depend on changes in the comparative situation of the countries concerned. On economic grounds net repayment of foreign loans will not take place until and unless the fundamental conditions of the two economies reverse themselves so that in the creditor economy the propensity to save falls short of domestic investment needs and the opposite occurs in the debtor economy. At least the interest differential that gave rise to the capital outflow must be reversed before a net return flow can be induced by the motive of maximizing income from capital. Such changes are bound to be gradual. Capital cannot be repaid suddenly in vast amounts, except in abnormal circumstances due to war, as in 1939–45, when Britain's debtors encountered no transfer troubles in liquidating their debts.

The legal forms in which capital movements occur can create some trouble in this respect. A capital exporting country has no legal obligation to grant new loans; it may stop granting new loans, and this, combined with the legal amortization requirements on the old loans, will induce not simply a cessation, but actually a reversal of the capital movement, a return flow which may be quite unrelated to any change in the basic economic conditions. The case is still worse with short-term credits that can be withdrawn on demand or at short notice. Such funds cannot be used for economic development at all. During the international financial crisis twenty years ago, it was a popular joke in some countries to compare foreign credit to an umbrella which a man is allowed to borrow as long as the weather is fine, but which he has to return the moment it starts raining. Under these conditions the umbrella is never of much use to him.

On the question of the return flow of interest and dividend earnings, the first thing to note is that in the economy of the creditor country these receipts have a positive income effect which should not be overlooked. The fact is that the multiplier theory bears upon invisible items in the current account of the balance of payments just as much as on merchandise trade. In theoretical illustrations it is usually confined to receipts from merchandise exports, but it applies in exactly the same way to interest receipts, which also are a current payment which people in a country receive, which they will spend, and which thus will tend to produce a more than equal increment in aggregate money income. The appearance of a merchandise import surplus need not be a depressive factor if it is accompanied by an increase in an invisible positive item such as interest receipts. On the contrary the interest receipts will have an expansive effect on aggregate money income, which will induce a quite ' painless ' increase in imports. The trouble is that, because of the saving propensity of the interest receivers and the possible saving leakage in the rest of the economy as well, the expansive effect is not likely to be sufficient to induce an increment of imports equal to the inflow of interest receipts. The remaining part of the necessary trade adjustment is likely to be ' painful ' to the creditor country. The debtor may have to resort to exchange depreciation or trade restrictions which will tend to have a depressive effect on the creditor economy. But whether this depressive effect is greater than the expansive effect due directly to the interest receipts is not absolutely certain.[1] And even if there is a net depressive influence, it can be offset, as mentioned before, by compensatory domestic policies in the creditor country.

So much for the income effects of the return flow in the creditor country. From the point of view of the debtor country, the payment of interest involves two things : first, a budgetary or

[1] Paul A. Samuelson, ' The Simple Mathematics of Income Determination ' (op. cit.), p. 150.

collection problem and, secondly, a transfer problem. The distinction became familiar in the German reparations controversy in the 1920's; it is fully applicable to the present case. The 'budgetary' problem of collection within the debtor country must be solved before the transfer part of the task can be tackled. The budgetary problem in the present case is that of securing a return in the domestic currency in the country in which the investment has been made, and this depends directly or indirectly on the productivity of the investment. It does not have to be a direct commercial return; it may arise in the form of increased taxable capacity. Anyway, two conditions must be met for the successful accomplishment of the transfer, and the first is that the debtor country shall use the foreign loan for productive purposes which increase the real national income and provide the return in domestic currency out of which interest can be paid.

The second condition involves the creation of an export surplus from which the foreign exchange will be available to service the loan. Now this is a matter that depends on the creditor no less than the debtor country. On the creditor's side, while a liberal commercial policy used to be stressed in the past, more recently great emphasis has been placed on the need for the creditor country to keep up its business activity and to offset any depressive effect of the return flow by domestic measures of expansion.

On the debtor's side, it is not in my opinion necessary that a project financed by foreign borrowing should itself make a direct contribution to the balance of payments by increasing either the debtor country's export capacity or else its production of import substitutes, by an amount equal to the interest charges. On the one hand, the particular projects in which foreign investment takes place are naturally determined by the marginal productivity of capital. In accordance with the basic rules of good housekeeping, when additional capital becomes available to a country, the country will want or should be urged to invest it in the form that yields the highest possible return, taking into account any external economies created by the project as well as the direct commercial yield. On the other hand, the particular goods through which the interest is transferred abroad are determined by the scale of comparative costs in international trade (though this scale need not be regarded as fixed and may well change as a result of the investment itself). No particular relation is required between the marginal-productivity-of-capital schedule and the comparative-cost schedule. So long as the two conditions stated above are met, there is no inherent difficulty in the servicing problem from the debtor's end.

This was the view I expressed five years ago[1] on the question as to whether or not foreign investment had to make a direct contribution to the future balance of payments of the debtor country if transfer of the return flow was to be accomplished without trouble. The doctrine that foreign investment was bound to come to grief unless it did make a direct contribution had at that time gained new advocates, but can be found in many earlier writings. Thus an authoritative British report in 1937 made the following weighty pronouncement: 'It is . . . a fundamental condition of sound international finance that a country should only borrow from abroad for the purpose of its capital development, if this development is of a type which is likely to improve its balance of payments in the future.'[2] I have always found it hard to reconcile this doctrine with elementary economic principles.

Under the influence of the income approach, an ingenious argument was developed to the effect that, once a project financed by foreign investment had been completed, its productive operation was subsequently bound to create new incomes for the factors engaged in it, and that these incomes would be spent partly on imported goods. This would produce a strain on the balance of payments, unless the project itself produced new exports or substitutes for imports. A recent study by Albert E. Kahn[3] shows that this pessimistic view was only one side of the matter. The other side is that the people who buy the new product in the home market, as long as they buy it out of their income and not from inflationary sources, must necessarily divert their

---

[1] *The Course and Control of Inflation* (League of Nations, 1946), p. 82.
[2] *The Problem of International Investment*, op. cit., p. 67.
[3] ' Investment Criteria in Development Programs,' *Quarterly Journal of Economics*, February 1951.

expenditure from other goods, including imported goods. There-fore, even if the industry does not produce anything that replaces goods previously imported, but produces a net addition of new goods for sale on the domestic market, there is no inherent reason for balance-of-payments difficulties to arise, always provided that the sale of the extra goods is not financed by means of inflation. There is no reason why foreign investment should be deliberately kept away from industries producing additional goods for the domestic market.

In fact, foreign business investment in the past tended spontaneously to keep away from industries working for the domestic market in economically backward countries. But this was not always—especially not before 1914—due to fear of transfer difficulties. It was chiefly due to the low incentive to invest in industries working for the poor local population, in contrast to those working for export to the growing manufacturing centres hungry for more materials and foodstuffs. It was in accord with the play of private profit motives under the influence of foreign market demand. In these circumstances, the private marginal productivity of capital in low-income countries was naturally higher in the export industries than in production for the home market. This leads back to a point that arose in the first chapter and that serves, I believe, as a basic, though of course only partial, explanation of the behaviour of private foreign capital in the past—and in the present also.

But this point applies mainly to private entrepreneurial investment. There is nothing in the market difficulty that militates against international capital movements in the form of foreign borrowing by public organizations in underdeveloped areas for the construction of overhead public installations or the establish-ment of manufacturing and farming activities catering to local needs. Even in the nineteenth-century environment of private international investment, which collapsed in the late 1920s, it was possible for this type of capital movement to materialize and, on occasion, to produce impressive results. Let us by all means welcome any private business capital that may come for-ward for investment in the world's poverty-ridden areas. But, to avoid disillusionment, let us recognize the handicap with which it is faced : the poverty of consumers in those areas. This handicap need not impede investment of the ' autonomous ' sort. If there is any hope for a revival of international investment for economic development, it is largely on this type of investment that I myself would place it.

CHAPTER VII

ACTION ON THE HOME FRONT

EXTERNAL AND DOMESTIC SOURCES

THE trouble with 'autonomous' international investment is that its effectiveness depends on domestic action; only with strong domestic policies directed to this end is there any assurance that it will go wholly into added accumulation rather than consumption. That is the trouble with all external sources of capital except the ' colonial ' form of direct investment.

It is most obviously true of inter-governmental grants-in-aid. These can easily be swallowed up directly or indirectly by increased consumption unless they are fitted into a comprehensive domestic programme of saving and investment.

We have seen that, without the complementary domestic saving enforced, if need be, by fiscal and monetary policies, import restrictions on consumer goods cannot be truly effective as a means of capital formation through imports of equipment from abroad.

Similarly, we have seen that domestic action is indispensable if an increased rate of accumulation is to result from an improvement in the terms of trade. No doubt such an improvement puts at the country's disposal fresh resources that can be used to promote economic growth. Without the corresponding domestic saving, however, this increment in current income derived from foreign trade cannot lead to any net increase in investment. Here again the real task is not to extract more capital goods from foreign trade but to extract more saving from the national income.

In all these cases capital formation depends on complementary domestic policies. External resources, even if they come in the most desirable forms, are not enough. They cannot automatically provide a solution to the problem of capital accumulation in backward areas. Domestic action is essential for the effective use of external contributions as well as for the tapping of potential domestic sources. There is no solution to the problem without steady and strenuous effort on the domestic front. In a sense, therefore, it all boils down to this : capital is made at home.

At the same time the advanced countries, as we have seen, can probably get along without having to export capital for the sake of domestic employment.

My intention is by no means to deny the desirability of external sources of capital or to underrate the degree to which they can reduce the pains of material progress in areas starting from abysmal levels of poverty. Foreign funds can certainly speed up the process and make it less arduous, less violently disruptive socially, and less likely to produce despotic forms of government. All this is widely appreciated, and I completely agree with it. Yet we must reject the common notion that foreign capital is something like a panacea. What needs to be stressed above all is that external sources can scarcely make a significant contribution to economic growth unless there is complementary action on the home front, along the lines indicated earlier.

But if a nation has enough control over its economy to implement the domestic policies required for the productive use of outside aid, then it ceases to be wholly or even partly dependent on outside aid for its capital supply. For then there is no reason why it should not employ the same means of fiscal and monetary control for the mobilization of potential domestic savings.

Potential savings may already exist in the form, for instance, of disguised unemployment on the land or of non-functional conspicuous consumption among privileged groups. If not, they can be created. The elementary formula for this is increased farm productivity (and conceptually the formula covers even the use of disguised unemployment since this, by definition, leads to increased output per worker remaining on the land).

In a poor community, just as food accounts for nearly all personal consumption, so the struggle for food absorbs most of man's energy. Greater efficiency in food production is the basic way of releasing human energy for capital construction. The domestic saving potential consists here in an increment of real income, and the task of mobilizing it is to withhold the highest possible proportion of this increment for investment purposes.

Improved farm productivity is the basic need in the early

stages of development. But as development proceeds, the capital accumulated will itself help to produce an increase in real income, of which again as much as possible is to be ploughed back into the country's capital stock.[1] The importance of output expansion exceeding the rate of population growth is widely realized in this connection and needs no further emphasis.

The general problem is to maximize the marginal saving ratio, *i.e.*, the proportion of any increment in income that is saved. The rise in productivity, in so far as population growth does not erase it, creates an opportunity for increased saving. The opportunity can be grasped—or missed. Its realization depends on the ways and means of extracting the saving out of the increased income. In the ideal case the whole increment goes into saving. This is perhaps a perfectionist view; some immediate relief of the crushing weight of poverty is probably unavoidable and may even be desirable for the sake of development itself.[2] How much to allow on this account is hard to know. The pressures for making some allowance are only too insistent. It should be comforting enough that the domestic sources of capital need not involve any belt-tightening but can come rather from the ploughing-back of output gains. If even this resort is seriously compromised little hope may remain for development.

The Role of Public Finance

The country's incremental saving ratio—or to vary the jargon, the marginal propensity to save—is the crucial determinant of growth. It is not something that takes care of itself; it does not maximize itself automatically. On the contrary, all the ' automatic' forces, including population increase, make for the additional income going into consumption. A serious question that arises here concerns the degree to which reliance can be placed on voluntary saving, especially in view of the demonstration effect of advanced consumption standards.

---

[1] A ' colonial ' piece of direct investment can equally result in an investible increment in national income, even if its profits are all returned to the creditor country. For it can hardly fail to increase the demand for local labour and materials, quite apart from any possible royalties or taxes accruing to the local economy.

[2] Cf. H. Mendershausen's comment, *American Economic Review, Papers and Proceedings*, May 1952, p. 601.

Consider Japan's experience. She remained isolated from the western world as regards consumption patterns. Her people were indoctrinated in the virtues of thrift and austerity; business firms were urged to reinvest their profits and to hold down dividends; wages were kept low. Yet all this was not enough. Much had to be done through public finance : taxation and forced loans.

I believe that public finance assumes a new significance in the face of the problem of capital formation in underdeveloped countries. However, the technical complexities of public finance are formidable, and I can attempt to make only some general observations.

According to one school of thought, the state should confine itself to keeping money income at a level corresponding to full employment without inflation, and should let individuals make their choice between consumption and saving out of that volume of income. Some average rate of saving greater than zero may result, and again it may not. To assume that if we only leave people alone they will save a sizable portion of their income, or even a sizable part of an increment in their income, may be unduly optimistic. In the poorer countries in the world to-day the propensity to consume is continually stimulated by the attraction of consumption patterns prevailing in advanced countries. This tends to limit the capacity for voluntary saving in the poorer countries. It creates a handicap which public finance should endeavour to offset.

It is generally true to say that the demonstration factor itself tends to breed political difficulties inhibiting the use of public finance for this purpose. But if we leave it at that, we yield to the vicious circle of poverty. It is just at this point—collective action through public finance—that there may be some hope of breaking the circle.

In fact, there is a widespread tendency for the state to take over a greater responsibility for the direction of the process of capital formation. In this situation the rate of accumulation no longer reflects the sum of individual preferences and propensities in regard to saving and current consumption, but is increasingly determined by governments on grounds of national policy.

It can be plausibly argued that the contemporary emphasis on government planning for economic development is to a great extent an outcome of the failure of nations under laissez-faire conditions to accumulate capital rapidly enough for the desired rate of growth.[1] Appropriation by the state of a greater share of the national income for investment activities does not have to interfere in any way with the freedom of consumers to spend their disposable income on the goods and services of their choice. It is the choice between saving and consumption that is assumed more and more by the state. Taxation is used increasingly as an instrument of compulsory saving.

It is interesting to note that Bentham, who introduced the concept of forced saving into economic literature in an essay written in 1804, included in it not only the levy that may result from inflation, but also the compulsory saving that can be brought about by government taxation.[2] This second meaning of his term ' forced frugality,' which was completely lost to the nineteenth century, may now be coming to the forefront, whereas the inflationary method of involuntary saving is generally discredited.

Inflation, when it passes beyond a certain rate, is apt to set up expectations and behaviour patterns such that it completely loses its power to create forced saving. In an advanced stage, inflation may even become a cause of capital consumption in a country's economy. These, however, are extreme conditions. We must admit that, over a wide range, inflation can be effective as an engine of forced saving, and is being effective in this sense in a number of underdeveloped countries to-day. But it frequently leads to a misdirection of the saving it creates, favouring investment, for example, in luxury industries and leaving essential

[1] J. J. Spengler, op. cit., p. 46.
[2] The following is an excerpt from Bentham's lengthy discussion of forced saving through taxation: ' By raising money, as other money is raised, by taxes (the amount of which is taken by individuals out of their expenditure on the score of maintenance), government has it in its power to accelerate, to an unexampled degree, the augmentation of the mass of real wealth. By a proportionable sacrifice of present comfort, it may make any addition that it pleases to the mass of future wealth; that is, to the increase of comfort and security.' Bentham adds, however, this cautionary note: ' But though it has it in its power to do this, it follows not that it ought to excercise this power to compel the community to make this sacrifice.' See F. A. von Hayek, 'A Note on the Development of the Doctrine of Forced Saving,' Quarterly Journal of Economics, November 1932, p. 124.

public facilities to decay. The shifts in income from the poor to the rich, which are a normal part of the process of inflation, make it a wasteful form of forced saving, since the rich may consume some of the extra income coming to them and not save all of it; better tax the poor and invest the proceeds without the intermediary of the rich. Above all, inflation is a source of social discontent and disruption, hence a powerful ally of extremist political movements. Inflationary pressures are inherent in the process of investment, but the way to stop them is not to stop investment. There are other ways: chief among them the powerful method of fiscal policy.

Objections to the use of taxation as an instrument of forced saving arise, first, on the score of its effect on the incentive to provide voluntary saving. They would carry greater weight if the flow of voluntary saving were considerable. Actually, in most of the poorer countries the flow is very meagre. The appeal to spare the goose that lays the golden eggs is not very strong when the goose is not laying many eggs of any kind. It is important to maintain and indeed increase the private incentive to save. However, economic considerations alone provide no ground for categorical imperatives in this regard, but point rather to the need for weighing (a) the social cost of providing the incentives, in relation to (b) the current or anticipated ' returns ' in the form of private voluntary saving. The economic calculus, though difficult to apply, has its place here too.

A more specific objection to compulsory saving through taxation is that it may lead private people to reduce their saving or actually to dissave. The result would be a cumulative tendency for more and more taxation, and less and less private saving. The state comes forward trying to increase the flow of saving through the compulsory method of taxation, the public responds by reducing its contribution to that flow; the state gives another turn to the screw, the public withdraws still further; and so on. That this might be the trend of events was feared by some in Western Europe after 1945. The very considerable flow of local resources into rebuilding Europe's capital equipment was brought about largely by the state, to some extent also by private business saving, but to an almost negligible extent through voluntary personal saving. However, the cumulative tendency for the displacement of personal saving by compulsory collective saving is not likely to be a real danger in the long run. It is not safe to generalize from the peculiar post-war conditions of Western Europe, where a certain amount of dissaving was perfectly natural since the war-time saving had been merely a temporary deferment of consumption, not intended to be permanent. In normal times some demand for new assets to hold and hence some saving to satisfy the demand, at any rate by the wealthier people, is likely even at sizable rates of taxation.

For the sake of the incentive to save, taxation should not be on personal income, but rather on expenditure. As it is, some taxation is always levied on expenditure through excise and other indirect taxes, which usually bulk large in the fiscal systems of underdeveloped countries, but the proposals for a comprehensive tax on personal consumption expenditure in place of the personal income tax may be worth reconsidering. The same effect might be obtained to some extent by exempting from the income tax that part of a man's income which he saves. In one form or another this has actually been done in some countries. Japan, for example, has permitted life insurance premiums to be excluded from the income subject to tax. All this is liable, however, not only to administrative difficulties but also to objections of principle.

Consideration must be given to the effects of taxation on the incentive to work, as well as the incentive to save. Since individuals are interested not only in their current consumption but also in the size of their asset holdings, there is a case for forced loans as an alternative to taxation. They may be little more than tax receipts and yet make a difference to the incentive to work and to produce, as was found during the war period, when the unspendable cash reserves, accumulated as a result of rationing, made consumers feel much better off. Forced loans in place of taxation would be a method of forced saving in form as well as substance.

The general economic problem, to repeat, is to direct as much as possible of the increment in real income into saving and to allow as little as possible of it to go into an immediate increase in consumption. One might think that, as income increases, there would be an automatic growth of tax revenue (and thus of compulsory saving collected through taxation). But tax revenue is not likely to grow by the whole amount of the increment in income. Nor is it certain even to increase in the same proportion as income. All depends on the methods of taxation in force. With a poll tax or an excise duty on necessities, revenue may not respond at all to an increase in national income. There is no automatic mechanism by which a high share of any increment in income is absorbed by taxation for the purpose of capital formation. If this result is to materialize, tax methods must be devised accordingly.

There is need for a fresh approach to the methods of public finance. The conventional precepts are not always relevant to the problem of capital formation in backward economies. Let us glance at three different approaches used in the past.

First, there have been and still are people for whom the task of public finance is simply to keep government expenditure to a minimum and to raise the funds for this by taxing the public in the least troublesome way. A good name for this fiscal principle is the Canon of Innocuity.[1] This passive attitude is not very helpful here.

Secondly, even the idea, discussed a hundred years ago by John Stuart Mill among others, of using taxation as a means of mitigating the inequalities of wealth—a revolutionary and essentially socialist idea—appears rather old-fashioned now and in any case beside the point. Although we can still agree with Mill that ' the true idea of distributive justice consists not in imitating but in redressing the inequalities and wrongs of nature,'[2] attention has shifted to another objective. Not a change in the interpersonal income distribution but an increase in the proportion of national income devoted to capital formation is the primary aim of public finance in the context of economic development. This does not mean that the principle of ability to pay has lost its significance. On the contrary, it should be strictly applied in taxation for collective saving. It is precisely this that makes the

---

[1] Cf. Edwin R. A. Seligman, *Essays in Taxation* (New York, 1897), p. 381.
[2] *Principles of Political Economy*, op. cit., p. 805.

fiscal preferable to the inflationary method of forced saving, though the preference can also be defended on other grounds.[1]

Thirdly, even the Keynesian notion of functional finance is irrelevant here. A fiscal policy aimed merely at preventing deflation and inflation is not going to solve the problem of capital formation. Keynes, doubtless for aesthetic as well as economic reasons, tended before the war to ridicule the Victorian virtues of abstinence and thriftiness, but this again is not a helpful attitude in the less developed countries. Keynesian economics is a powerful and flexible tool of analysis. At any rate formally, it can be adapted to all kinds of different situations. Substantively, however, there is no doubt that Keynes's General Theory has a bias against saving and in favour of spending, a bias that arises naturally and legitimately from the particular circumstances of the older industrial countries in the 1930s, but one that is pernicious when transplanted to the conditions in which the underdeveloped countries find themselves.[2]

The use of public finance for capital formation in underdeveloped countries is not an academic and unrealistic notion. There exist important examples of it. Once more, look at Japan. In the initial period of development, especially in the 1870s and 1880s, the state dominated the scene in providing capital for public works and industrial expansion. How was this financed ? By stiff taxation, especially of the agricultural population; occa-

[1] On distributive as well as technical grounds, J. H. Adler's case for property rather than income taxes merits attention : ' Since the distribution of real property, both urban and rural, is in most underdeveloped countries more uneven than the distribution of income, it may well be that the incidence of a proportional property tax with a relatively high level of basic exemptions is more progressive than a personal income tax; besides, it is easier to administer. Furthermore, a higher level of property taxation may have some beneficial effects upon the prevalent habit of devoting private savings largely to the acquisition or construction of real property.' (' The Fiscal and Monetary Implementation of Development Programs,' *American Economic Review, Papers and Proceedings*, May 1952, p. 594).

[2] Except where income levels are so high that abstinence matters little, preoccupation with capital accumulation seems to be inseparable from an atmosphere of ' puritanism ' (of which the Victorian tone reportedly prevailing in matters of art, taste and convention in present-day Russia is perhaps another instance). Hence it may be that the Keynesian revulsion against the Victorian virtues is one of the sophisticated attitudes which backward nations cannot afford to take over from the advanced.

sionally by forced loans imposed on the commercial middle classes in the towns; and also by credit expansion, which was not inflationary in so far as it reflected an increase in the monetary sector of the economy. People who had not used money before performed saving in the very act of building up their cash balances. Japan achieved her industrial growth without much inflation.

The outstanding instrument of forced saving in Japan was the traditional land tax, which was drastically tightened up and reassessed in the 1870s, when it brought in about four-fifths of total government revenue. This was ' the device which was used to siphon off a part of the increment in productivity in agriculture, and these revenues were channelled directly into investment projects by government action.'[1] This was the way the requisite means of subsistence were mobilized for capital construction. In sharp contrast to agriculture, manufacturing industries were lightly taxed or even subsidized. So the squeeze on agriculture did not have to affect investment incentives in industry and public works— a point of general significance. Later the picture gradually changed, though at the end of the century the land tax still accounted for nearly half of the total tax revenue.

Other examples can be found in more recent times. Latvia, a war-ravaged as well as underdeveloped country that received practically no foreign loans, kept government revenue at a high level in the 1920s in order to finance budgetary appropriations for investment expenditure by private as well as public organizations. In addition, large funds were collected in the form of budget surpluses and deposited with the central bank. Government deposits at this bank in the 1920s showed a remarkable increase, the counterpart of which was a roughly equal growth in the bank's loans and discounts to traders, farmers and industrialists. In short, the central bank in this case served as a reservoir through which the saving collected by the state was made available for capital outlay throughout the economy.

It should be added, however, that in this case the effectiveness of the fiscal system may have been partly due to accidental circumstances. In the early post-war period after the first world war

[1] Bruce F. Johnston, 'Agricultural Productivity and Economic Development in Japan,' *Journal of Political Economy*, December 1951.

the paper currency circulating in the country was that left behind by foreign occupation authorities and its quantity could not be increased. For a time the government had no printing press, and it may have been this little technical difficulty that forced it from the start to institute a fairly rigorous revenue system, which later proved so poent a collector of investible funds.[1] Besides, Latvia was helped by good export markets for her flax and timber, just as Japan had earlier been helped by the foreign demand for her raw silk. But other countries, including some with large petroleum reserves, have been presented with similar opportunities without deriving similar benefits from them.

While the Latvian episode is relatively unknown, the Polish case has attracted some attention. In Poland during the inter-war period it was not the central bank so much as two government banks (one for agriculture, the other for industry) which received budgetary appropriations from the government. Here too, the government actually realized budget surpluses over a number of years, and these were passed on to the two government banks, which re-lent the funds to private firms and government corporations for investment.[2] Turkey has had a similar system, which is even more familiar, and which I need not attempt to describe.

The country that affords the most notable instance of forced collective saving is Soviet Russia under the five-year plans since 1928. In this case private investment activity was entirely suppressed. This example will not be relevant to nations living under a régime of political freedom and individual rights. I mention it along with the others only in order to bring out the point that in countries with widely different political ideologies the system of collective saving appears to have arisen from basic economic needs which those countries had in common. It worked of course imperfectly, being man-made; but it worked nevertheless. It became very prominent in the post-war reconstruction effort of Western Europe in the 1940's, but that is an example that does not come from an underdeveloped area.

We can readily concede that public finance has only too often

[1] See *The Course and Control of Inflation*, League of Nations, 1946, pp. 23–4, 56–7 and 63.

[2] Ibid., p. 57. Cf. also J. Taylor, *The Economic Development of Poland, 1919–1950* (Ithaca, N.Y., 1952), Chapter 5.

been distinguished by waste in such forms as overstaffed services, ostentatious buildings and military establishments. All we have done is to illustrate the possibility of collective saving. That this has not been the typical form of government operation is not to be wondered at, for in the past it has not even been a recognized aim of public finance to any great extent.

From the examples quoted, as well as from general considerations, it should be clear that the fiscal method of compulsory saving is entirely compatible with private investment.[1] It is the act of saving which the state enforces. The act of investment can be left in private hands. A variety of institutional forms is conceivable (state loans, capital subscriptions, mixed companies, development finance corporations, investment trusts, etc.). New institutions may not actually be needed if banks of some kind already exist. The savings collected by the government could be deposited with the banking system or applied to the reduction of government debt held by the banking system. This would permit the banks to extend credits to private entrepreneurs without inflationary effects, leaving to private firms or individuals the execution of the investment projects as well as their subsequent operation. The two components of capital formation, saving and investment, depend on thrift and enterprise; there is nothing to prevent collective thrift from being combined with individual enterprise.

Most underdeveloped countries will need a combination of private and government action in the field of saving and investment. Each country must work out its own mixture in accordance with its own particular needs and opportunities. There can be no standard recipe of universal applicability. The fact that I have thought it useful to make a short excursion into the field of public finance does not mean that I would place anything like exclusive reliance on fiscal methods for a solution of the problem of saving. After all, in an underdeveloped country the fiscal machinery is likely to be underdeveloped also. It is too easy for an economist to dump all unsolved problems on the shoulders of ' the govern-

[1] Cf. Howard S. Ellis, *The Economics of Freedom*, p. 40.

ment.' Who are 'the government'? We know, however, that certain things are peculiarly difficult, if not impossible, to achieve without some form of collective action; and one of them, it seems to me, is the mobilization of domestic saving potentials in economically backward areas.

SOCIAL OVERHEAD CAPITAL

If there is a place for government activity on the investment side, it is by almost general consent in the field of essential public works and services, ranging from roads and railways to telegraph and telephone systems, power plants, waterworks and—last but not least—schools and hospitals. We have noted that in the absence of these basic facilities, which in advanced countries can be taken for granted, the yield of any injection of private capital may turn out disappointingly small. While a large foreign corporation might construct some of these things itself in order to carry on its business, small-scale individual enterprises cannot be expected to do so.

It is the need for this type of investment that makes capital building in a backward country such a 'lumpy' process. This is what renders the concept of marginal productivity of capital so difficult to apply in underdeveloped areas where, as H. W. Singer remarks, the 'problem is not at all that of marginal additions but one of structural change and all-round growth.'[1] In such circumstances, contrary to the motto of Marshall's Principles, change is apt to be, in the nature of the case, saltatory.

Once a minimum structure of social overhead capital exists, any private firm can make use of it at small or zero additional cost not only to itself but to the community. And naturally those communities will be at an advantage that can give full employment to such facilities. Here again, if we want to see a circle we can see one. In a poor country an overhead capital structure may not initially have enough work to do to justify its existence and can then justify itself only by faith in the future.

The great importance of public overhead capital may warrant

---

[1] See the discussion in *American Economic Review, Papers and Proceedings* May 1952, p. 608.

some interference with the composition of the existing flow of investment.[1] The actual composition may be shaped by the country's backwardness itself, and it would be rash to assume that it cannot be improved upon. In the overcrowded peasant economies of Eastern Europe, for instance, the peasant generally did some saving, but he preferred to keep the investment process in his own hands. The result was a relative over-supply of the kind of capital goods used by the individual farmer under existing conditions (barns, carts, primitive implements, draught animals, etc.) and a lack of the large-scale capital construction that would have promoted a change in those conditions. There was an obvious need for co-operative rural investment, and at least in Bulgaria some promising attempts in this direction were made before the war.[2]

While the American economy to-day impresses the world mainly by its mass production methods, in the early nineteenth century it distinguished itself above all by the way it was building up 'social overhead capital.' Even that critical English visitor, Frances Trollope, wrote in 1832: 'There is no point in the national character of the Americans which commands so much respect as the boldness and energy with which public works are undertaken and carried through.' We are too apt to forget how large a part public investment played in this development. A series of essays by Carter Goodrich has furnished some useful reminders. In the first half of the nineteenth century 'the proposals to construct canals and turnpikes and other improvements, and later the railroads, at the public expense, were among the most important policy questions of the time.'[3] The ambitious Gallatin Plan of 1808 was rejected not to safeguard private enterprise, but only because eventually the belief gained ground that 'the state rather than the federal government was the appropriate agency for internal improvement.'[4] In fact, 'the conspicuous features [of the movement for internal improvements] down to

---

[1] J. H. Adler, op. cit., p. 585.
[2] Cf. Doreen Warriner, *Economics of Peasant Farming* (London, 1939), pp. 161–67.
[3] Carter Goodrich, 'National Planning of Internal Improvements,' *Political Science Quarterly*, March 1948, p. 17.
[4] Ibid., p. 30.

the Civil War were the extent of government activity and the extraordinary intermingling of public and private enterprise.'[1]

In somewhat similar ways the German principalities, as Schumpeter has pointed out, endeavoured to prepare a favourable environment for private enterprise by canal and road building and the like.[2] Australia, as we have seen, provides another good example of state investment in public works in the early stages of development.

The building of the overhead capital structure, more than any other form of investment, requires long views and steady pursuit. While it is peculiarly suited to collective or co-operative action in underdeveloped countries, it is particularly vulnerable to political change. This is an argument for placing it under some independent and continuous body, unaffected, if possible, by shifting cabinets and parliamentary fortunes. In a number of countries permanent economic councils or development corporations have been set up for this purpose. The accumulation of social overhead capital is an expensive and long-term investment which should not be continually exposed to short-term variations in the political weather.

Lastly, let us remember that social overhead capital means a social overhead charge; it does not pay for itself. It cannot be an economic success unless the more specialized activities which it is meant to serve do come into being. It provides a skeleton structure into which the economy must be encouraged to grow through less lumpy and more widely diffused investments of capital, and, above all, through the endeavour and enterprise of individuals.

INDIVIDUAL EFFORT: THE GROUNDWORK

In the growth of Western industrialism the application of capital to the processes of production has been for the most part in the hands of individual entrepreneurs. Some of the industrially backward communities to-day may reject this recipe on principle

---

[1] Carter Goodrich, ' Public Spirit and American Improvements,' *Proceedings of the American Philosophical Society*, Vol. 92, No. 4, October 1948. See also a further paper by the same author, ' The Virginia System of Mixed Enterprise,' *Political Science Quarterly*, September 1949.

[2] Joseph A. Schumpeter, *Business Cycles* (New York, 1939), Vol. I, p. 235.

or think it inapplicable to them. It would be unreasonable, however, to close one's eyes to a central feature in the greatest spurt of
economic expansion the world has seen. The debate between
planners and anti-planners is not our concern here. Besides, one
cannot realistically treat the problem as one of exclusive choice
between state action and individual enterprise. In the familiar
case for the private exercise of the investment function their are
just one or two points that I wish to pick out as material for our
concluding reflections.

In reality, of course, the investment function is not separated,
or even separable, from other economic functions. It is the
private ownership and operation of business that makes for the
private exercise of the investment function as a by-product.
What we are looking at is therefore only one facet of a large and
complex topic.

Leaving investment to the individual entrepreneur can have
the advantage of providing the machinery for saving the increment
of income which capital investment creates. If there is any
hope for substantial private saving it lies mainly in the reinvestment of entrepreneurial profits. In a backward country, who but
the businessman can have any strong inducement as well as the
capacity to save ? Saving and investment incentives are closely
tied together in the person of the entrepreneur, in his past achievement and future ambitions. The ploughing-back of entrepreneurial profits was historically the major source of capital accumulation
in Western economic growth and as such occupies a central place
in Schumpeter's theory of development. If the pattern can be
repeated elsewhere, it would be an effective and almost automatic
way of maximizing a country's marginal saving ratio.

Capital formation can be permanently successful only in a
capital-conscious community, and this condition, which is just as
important for the continued maintenance as for the initial creation
of capital, is promoted by a wide diffusion of investment activity
among individuals. Nothing matters so much as the quality of
the people. The personal habits and traits associated with the
use of capital—among them initiative, prudence, ingenuity and
foresightedness—give a deeper and surer base to a nation's
economic advance than the blueprints of a planning commission.

Therefore it is well for the state to leave scope for the exercise of these qualities and to reduce barriers to their development. The state might withdraw from areas where individual enterprise has learned to stand on its own feet and turn its attention to other fields where its powers are needed to clear the way. This is what Japan, for example, did at the end of the last century and it looks as though Turkey, after two decades of governmental predominance in investment activity as well as saving, were following a similar sequence.[1] There may be other ways in which capital can be made to enter into the social culture of an industrially backward people, but opportunity for private investment may be the most effective in the long run.

A nation cannot be strongly capital-conscious unless the individuals that compose it do some saving of their own and can see from their own experience the point of roundabout methods of production. If this requisite is not fulfilled foreign business capital is apt to remain a mere projection of the creditor economy. Direct foreign investment in these circumstances is not always a happy form of cultural contact, and this aspect of it may lie at the root of some of the trouble in which it has often resulted.

From a view-point broader than that of pure economics, capital is well described as ' a social heritage dependent upon the institutions and habit-patterns of thought and action of individuals in society . . .' And 'that is why capital cannot be . . . "transferred" from one situation to another without the individuals who will re-adapt and "re-fashion" it for use in a new pattern of activity.'[2] It is no accident that nineteenth-century foreign investment scored its greatest successes in the ' empty ' plains of the temperate regions where it went together with large numbers of people. These people took with them the ideas they had inherited.

' Ideas,' said Marshall, ' whether those of art and science or

---

[1] Cf. *The Economy of Turkey*, Report of a Mission, International Bank for Reconstruction and Development, Washington, D.C., 1951. For some interesting general comments, see also Bernard Lewis, ' Recent Developments in Turkey,' *International Affairs*, July 1951, p. 324, and Richard D. Robinson, ' The Lesson of Turkey,' *The Middle East Journal*, Autumn 1951, p. 424.

[2] S. Herbert Frankel, *Some Conceptual Aspects of International Economic Development of Underdeveloped Territories* (Essays in International Finance, Princeton University, May 1952), pp. 14–15.

those embodied in practical appliances, are the most "real" of the gifts that each generation receives from its predecessors. The world's material wealth would quickly be replaced, if it were destroyed but the ideas by which it was made were retained. If, however, the ideas were lost, but not the material wealth, then that would dwindle and the world would go back to poverty."[1] The ways and uses of capital investment are among the ideas to be disseminated if the backward parts of the world are to be delivered from their present poverty.

We have reached a field of sociological rather than economic considerations, and at the border of this field I will stop. That we have come to it is not surprising, for the advancement of the backward countries is far more than an economic problem.

[1] *Principles of Economics* (8th edition), p. 780.

INDEX

Ability to pay, 78–9, 100, 108, 147
Abstinence, 110, 148
Acceleration principle, 26
Adler, J. H., 148, 153
Advertising, 8, 62
Africa, 64, 80, 90, 128
Agriculture, 21, 23, 32, 35–6, 87
  and industry, 51, 54–5, 108, 149
  improvements in, 52–6, 66, 141
  investment in, 46, 50, 91, 153
Algeria, 80
American (*see also* United States)
  aid, 96–7
  capital, 83, 131
  consumption patterns, 62, 67
  direct investments, 24, 28, 82, 85, 87
  standard of living, 20, 63
Amortization, 82, 92, 130–34
Argentina, 64, 86–7, 99
Asia, 64
  South-eastern, 32, 34, 35, 48, 50
Australia, 51, 64, 86, 91, 109
Austria, 96

Balance of payments, 58, 121, 132, 135–7
  disequilibrium in, 70–75, 81, 92–3, 95, 118
Balogh, T., 73, 79
Banking system, 101, 151
Belgium, 97
Bentham, J., 16, 49, 144
Bloomfield, A. I., 125
Bolivia, 51
Brazil, 78, 85, 107
British (*see also* Great Britain)
  capital exports, 28–9, 74
  Commonwealth, 107
  foreign investment, 24, 79, 83
Brown, A. J., 86
Buchanan, N. S., 46, 132
Bulgaria, 153
Burma, 34
Business cycle, 12, 13, 29, 126–7

Campos, R. de Oliveira, 126
Canada, 22, 24, 28, 64, 78, 83, 85, 86, 106–7
Capital,
  demand for, 4–6, 12, 30, 48, 107, 109
  intensity, 7, 9, 10, 45, 51
  lack of, 5, 17, 57, 67, 93, 130

Capital,
  marginal productivity of, 14–5, 27–8, 30, 136–8, 152
  per worker, 13, 48–9
  supply of, 4–5, 31–2, 49–51, 75, 105, 107, 116, 130
  use of, 12, 18, 108, 154
Chile, 7
China, 8, 19–20, 90, 107
Clark, C., 63, 98
Classical economics, 17, 70
Cleland, W. W., 35
Colombia, 19
Colombo Plan, 48
Colonies, 79–80
Communication, 64–5, 66–7, 76–7
Comparative advantage, 21, 22, 69, 84, 123
Comparative cost, 71, 120, 137
Complementary industries, 11, 15, 27
Construction,
  capital, 95, 115, 141, 149, 153
  public, 55, 138
  residential, 114, 117
Consume, propensity to, 58–9, 61-2, 67, 72, 92–3, 95, 118, 143
Consumption
  and investment, 38, 103, 115
  and saving, 60, 67, 70, 111, 143–4
  'conspicuous,' 37, 58, 61, 68, 141
  pattern of, 59–61, 65, 67, 75, 118–9, 143
  productive and unproductive, 37–8
Copland, D. B., 91
Credit expansion, 26, 106, 112, 117, 149
Customs unions, 19

Demand elasticity, 9, 10, 14, 22, 71, 73
Demonstration effect, 58, 63–7, 73, 76, 81, 95, 118, 142, 149
Denmark, 51
Dernburg, H. J., 83
Disguised unemployment, 32–7, 40, 43–5, 47, 49, 50, 54–5, 66, 103, 141
Diversification, 21
Dividends, 134, 135, 143
Dollar shortage, 62, 70, 71, 73, 93
Domar, E. D., 132–3
Duesenberry, J. S., 58, 60

E.C.A. (Economic Co-operation Administration), 95–7

Ecuador, 19, 67
Education, 2, 47, 48, 64-5, 88
Effective demand, 17, 21, 124-5
Egypt, 34, 35, 36
Ellis, H. S., 71, 76, 97, 151
Emigration, 47-8
England. *See* Great Britain.
Enterprise,
    foreign, 84, 88
    individual, 10, 16, 151, 154-6
    public, 154
    qualities of, 10, 17
Equipment, 2, 5-7, 9, 10, 62, 114
    imported, 42, 45-6, 97, 109-16, 140
Europe, 109, 121, 130
    Eastern, 35, 64, 153
    South-eastern, 32, 34
    Western, 17, 21, 24, 28, 64, 145-6, 150
European Recovery Programme, 95-7
Exchange control, 73, 82, 83, 93
Exchange depreciation, 135
Exchange rate, 71, 73
Export
    prices, 73, 97-9, 101
    proceeds, 97-101, 111, 112, 127
External economies, 14-5, 86, 136
Extractive industries, 24, 25, 29, 83-4

Farming. *See* Agriculture
Feis, H., 89
Financial organization, 3, 26
Fiscal policy, 15, 96, 119, 129, 133, 140, 145
Food, 9, 23, 36-9, 42-3, 52, 141
    crops, 35, 39
    deficit, 39, 42
    production, 50, 53-4, 141
    requirements, 42, 44
    surplus, 38, 40-41, 43
Foreign aid, 44-5, 66, 77, 93-5
Foreign investment, 24-30, 57, 66, 79, 82-9, 120-39, 156
    business, 25, 75, 92, 106, 138
    'colonial' type of, 25, 29, 90, 140, 142
    direct, 25, 28, 82-92, 156
Foreign loans, 42, 46, 48, 82, 95, 126, 136
    to public authorities, 24, 28, 89-91, 128
France, 80, 89
Frankel, S. H., 90, 128, 156
Full employment, 102, 111, 129, 143
Functional finance, 148

Gallatin Plan, 153
Germany, 89, 128, 136, 154

Gold movements, 121-2
Gold standard, 72
Goodrich, C., 153-4
Government expenditure, 65, 78, 102, 103, 106
Gray Report, 77, 82
Great Britain, 21, 74, 86, 87, 89, 107, 110, 128, 134
Gudin, E., 100
Gutmann, P. M., 42

Haberler, G., 71, 73, 96, 123
Haddon-Cave, C. P., 91
Hamilton, A., 104
Hansen, A. H., 48
Harrod, R. F., 125
Havana Conference, 129
Health, 2, 4, 47, 48
Hilgerdt, F., 21, 51
Hoarding, 26
Hobson, J. A., 127

Import
    prices, 97, 102
    restrictions, 73, 100-1, 104-19
Imports of capital goods, 97-101, 109-17, 127, 140
India, 8, 34, 48, 65, 98, 105
Industrialization, 23, 51, 53, 55, 75, 109
Industry, 16, 22, 28, 46, 50-1, 55, 85
Infant industry, 104-5, 108-9, 118
Inflation, 100-1, 106, 113-4, 116-7, 144-5
Innocuity, Canon of, 147
Innovation, 13
Interest, 82, 92, 125, 132-6
International Bank for Reconstruction and Development, 156
International economics, 68, 70, 121, 131
International grants, 42, 48, 80-1, 89, 92-8
International trade, 20-23, 71, 74, 98, 120-23
Inventory profits, 28
Investment,
    autonomous, 29-30, 92, 139, 140
    domestic, 66, 113, 133, 134, 140
    extensive, 48-50
    governmental, 79, 91, 103, 156
    incentives, 5-6, 11-14, 17, 26-7, 30-1, 105-7, 117, 138, 155
    induced, 29
    intensive, 48-50
    international. *See* Foreign investment
    private, 43, 101, 151, 155-6
    public, 16, 30, 153

Israel, 64
Issawi, C., 35
Italy, 97

Japan, 15, 16, 43, 89, 90, 91, 143, 146, 148-9, 156
Johnston, B. F., 149

Kafka, A., 116
Kahn, A. E., 79, 137
Keynes, 10, 38, 123, 124, 148
Keynesian economics, 17, 21, 124, 128-31, 148
Kindleberger, C. P., 73
Knapp, J., 125
Knight, M. M., 79-80
Korea, 87, 97
Kurihara, K. K., 126
Kuznets, 59, 61

Lary, H. B., 132
Latin America, 7, 34, 64, 65, 66, 90, 117
Latvia, 149-50
League of Nations, 27, 72, 80, 137, 150
Leakages, 39, 40, 47, 55, 74, 102, 112, 135
Leisure, 64, 73
Lenin, 127
Lewandowski, M., 87
Lewis, B., 156
Link, R. G., 10
List, F., 104
Luxemburg, R., 127
Luxuries, 62-3, 65, 111, 114, 116-7

Machlup, 124
Maintenance, 113, 115, 155
Malaya, 98
Management, 14, 28, 82, 88
Mandelbaum, K., 35
Manufacturing, 24, 46, 52, 83-5, 106, 149
Marginal saving ratio, 113, 142, 155
Marsh, D. B., 57
Marshall, 14, 15, 152, 156-7
Martinez, A. B., 87
Marx, 127-8
Mass production, 20, 45, 153
Mendershausen, H., 80, 142
Metzler, L. A., 126
Middle class, 17, 64, 74, 149
Middle East, 68
Migration, 94, 130, 131, 156
Mill, J. S., 11-2, 16, 24, 74, 121-2, 147
Mining, 83, 90
Mintz, I., 125
Monetary expansion, 6, 8, 17, 36, 106, 129

Monetary policy, 15, 96, 129, 133, 140
Monopoly, 47, 128
Multiplier, 40, 41, 74, 124, 135

National income, 36, 63, 111, 136
and foreign aid, 77, 94
and foreign investment, 133
and foreign trade, 23
and saving, 42, 115, 140
share of capital formation in, 59, 75, 76, 90, 117, 144, 147
Natural resources, 1, 6, 12, 130
New Zealand, 51, 64, 99

Obsolescence, 110
Ohlin, B., 121, 123-4
Oil fields, 24
Organization of farming, 33, 35, 46
Overhead capital, 10, 47, 85, 91, 117, 128, 152-4

Peru, 19, 86
Pesmazoglu, J. S., 28
Petroleum, 23, 83, 150
Philippines, 95
Point Four, 77, 82
Polak, J. J., 94
Poland, 150
Population, 1, 8, 12, 18, 21, 36, 41, 56
agricultural, 32, 34-5, 41, 148
excess, 32-4, 49, 51, 55
growth of, 21, 36, 47-50, 87, 131, 142
Portugal, 69, 80
Prebisch, R., 57, 67
Preiser, E., 125, 126, 128
Prest, A. R., 34, 43
Prices, 71, 99, 110, 121, 122, 124
and productivity, 8
of raw materials, 97
rise in, 6, 17, 36, 102, 113
Primary production, 21, 24, 53, 84, 87
Productivity, 19, 20, 27, 66-9, 87
and balance of payments, 70-72, 74
and population, 18, 142
and purchasing power, 8, 17, 22, 28, 85
in agriculture and industry, 51-6
108, 141, 149
through capital investment, 9, 10, 13, 21, 23, 133, 136
Profits, 27, 28, 84, 99, 105, 110, 111, 142
reinvestment of, 86, 143, 155
Public finance, 44, 70, 115, 118, 143, 147, 150
Public utilities, 24, 29, 47, 84, 85, 89
Public works, 78, 85-6, 102, 113, 126, 148, 152-4
Puerto Rico, 34, 80

Railways, 10, 29, 36, 80, 85–7, 91, 117, 152–3
Remer, C. F., 90
Replacement, 110, 113, 114, 130
Reubens, E. P., 75, 90
Ricardo, 69, 120
Robertson, D. H., 23
Robinson, R. D., 156
Robinson Crusoe, 6
Rockefeller Report, 78, 82
Rosenstein-Rodan, P. N., 9, 35, 63
Royal Institute of International Affairs, 26, 90

Salter, A., 27
Samuel, A. M., 79
Samuelson, P. A., 72, 125, 135
Saudi Arabia, 86
Save, propensity to, 60, 65, 74, 117, 127, 134–5, 142–3
Saving,
  abortive, 37
  business, 145
  collective, 43, 146–7, 151
  complementary, 40, 42, 140
  compulsory, 37, 44, 65, 100, 101, 115, 118, 144–5
  effective, 37–8
  excessive, 9, 127
  forced, 102, 106–7, 112–13, 116–17, 144–49
  potential, 37–43, 48, 49, 54, 95, 141, 152
  temporary, 114, 146
  virtual, 37–8, 43
  voluntary, 37, 40, 65, 70, 101, 105, 115, 142, 145
Say's Law, 8, 9, 11
Schumpeter, 11–13, 15, 154, 155
Seligman, E. R. A., 147
Senior, Nassau, 58
Singer, H. W., 24, 30, 84, 152
Skills, 2, 15, 47, 86, 104
Smith, Adam, 6, 18
South Africa, 64
South America, 50, 52
Soviet Russia, 43, 64, 76, 109, 110, 150
Spengler, J. J., 15, 17, 144
Stagnation, 11, 15, 76
Staley, E., 75, 89
Subsistence fund, 39, 40, 42, 44
Sudan, 43
Sweden, 19
Switzerland, 19

Tariff, 18–22, 74, 104–9, 118
  factories, 106
  preferences, 18, 107
Taussig, 124
Taxation, 37, 43, 99–103, 108, 143-48
  double, 82
  indirect, 43
  progressive, 78–80
  property, 148
  proportional, 78–9
Taylor, J., 150
Technical discontinuities, 2, 9, 10, 12
Technical progress, 2, 3, 33, 61–2
Techniques of production, 12, 15, 32, 45–6, 62, 88
  agricultural, 32–4, 43, 46, 52–3, 66
Technology, 2, 82, 88–9
Terms of trade, 42, 97–103, 122–3, 140
Thrift, 143, 148
Training, 37, 45, 47, 88
Transfer difficulties, 83, 138
Transfer mechanism, 121, 123
Transport costs, 18–9, 39–42, 122
Transport facilities, 2, 15, 18, 47, 94
Trinidad, 34
Trollope, F., 153
Truman, President, 65
Tsuru, Shigeto, 15
Turkey, 150, 156

United Kingdom. *See* Great Britain
United Nations, 18, 19, 24, 53, 63, 66, 83, 97, 117
United States, 17, 23, 34, 49, 97, 125, 128
  foreign aid, 77–8, 94, 96–7
  foreign investment, 27, 82–4, 129, 131
  mass production, 20, 45, 153
  trade policy, 87, 109
Uruguay, 64, 66–7

Veblen, T., 58, 61
Venezuela, 19, 23
Vicious circle, 4, 10–11, 57, 70, 85, 143
Victorian virtues, 148
Viner, J., 16, 94

Warriner, D., 35, 153
Welfare, 47, 78, 79, 94
Whale, B., 74
Williams, J. H., 24, 27, 121
Wythe, G., 7

Young, A. A., 6

PATTERNS OF TRADE
AND DEVELOPMENT

THE WICKSELL LECTURES ARE SPONSORED BY
THE WICKSELL LECTURE SOCIETY
IN COOPERATION WITH
THE SOCIAL SCIENCE INSTITUTE, STOCKHOLM UNIVERSITY
THE STOCKHOLM SCHOOL OF ECONOMICS
THE SWEDISH ECONOMIC SOCIETY

These lectures were delivered in Stockholm on April 7th and 10th, 1959, and are reprinted by permission of the Wicksell Lecture Society

CONTENTS

Introduction by Professor Erik Lundberg, 167

Preface, 169

FIRST LECTURE, APRIL 7, 1959

Contrasting Trends in 19th and 20th Century World Trade, 171

Trade Expansion and the Transmission of Economic Growth, 171

The Role of the New Countries in World Trade and Investment, 173

The Current Lag in Exports of the Poorer Countries, 178

Trade Trends and International Investment Incentives, 187

SECOND LECTURE, APRIL 10, 1959

The International Economy and the Problem of Growth, 193

Past and Present Development Patterns, 193

Industrialization for Export Markets, 197

The Pattern of Home-Market Expansion, 203

Summary and Conclusion, 210

Appendix: Dynamic Aspects of Trade Theory, 215

Index of Authors, 227

INTRODUCTION

LAST year Professor Lindahl inaugurated the Wicksell Lecture
Society. On that occasion, he outlined the background and the
aims of this Society. I can therefore make my introduction very
brief.

The purpose of the Wicksell Lecture Society—the distinguished
character of which is illustrated by its being linked to the name of
Knut Wicksell, our greatest and most well-known economist—is to
invite to Stockholm each year an outstanding economist to lecture
on economic questions, especially in the field of international trade
and finance. The lectures are published as a special series by the
Swedish Economic Society in Stockholm.

This year, as well as last, we were fortunate enough to have as
our guest an economist of world fame—Professor Ragnar Nurkse
from Columbia University, New York. Professor Nurkse had as
early as in the middle of the 1930s published a book in Vienna on
international capital movements. As research worker in the
League of Nations' economic department he was active in this field
for many years and one most important result of his work was a
League of Nations' publication ' International Currency Experience ' published in the year 1944. I consider this study to be the
best available one we have of the lessons of international monetary relations during the inter-war period. During the post-war
period Professor Nurkse was intensively studying problems of balanced and unbalanced economic growth with special regard to
international repercussions. He has written a great number of
articles on business cycles, economic growth and balance of
payments' problems of various countries, and he published an
outstanding book on problems of capital formation in ' underdeveloped ' countries. In all Professor Nurkse's writings on international economics we cannot help but observe and enjoy the
particularly clear way in which he presents the problems, the deli-
cate manner in which he uses—but does not over-use—available
statistics, as well as his sense for finding balanced proportions be-

tween theory and historical facts in interpreting the trends of economic development.

As Professor Nurkse was spending this year in Geneva we took the opportunity of inviting him to Stockholm as this year's Wicksell lecturer.

He delivered two lectures to the Society, on the 7th and the 10th of April, the first dealing with ' Contrasting Trends in 19th and 20th Century World Trade ' and the second with ' The International Economy and the Problem of Growth '. After returning to Geneva Professor Nurkse wrote an appendix to his lectures (' Dynamic Aspects of Trade Theory '), giving more precise formulations to some important points discussed therein.

Professor Nurkse died a few days after having finished this appendix. No-one could possibly have suspected that these lectures —so penetrating and forcefully delivered before an intent audience of businessmen and economists—would be his last. We had a strong impression that we were listening to a hard-working scientist, deeply engaged in a most important field of research, who was assuring us that this work of his would go on for many years to come. We did not know the tragic fact that Professor Nurkse was imposing too great a strain upon his health and that the line of research he was carrying out—and I feel there is no other economist who could do this work as well as he—would be abruptly cut off.

Professor Nurkse had since the 1920s been very interested in Sweden and after many visits he had acquired a wide knowledge of Swedish culture as well as of Swedish economic thinking. He had many friends and admirers in Sweden, and his knowledge of the Swedish language was admirable. I feel that in publishing his lectures in the Wicksell Society Series we are honouring Professor Nurkse and his memory in the best possible manner.

The high quality pervading the whole of Professor Nurkse's impressive list of writings is only too evident in the lectures presented in this volume; and it is this, above all, that makes his work an achievement of the very highest order, which in my opinion could be equalled by very few economists indeed.

ERIK LUNDBERG

PREFACE

I should like to express my sincere thanks to the members and sponsors of the Wicksell Society for providing the most agreeable and stimulating conditions ever enjoyed by a visiting lecturer. I cannot begin to name the many individuals to whom I am indebted, but my special thanks are due to Professor Erik Lundberg for his unfailing assistance, advice and encouragement during my visit to Stockholm. To Dr. Karl-Olof Faxén I am grateful for undertaking the thankless task of seeing these pages through the press.

The combination of economic history and theory is one of the most difficult *genres* in economic literature, and produces only too often results that fall between two stools. Yet it is precisely this form of discussion that I am foolhardy enough to attempt in the following pages. The relations of trade to development are a subject that strongly invites such treatment, but still affords no protection against the particular peril involved. I cannot, of course, pretend to have done more than scratch the surface of a fascinating field of study.

In the preparation of these lectures I have made some use of work done under a research professorship made possible by a grant from the Ford Foundation to Columbia University. I am grateful to my friends and colleagues at Columbia for having given me a respite from teaching obligations and a chance to pursue certain studies in the international economics of growth. This work has greatly benefited from the facilities which Dr. A. Breycha-Vauthier, Director of the United Nations Library in Geneva, has kindly placed at my disposal, and from the help which Dr. Robert M. Stern has given me with trade statistics and other source materials.

R. N.

Geneva,
April 26, 1959.

CONTRASTING TRENDS IN 19TH AND 20TH CENTURY WORLD TRADE

IN THE Western world today some widely accepted doctrines of trade and development are still to a large extent influenced by the experience of the 19th century. It is inevitable that economic thought should lag behind the facts of economic history. Even economists are human; our mental activity is, and indeed should be, shaped in some measure by limits set by experience. When conditions change, however, conceptions and preconceptions derived from earlier experience can become a shell that inhibits the development of thought as well as action. Thus the 19th century model of world trade is one which many of us still tend to carry in our minds as something like the normal or ideal. As it recedes in time, it appears more and more clearly to have been the product of very peculiar circumstances. We economists should always be ready to adapt the framework of our thinking if our work is to have relevance to the changing real world. It is in this spirit, and with these preoccupations as a motive force, that I venture to attempt a comparative sketch of long-term trends in international trade.

TRADE EXPANSION AND THE TRANSMISSION OF ECONOMIC GROWTH

The volume of world trade reached an all-time record level in 1957, but this is not surprising since nearly everything is bigger now than ever before. In relation to world production, international trade is smaller than it was some fifty or a hundred years ago. If we assume, as seems in fact to be the case, that roughly one-tenth of the value of commodities produced in the world now enters into international trade, this proportion was probably something like one-sixth in the years before the first world war.

But it is not just the *average* ratio of world trade to world production that adequately measures the relative weight of international trade in world economic affairs. More important was the *incremental* relationship between trade and production a hundred years ago. Trade played a crucial part in the economic growth not only of the ' new ' countries overseas but also of the ' old ' countries in Europe. In England at the time of Ricardo the margin of cultivation was creeping up the hillsides into poorer and poorer land and it is clear that without the burst of external trade which occurred soon afterwards, the struggle for food would have prevented industrialization from going as far as it did in Britain and elsewhere in Western Europe.

Trade was an ' engine of growth ' in the 19th century. Sir Dennis Robertson, from whom this phrase is borrowed, observes in passing that it was not just a matter of optimum allocation of a given stock of resources.[1] It was certainly that, but it was something more as well. As I see it, it was also a means whereby a vigorous process of economic growth came to be transmitted from the center to the outlying areas of the world. This aspect of 19th century experience was more or less neglected by the traditional trade theory, which focussed its powerful spotlight on the beneficent specialization of productive activities that results when two economies previously isolated enter into contact with each other. The theory of international specialization, static though it is, is none the less fundamental; and it was in fact a highly relevant theory at a time when economies were opened up to one another by revolutionary improvements in transport, reductions in tariffs and by other means (as in the case, for example, of Japan). Yet it left something out. Trade was an engine of growth transmission as well as a means of improved allocation of existing resources. The classical trade theory derived a great deal of prestige from the brilliant record of 19th century trade and development, even though it paid little or no attention to an essential aspect of that experience, namely, the dynamic spread of economic growth through trade. Why was this aspect neglected ? Perhaps because economic growth was taken for granted, like the air we breathe. As it was going

---

[1] D. H. Robertson, ' The Future of International Trade ', in *Essays in Monetary Theory* (London, 1940), p. 214, reprinted in the American Economic Association's *Readings in the Theory of International Trade* (Philadelphia, 1949).

on at a pace satisfactory for both the new countries and the old, it seemed a matter of no particular interest compared with the fascinating theoretical problem of 'entry into contact'. Once economies had entered into contact through trade and reallocated their resources for increased specialization, what happened after that ? Well, of course, they just grew and progressed, as everything did in the 19th century.

The focal center of economic expansion was initially Great Britain, whose population, despite heavy emigration, trebled in the 19th century while her real national income appears to have increased about ten-fold and the volume of her imports more than twenty-fold. (For our purposes the 19th century starts, in principle, in 1815 and ends in 1914.) The ratio of British imports to the national income was only about 12 per cent at the beginning, but in the latter part of the century had increased to about 30 per cent.[1] The change in commercial policy may be an important proximate explanation, but basic conditions helped to force the change. The industrial revolution happened to originate on a small island with a limited range of natural resources, at a time when synthetic materials were yet unknown. In these circumstances economic expansion was transmitted to less developed areas by a steep and steady increase in Britain's demand for primary commodities which those areas were well suited to produce. Local factors of production overseas, whose growth may in part have been induced by trade, were thus largely absorbed by the expansion of profitable primary production for export. On top of this, the center's increasing demand for raw materials and foodstuffs created incentives for capital and labor to move from the center to the outlying areas, accelerating the process of growth-transmission from the former to the latter.

THE ROLE OF THE NEW COUNTRIES
IN WORLD TRADE AND INVESTMENT

This pattern of 'growth through trade' affected particularly the new countries or, as the late Folke Hilgerdt used to call

[1] See E. A. G. Robinson, 'The Changing Structure of the British Economy', *Economic Journal*, September 1954. As everyone knows, the rate of Britain's growth slowed down after 1870, but it still remained of central importance in the international economy until the eve of World War I.

them, the ' regions of recent settlement ' in the world's temperate latitudes: Canada, Argentina, Uruguay, South Africa, Australia, New Zealand. No doubt the United States, too, belongs substantially to this group, though Hilgerdt did not usually include it, since the United States is so big a trader and producer as to be in a class by itself for most purposes. These regions had certain essential characteristics in common, but in the present context what matters is their high, though varying, dependence on growth through primary commodity exports and on the private foreign investment which, directly or indirectly, was thereby induced.

Alfred Marshall referred to ' the splendid markets which the old world has offered to the new. '[1] He forgot to mention that these were *growing* markets, but this he seems to have assumed as a matter of course. The second-last chapter of his *Principles*, which deals with ' General Influences of Economic Progress ', begins as follows: ' The field of employment which any place offers for labor and capital depends, firstly, on its natural resources; secondly on ... knowledge and organization; and thirdly, on ... markets in which it can sell those things of which it has a superfluity. The importance of this last condition is often underrated; but it stands out prominently when we look at the history of new countries. '[2] It is perhaps significant that such remarks, though true almost to the point of platitude, were left unrelated to the traditional theory of international trade.

It was no doubt under the impression of contemporary experience that Marshall declared that ' the causes which determine the economic progress of nations belong to the study of international trade '.[3] In the second half of the 20th century this may seem to us a curious statement. It can be understood only in the light of historical conditions. It embodies the particular experience of Britain's economic relations with the new countries overseas. Economic progress in these areas was due not to international specialization alone but also to the fact that the rapid growth which was taking place in the center was transmitted to

[1] *Principles of Economics* (8th ed.) pp. 668.
[2] *Principles of Economics* (8th ed.) pp. 668.
[3] *Principles of Economics* (8th ed.), p. 270.

the outlying new countries through a vigorous increase in demand for primary products. This was perhaps the most spectacular feature of the 19th century trade.

The new countries seem to have greatly increased their share in the rapidly growing total volume of world trade. At any rate their share in British imports rose from 8 per cent in the middle to 18 per cent at the end of the 19th century.[1] This does not include the United States, whose share in British imports during that period remained fairly constant at just under 20 per cent. The great increase in the U.S. share in British trade had taken place earlier.

While trade all over the world was expanding at a rapid pace, there is no doubt that the exports of the new countries enjoyed a particularly vigorous increase in demand. Correspondingly the outflow of British capital went mostly to these favored areas. The year 1870 is the earliest for which we can determine with any degree of confidence the geographical distribution of British capital invested overseas. The share of the 'regions of recent settlement' in the British foreign-investment total outstanding rises from less than one-third in that year to just about two-thirds in 1913. Again the share of the United States in that total remains constant at about one-fifth, while that of the other new countries shoots up from about 10 per cent in 1870 to 45 per cent in 1913.[2] But again we must remember that the rise in the U.S.

[1] The percentage distribution of British imports by countries of origin may be summarized in the following figures, which I owe to the assistance of Dr. Robert M. Stern:

	1857–59	1911–13
United States	19	19
Other ' new ' countries (a)	8	18
Industrial Europe (b)	21	23
All other areas	52	40
Total	100	100

(a) Canada, Argentina, South Africa, Australia, New Zealand.
(b) Germany, France, Italy, Belgium, Netherlands.

[2] The total (gross) amount of British capital overseas increased from about £ 1,000 million in 1870 to about £ 4,000 million in 1913, and its percentage distribution by regions may be roughly indicated as follows:

	1870	1931
United States	20	20
Other ' new ' countries	10	45
Europe	50	5
All other areas	20	30
Total	100	100

share in British capital exports occurred in the earlier part of the century, for which the data are too poor to permit any confident statistical estimates.

The growth in British imports of primary products induced British capital exports to most if not all primary producing countries, but it is clear that the R.R.S. group was specially favored by the flow of capital as well as the rise in demand for its exports. Evidently there was a connection between the two phenomena. Private international investment in undeveloped areas was fundamentally, if not directly, induced by the growth in demand for essential foodstuffs and raw materials. The connection was not always a close one with regard to timing. Thus the 1880's were a period of active capital exports even though trade in agricultural products was relatively depressed. All the same, in that decade and on other occasions also, foreign investment was supported by a long-run prospect of expanding demand in the industrial centers for the raw materials whose supply it went out to augment.

These circumstances illustrate the essentially cumulative nature of economic growth. ' To those who have shall be given ': there is good reason for calling this ' the first law of development '.[1] It was Wicksell, whose great name we here commemorate, who originated the idea of ' cumulative process ' in the theory of short-term business fluctuations. This notion is based on the reciprocal stimulation of consumption demand and capital investment. When consumer buying increases, business investment appears more profitable, and vice versa; the two elements reinforce each other in the upward as in the downward direction. But cumulative causation need not confine itself to the short run. The notion can be fruitfully applied to long-run growth also, as Myrdal and Svennilson have suggested.[2]

In our particular case a cumulative process of development was produced by the relation between export demand and foreign investment. Areas that had natural resources whose products were in growing demand abroad received capital with which

---

[1] This remark has been made by Prof. A. K. Cairncross.

[2] Cf. Gunnar Myrdal, *Rich Lands and Poor* (New York, 1957) and Ingvar Svennilson, ' Den ekonomiska tillväxtens problem ', *Ekonomisk Tidskrift*, 1954, p. 29.

to exploit those resources and to increase the supply of those products. An increase in export demand alone is a favorable factor: it may improve the terms of trade, but even if it does not, it draws any increments in local capital and labor into lines in which the country enjoys a comparative advantage, so that increased supplies of imported goods in great variety can be got in exchange. If on top of this foreign capital comes in, this may lead not only to an enlargement of the export sector itself but also to the building of overhead facilities essential to the expansion of domestic activities as well. In fact, railways were the principal object of external investment in the areas of recent settlement. These areas include countries that are now among the most prosperous in the world. It is not suggested that the trade-and-investment relationship is the only explanation of their rapid growth in the past. There are other factors, but these lie outside our present subject.

Economists like Marshall and Robertson in contemplating the 19th century scene spoke of the old countries (in Europe) and the new countries (overseas) as the world's workshops and granaries respectively. This was of course an incomplete view of the world. It ignored the exotic countries, the ' outsiders'. Such areas as China, India, tropical Africa and central America were not unaffected by the forces of growth through trade, but compared with the newly settled countries they were relatively neglected by the expansion of export demand as well as the flow of capital. And in places where both trade and capital flows were exceptionally active, as in parts of South-East Asia, the outcome was sometimes a ' dual economy ' in which a well-developed export sector coexisted with a primitive domestic economy. This lopsided pattern of development was surely better than no growth at all, yet it did show up the limitations of the external trade-and-investment engine when other conditions of progress were absent.

It is interesting to notice that J. A. Hobson in his influential study on *Imperialism* was perfectly aware that, with one exception (Malaya), the British colonies acquired in the second half of the 19th century—the products of the ' New Imperialism '—took a relatively insignificant share in the expansion of Britain's trade. In the course of a dispassionate study of statistical evidence he found that Continental Europe and the new countries overseas took the major share in this expansion. What then, he asked, was the economic motive of the New Imperialism ? His answer was : foreign investment—the desire of a capitalist society to find an offset to its surplus savings, to gain exclusive control of colonial markets and to dump excess supplies in primitive economies. This is his economic explanation of imperialism.[1] But it contradicts in effect his earlier analysis of the pattern of trade expansion. Here the spirit of rational empiricism forsakes him; he cites no evidence. Had he tried to do what he did for trade, that is, to show the geographical distribution of overseas investment, he would have found that British capital tended to bypass the primitive tropical economies and flowed mainly to the regions of recent settlement outside as well as inside the British Empire.

These fertile temperate regions, though now all more or less industrialized, became indeed, and still are, the world's principal granaries. They dispelled the Malthusian spectre of world food shortage, at any rate for a century or two. This turns out to have been the main object and achievement of British capital exports.

THE CURRENT LAG IN EXPORTS OF THE POORER COUNTRIES

In the twentieth century we observe first of all a marked slackening in the rate of world trade expansion. A period of about 30 years is generally sufficient to disclose long-term trends or changes in trend. In the period from 1928 to 1958 the quantum of world trade (outside the Soviet area) has increased by 57 per cent. A hundred years ago the pace of trade expansion seems to have been roughly five times faster.[2]

[1] To Hobson the underconsumptionist it looked as if a part of Great Britain's current saving had to be continually invested abroad—so as to maintain business profits and activity at home—because oversaving and underconsumption kept down investment incentives in Great Britain. In reality a part of British saving was invested abroad because the growth of British consumption expenditure, including expenditure on imported goods, created inducements to invest overseas as well as at home.

[2] The following indications of percentage changes in the volume of world trade are available and may be quoted for comparison, though for the earlier periods they naturally rest on shaky statistical foundations:

This slackening has occurred in spite of the fact that in the world as a whole economic growth is now taking place at probably a faster rate than ever before. It is true that in the last five or six years world trade and output have just about kept pace with each other, but this is too short a period on which to base a trend. In at least the latter half of the 19th century trade was growing faster than total production, though not quite so fast as manufacturing production.

The lag of international trade behind the growth of world output since 1928 is partly due to the fact that production has increased especially in countries such as the United States whose relative weight in world output is greater than in trade. Even if the United States had maintained its own, relatively low, ratio of imports to national product the rise in the U.S. share in world output would have reduced the average ratio of world trade to world production. In fact, America's own import ratio has declined, which has further contributed to the lag of world trade in relation to world output.

No doubt trends in commercial policy have also had something to do with the change in the overall ratio of trade to world production. But they cannot entirely account for certain shifts that have occurred in the internal proportions of world trade. In the years before 1914 exports of primary products were expanding more rapidly than exports of manufactured goods, in spite (or because?) of the rapid spread of manufacturing. In the mid-twentieth century we find, by contrast, a tendency for food and raw material exports to lag behind exports of manufactured goods. More specifically we observe a lag in the exports of primary producing countries compared with those of industrial countries, although as may be seen from the following indices

---

	1850–1880	1880–1913	1928–1958
Changes in volume of world trade :	+270%	+170%	+57%

The percentages for 1850–80 and 1880–1913 are based on an index that was used by Professor Bertil Ohlin in *International Economic Reconstruction* (Joint Committee, Carnegie Endowment and International Chamber of Commerce, 1936), p. 29. The figures are necessarily uncertain and can only serve as a rough indication, but they are not out of line with the volume indices for British trade now carefully revised in A. H. Imlah, *Economic Elements in the Pax Britannica: Studies in British Foreign Trade in the Nineteenth Century* (Cambridge, Mass., 1958), pp. 96–98. The figure for 1928–58 is based on GATT and UN indices excluding the Soviet area.

the lag is really significant only if we exclude petroleum, the twentieth-century boom commodity:

Indices of Export Volume, 1928 = 100

	1955	1957
Exports from Industrial Countries (a)	139	162
Exports from Non-industrial Countries (b)	138	151
of which : 1) Petroleum	479	...
2) All other primary products	118.5	...

(a) OEEC Europe, United States, Canada and Japan.
(b) All other countries outside the Soviet area.
Source : *Trends in Internationl Trade,* GATT, Geneva, 1958.

The exclusion, or at any rate separate treatment, of petroleum seems justifiable on the grounds that oil deposits are unevenly distributed gifts of nature, that they are exploited for export in only a limited group of countries, and that the great majority of underdeveloped countries have no means of benefiting from the present petroleum boom. This applies to other minerals too, but other minerals as a group have not enjoyed a trade expansion much above the average increase in world trade since 1928.

Although divergent price movements might be expected to change the picture, in fact the terms of trade between crude and manufactured products are now just about back to where they were in 1928. So we reach much the same conclusion if we look at the share of primary producing countries in the value of world trade:

Percentage Share of Non-Industrial Countries in the Value of World Trade (a)

	Including oil-exporting countries :		Excluding oil-exporting countries :	
	1928	1957	1928	1957
Exports	33.8	31.3	32.2	24.4
Imports	28.0	35.0	26.9	30.4

(a) Excluding all Soviet area imports and exports. Source: *Trends in International Trade, op. cit.* The figures for imports as well as exports are based on f. o. b. values.

If the oil countries are included, the fall in the export share of the less developed countries is hardly significant. Here again an appreciable lag in exports is observed only if the petroleum countries are left out of account. On the import side we find in either case a rise in the share of primary producing countries. The gap which appears between the import and export figures for 1957, reflecting capital transfers and other invisible receipts, will concern us later. We shall find that the lag in the export trade of the less developed countries is quite troublesome enough, even though it seems to be counterbalanced by a ' lead ' on the import side.

But first we should notice that the figures just given cover the trade of primary producing countries with each other as well as their trade with the industrial countries. If we separate these two types of trade flows and if we apply the same distinction to the trade of industrial countries, we obtain an interesting *Tableau économique* of world trade at the present time (1957):

Exports of :

Industrial countries to each other	(AA)	43 %
Industrial to non-industrial countries	(AB)	26 %
Non-industrial to industrial countries	(BA)	22 %
Non-industrial countries to each other	(BB)	9 %
Total exports (excl. Soviet area) :		100 %

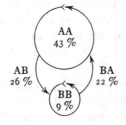

On the whole the industrial countries, which we may denote as group A, are high-income countries, while the non-industrial countries—group B—are almost all in the low-income class. Countries such as Australia, New Zealand and even Argentina, which in the figures used here, computed from the latest GATT report, are classed with the B group, are exporters of primary commodities, yet internally are quite highly industrialized and definitely not low-income countries. But these few exceptions do not seriously affect the picture.

The picture is one that mirrors the basic lopsidedness of the world economy. The twenty countries in group A are each others' best customers. The more than a hundred countries in group B, containing two-thirds of the total population of the A and B groups combined, have very little trade with each other—as a result, no doubt, of their low purchasing power and low productivity. Their exports to the A group are two-and-a-half times as great as their exports to each other. By contrast, the A countries' exports to each other are far greater than their exports to the B group. It will be useful in what follows to keep in mind this unsymmetrical character of trade relations between advanced and backward economies.

There is no suggestion that the topheavy structure of world trade is something new. On the contrary, trade in the 19th century seems to have been still more highly concentrated in the relatively advanced areas, as is clear from a useful though somewhat incomplete world trade matrix which Professor Lewis has tried to construct for the year 1887.[1]

The focal center of economic growth in the non-communist world today lies predominantly in North America and Western Europe, or in what we may conveniently call the North Atlantic area. On closer inspection we should have to note that each of the two main parts of this center has its own dependent area of raw-material supply to the south, in the western and eastern hemisphere respectively. But here we have no time for such details.

The main point we must recognize is that this focal center, in terms of real income per head, is advancing vigorously, but is not transmitting its own rate of growth to the rest of the world through a proportional increase in its demand for primary products. The reasons for this are well known. 1) The composition of industrial production in the advanced economies is shifting away from ' light ' industries in favor of ' heavy ' industries (such as engineering and chemicals), that is, from industries where the raw material content of finished output is high to those where it is low. 2) As a special case, the rising share of services in the total output of advanced industrial countries tends to cause their raw-material demand to lag behind the rise in their national product. 3) The income elasticity of consumer demand

[1] W. A. Lewis and P. J. O'Leary : ' Secular Swings in Production and Trade, 1870–1913 ', *The Manchester School*, May 1955. The intra-trade of Europe and the U.S.A. represented as much as 64 per cent of the (incomplete) total of world exports in 1887. Intra-trade in Asia, Africa and South America is not known but was probably small and would not have made much difference to the percentage share of the advanced area's intra-trade.

for many agricultural commodities tends to be low.   4) Agricultural protectionism has adversely affected imports of primary products from the A to the B group, though this point should not be exaggerated.   It affects especially Western Europe's imports from the R.R.S. rather than the North Atlantic's imports from the less developed tropics.   Besides, there is plenty of protectionism hampering also the trade in manufactures.   What we have to explain is a comparative lag in exports of primary producing countries.

5) Substantial economies have been achieved in industrial uses of natural materials (e.g. through electrolytic tin-plating and through systematic recovery and reprocessing of metals).   6) Last but not least, the leading industrial centers have tended more and more to displace natural raw materials by synthetic and other man-made substitutes produced from a few basic elements of mostly local origin.   The demand for such staple commodities as crude rubber, silk, indigo, nitrates, jute, hemp, vegetable oils, hides and skins has certainly been held back and in some cases severely reduced by the growth of the chemical industry in the 20th century.   Among United States imports one of the latest technological casualties is said to be chicle, a vegetable product imported from Central America for the manufacture of chewing gum.   It appears that the United States chemical industry has developed a synthetic substitute that is just as good or even better.

These are among the main explanations of the lag in the export trade of the less developed countries at the present time. It has been estimated that, since the late 1920's, exports from the primary producing countries to the United States and Western Europe have fallen from about $3\frac{1}{2}$ per cent to rather less than 3 per cent of the combined gross national product of this industrial area.[1] If again we exclude petroleum the fall would be about $3\frac{1}{2}$ per cent to probably less than $2\frac{1}{2}$ per cent.   This means that over the last three decades most primary producing countries have suffered a marked shrinkage in the importance of their exports in relation to the output and income of the industrial world.

[1] ECE, *Economic Survey of Europe in 1957*, Chap. 4, p. 6.

If for a moment we consider the United States in particular, the fall in the ratio of U.S. imports to gross national product from about 6 per cent to 3 per cent over the last 50 years[1] contrasts sharply with the rise in the British import ratio in the 19th century. Professor T. W. Schultz of the University of Chicago has shown conclusively that the demand for raw materials as a whole, not only those imported, has lagged far behind the expansion of output in the American economy.[2] What we are considering therefore is merely the international aspect of a fairly general tendency. In a country so well supplied with capital and technical know-how it is a natural tendency for investment in ' research and development ' to displace crude materials with synthetic products. Some economists are more inclined to stress the future prospect of expansion in U.S. imports of primary commodities. They may prove right, but it is never safe to engage in long-term predictions. The facts for the past few decades are sufficient to reveal certain changes in trends. The report of the ' Paley Commission ' in 1952 gave a famous projection of U.S. demand for raw materials in the year 1975, but for this purpose it had to assume that ' techniques of production do not change '.[3] This has always seemed, to some of us, like a performance of Hamlet without the Prince of Denmark.

It is true in a sense that the United States is becoming more dependent on foreign mineral resources. Many people have been impressed by the fact, brought out by the Paley Report, that over nearly half a century the raw material consumption of the

[1] According to Dr. W. Lederer, the economist responsible for U.S. balance-of-payments estimates, U.S. merchandise imports as a percentage of GNP have fallen from 5.70 per cent in the period 1896–1914 to 2.97 per cent in 1955. See *Review of Economics and Statistics,* May 1956, p. 184.

[2] In a paper on ' Economic Prospects of Primary Products ', presented under the auspices of the International Economic Association, Rio de Janeiro, August 1957, Professor Schultz has summed it up as follows : ' We explain the slow increase in consumption of primary products in the United States in terms of the income elasticity of demand. Put in its simplest terms, the demand schedule has shifted to the right at a rate which has exceeded only a little the growth of population. A more than doubling of per capita real income has added only about one-sixth to the demand for primary products ... On the supply side, we infer that enough additional output has been forthcoming to satisfy the increases in demand at about the same ... (relative) supply price, except in the case of forest products. '

[3] U.S. President's Materials Policy Commission, *Resources for Freedom,* Vol. 2, Chap. 22.

United States has increased by 98 per cent while its own production of raw materials rose only by 70 per cent. As a result, from a net exporter of raw materials at the beginning of the present century the United States has turned into a net importer. This change is sometimes referred to as the ' scissors effect '.[1] That the raw-material consumption of the United States has risen 40 per cent faster than its raw-material production is no doubt interesting and important. But even more impressive is the fact that the gross national product of the United States has, in its turn, increased about 150 per cent faster than its raw-material consumption. Most striking of all is the fact that United States manufacturing production has increased more than three times as fast as the American economy's intake of raw materials.[2]

Evidently the ' scissors effect ' has been overshadowed by the effect of raw-material economies, the growth of synthetics and the other factors mentioned. As for metals in particular, the tin, lead and copper we import do not all get lost in the United States. To the extent that they are used over and over again, imports are needed only as additions to a revolving stock of metals, not to support a given volume of manufacturing output.

It is therefore in no way surprising that, as an overall result, the increase of United States imports of primary commodities has failed to keep pace with the growth of the American economy. Similar tendencies are at work in Western Europe,[3] though in this

---

[1] Sir Donald MacDougall, *The World Dollar Problem* (London, 1957), p. 186.
[2] These developments in the U.S. economy are summarized in the following table :

	1904–13	*1944–50*	Percentage
	(Billions of dollars at 1935–39 prices)		change:
1. Raw Material Production	4.8	8.2	+70%
2. Raw Material Consumption	4.4	8.7	+98%
3. Gross National Product	43.7	149.0	+242%
4. Manufacturing (1935–39 = 100)	47	204	+335%

Items 1 and 2, which exclude agricultural foodstuffs and gold, are taken from the Paley Report. It should be noted that the production figures do not include secondary production of metals, derived from scrap, etc., the relative importance of which is increasing. Item 3 : the GNP figures come from a paper by R. F. Daly (in *Studies in Income and Wealth*, Vol. 14) and are cited by T. W. Schultz (op. cit.). Item 4 : Federal Reserve Board index linked to the NBER index constructed by S. Fabricant which goes back to the beginning of the present century.
[3] A. K. Cairncross and J. Faaland, ' Long-term Trends in Europe's Trade ', *Economic Journal,* March 1952, pp. 26–27.

area especially they have been masked to a large extent by the spectacular growth of petroleum imports in the last 30 years.

If the statistics of present-day world trade were considered in isolation, the lag in the primary commodity exports of the less developed countries might present something like a problem of ' identification ': has it been due to factors on the side of demand, external to these countries, or has it been due to limitations of supply in these countries themselves ? Being aware of the major background factors, we have treated it as mainly a reflection of relative sluggishness in external demand emanating from the great industrial consumers. It cannot be denied that domestic policies causing limitations on the supply side in producing countries have also been effective in certain cases. But such policies can sometimes be interpreted as reactions to relatively unfavorable demand conditions for primary export products. They may serve in effect to implement the terms of trade argument for protection by tightening up the supply of export products for which world demand is not only sluggish in expanding but also, at any given time, is apt to be price-inelastic in the lower ranges of the demand schedule.

It is possible that population pressure in certain countries such as India and Indonesia has hurt primary production for export by causing a reversion to subsistence production for local needs.[1] But this is not an inevitable result: an alternative is to maintain or increase the export crops as far as possible and to import the food needed for the growing population. And this is actually happening to some extent: the low-income countries are becoming an increasingly important outlet for the food poured out by the United States in competition with Canada, Argentina and Australia.

The causal predominance of demand conditions suggested by the survey of particular factors fits in very naturally with the unsymmetrical pattern of world trade between countries at different levels of development, which our chart has served to illustrate. In a world in which (outside the Soviet area) over nine-tenths of the manufacturing and over four-fifths of the total productive activity are concentrated in the advanced industrial

[1] This possibility is mentioned by H. Myint in his interesting article ' The ' Classical ' Theory of International Trade and the Underdeveloped Countries ', *Economic Journal,* June 1958, pp. 325 and 331.

countries, the ideas of symmetry, reciprocity and mutual dependence which we associate with the traditional theory of international trade are of rather questionable relevance to trade relations between the center and the periphery. Despite the population masses and the vast physical areas of the underdeveloped countries, we must try to realize their pitiable smallness in aggregate economic terms, by comparison with the giant industrial economies. In such a world the distinction between dominant and dependent economies is a vital one in any dynamic view of international economic relations. It does not contradict the idea of mutual dependence that lies at the basis of *trade* theory pure and simple. It belongs to a different order of discourse: to the international economics of growth.

TRADE TRENDS AND INTERNATIONAL INVESTMENT INCENTIVES

For perfectly understandable reasons, then, the world's industrial centers on both sides of the North Atlantic in the mid-twentieth century are not ' exporting ' their own rate of growth to the primary producing countries through a corresponding expansion of demand for primary products. With the growing refinement of technology it is only natural that the raw products of the soil should tend in general to become relatively less essential in an advanced industrial economy. Equally natural is the fact that it is precisely in such crude and simple products of the soil that the poorer countries generally tend to have a comparative advantage, at least on a static view of the matter. This disparity is one of the basic factors that lie behind the increasing discrepancies in income levels.

In the 19th century conditions were different: they happened to be such that the growth of the dominant economy, Great Britain, did tend to transmit itself to the periphery through an even more than proportional expansion in demand for crude materials and foodstuffs. Again the main reasons, already mentioned, are obvious. Neither experience can provide the basis for anything like a universal law. As Professor Hicks has put it, a change has taken place in the economic atmosphere of international trade from the 19th to the 20th century.[1]

---

[1] J. R. Hicks, ' An Inaugural Lecture ', *Oxford Economic Papers,* June 1953, p. 130.

The basic case for international specialization is not affected by this change. The point is merely that the forces making for the diffusion of economic growth from advanced to less developed countries are not as powerful in the trade field as they were a hundred years ago. The 19th century pattern of development in outlying areas was geared to export markets for primary staples. This mechanism of growth transmission is now in comparatively low gear.

Nor is this all. Conditions in the trade field have some influence on international investment. The vigorous expansion of demand for primary commodities induced a massive flow of private capital to peripheral areas in the past. Conversely, the lag observed at the present time in the export trade of most of the less developed countries provides a simple explanation for the lack of incentive for private foreign investment.

Movements of private capital for productive investment in less developed countries have always depended to a large degree on the growth of external demand for the export staples of such countries. The home market does not generally offer any strong inducements in a thinly settled or backward economy.[1] There are other economic reasons for the now limited volume of private capital flows to less developed countries. One of them is the highly progressive taxation in the advanced countries. There are also political reasons. For most people the Cold War is the reason for the absence of large-scale private capital exports to underdeveloped countries. But there was a cold war for many decades in the 19th century too, between Great Britain and Russia. (A cheerful thought, but let us beware: historical analogies can mislead). The cumulative interaction of raw-material demand and foreign investment so characteristic of 19th century experience is naturally weaker today, for the reasons we have noted. For us economists this may be a sufficient explanation.

If anything is needed to confirm this hypothesis just look at the petroleum countries today. These are the exception that proves the rule. Here is a primary commodity that has enjoyed

---

[1] By and large, it is only where the ' take-off ' has already occurred, as in some Latin-American countries, that the domestic market can offer substantial inducements for foreign direct investments to come in.

a tremendous expansion of world demand. The non-industrial countries exporting this commodity have considerably increased their share in world trade.[1] And quite naturally these countries have managed to attract the lion's share of private foreign investment, at all events of United States direct investment since the last world war.

A curious parallel emerges in this way between the 'new countries' of the 19th century and the 'oil countries' of the twentieth. Both show a rising share in world trade. Both exert a strong attraction for private foreign capital. Both happen to be, on the whole, sparsely populated. The new countries banished the world food crisis that worried Malthus. The oil countries have banished the fuel crisis due to the exhaustion of coal supplies which in England worried J. S. Mill and Jevons. These are only some of the similarities. The dissimilarities are too obvious to enumerate. It may be that, of the two types of areas, the case of the new countries will long remain the more important and interesting illustration of the trade-and-development nexus. Yet the main point stands: the oil countries today like the new countries a hundred years ago demonstrate a cumulative relationship between external demand for primary products and incentives for private international investment. It is the ancient rule again: Those who have (oil deposits) shall receive (foreign capital). If a wide range of primary commodities other than crude oil were enjoying an equally strong increase in world demands, is there much reason to doubt that a larger volume of private capital would be attracted to the underdeveloped countries, in spite of the political risks which, in varying forms and degrees, have always existed and will always continue to exist?

With things as they are in the trade field, governmental loans and grants are called upon to fill the gap left by the relatively modest level of private foreign investment. With the aid of such transfers as well as other non-commercial receipts (including American military expenditures overseas) the less developed

---

[1] The exports and imports of the main oil-exporting countries as a percentage of total world trade (excluding all Soviet area trade) have gone up as follows:

	1928	1957
Exports	1.6%	6.9%
Imports	1.1%	4.6%

countries have been able to increase their share in world imports and this, as we have seen, is true even if we leave the oil countries. The motive force of the mechanism is different; it has not come from market incentives to the same extent as in the past.

On this view of the matter there is a connection, then, between the lag in the export trade of most underdeveloped countries and the pressing need for official non-commercial transfers of funds from the richer to the poorer areas. It is this call for, and use of, non-commercial transfers that represents what is known as the Dollar Shortage, a phenomenon now limited, by and large, to the world's less developed areas. Perhaps a basic reason why we did not hear of a Sterling shortage in the 19th century was the rapid secular growth in Western Europe's and especially Great Britain's import demands for primary products and, on top of this, the stimulus so created for private capital exports to underdeveloped regions.

The governmental transfers on which we now have to rely are distributed not so much ' to those who have ', but rather, as Francois Perroux once remarked, ' to each according to his need ', though inevitably their distribution is influenced by political as well as economic considerations. As regards the magnitude of the total capital flow we find that, relatively to the value of merchandise imports of non-industrial countries, it is now not much less than it was at the crest of the last big wave of foreign investment in what was still effectively the 19th century, namely in 1913. In that year the net outflow of capital from Western Europe and the United States combined was equal to approximately 20 per cent of the rest-of-the-world's total imports from this industrial area.[1] All of this was private capital. In 1956–57 we find that the relative size of the total capital flow from advanced to less developed economies is just about the same—17 per cent—except that now it consists mostly of official grants and governmental (or government-guaranteed) loans.[2] Most of this is coming from the United States.

In sum, though the mechanism is not the same, capital re-

[1] Again I am indebted to Dr. Robert M. Stern for collecting the data and computing this estimate.

[2] See the GATT report, *op. cit.*, pp. 32–34. Departing slightly from the method apparently followed in that report, we compare the capital flows with the value

sources are moving from advanced to less developed areas much as before. The ratio of capital flows to import values may not be particularly significant. More interesting, though less certain, is the fact that the 5 billion dollars of private and official funds (including reinvested profits) which passed from the richer to the poorer countries in 1956 were probably equal to about one-third of the total capital formation going on in that year in all the less developed countries outside the Soviet area. In any case there is no doubt that capital funds are moving in considerable volume in the right direction. But the conditions of world trade in which they move are for the most part very different.

These are among the essential facts of life in the world today. What are their implications for the doctrines as well as the policies of international economics ? Can the 19th century prescription for growth through trade be as effective as it was in the past ? Given the altered conditions of world trade, what are the major patterns and openings that present themselves for economic growth outside the industrial centers ? Such are the questions we shall now attempt to consider.

---

of imports from the industrial into the non-industrial countries outside the Soviet area. The percentages for 1956–57 come out as follows :

Private capital	7%
Official transfers	10%
of which : Grants	(8%)
Net loans	(2%)
Total	17%

This does not include the reinvested profits of U.S. subsidiaries. If these were included the total percentage would probably rise from 17 to about 20 per cent, of which private capital would account for 10 instead of 7 per cent.

THE INTERNATIONAL ECONOMY AND
THE PROBLEM OF GROWTH

Second Lecture

Past and Present Development Patterns

The 19th century pattern of economic growth through international trade was one in which outlying areas of the world economy were favored by a rapidly expanding demand for their primary products. This tended in some cases to raise their real income directly by improving their barter terms of trade, which in a time of great reductions in transport costs was not incompatible with improving commodity terms of trade for the industrial centers as well. But changes in the terms of trade have perhaps received an exaggerated amount of attention in the trade and development literature. There were other ways in which the demand expansion for primary products helped economic growth in the outlying areas.

It gave, first of all, comparatively advantageous employment to any increases accruing in the domestic labor force or capital stock. Secondly, it may have tended to stir up dormant or idle resources and to draw them into economic activity for export production.[1] Thirdly, it could help by attracting to those areas a part of the increase in capital and labor that was going on in the dominant centers of growth. Buoyant conditions of external demand tended to encourage the application of capital and improved techniques to primary production for export. They helped in some countries—where other conditions also were suitable—to promote expansion in the domestic economy as well. All this constituted a pattern of ' growth through trade ' which was particularly characteristic of the 19th century.

It would be a serious mistake to think that all this belongs to

---

[1] This point is stressed by H. Myint, *op. cit.* One way in which trade could lead to an ' awakening ' of domestic resources was through the creation of new wants that made people work harder and produce more cash crops for export. This particular point is perhaps to be looked upon as a once-for-all change rather than a truly dynamic factor of a continuing nature. Nevertheless it was also possible for trade expansion, by opening up additional opportunities for the advantageous use of productive resources, to create continuing inducements for additional domestic resources to come forward.

the past. It has a part to play in today's world also. But if it
is true that, for reasons indicated earlier, there is a relative lag
in the industrial countries' demand for a wide range of primary
commodities, this pattern is bound to be less prominent than in
the past.

If there is such a lag—and the facts brought out by international economic organizations[1] suggest strongly that there has
been one in recent years—then what are the less developed
countries to do ? Consider the problem that faces countries
whose appetite for better living is rising, whose labor force and
even capital stock is growing, but for whose exportable crude
staples there is only a sluggish expansion of external demand. In
the face of such conditions it might be useless, perhaps even
worse than useless, to push the additional labor and capital into
the traditional export sectors, in view of the inelastic demand
which the traditional export staples are likely to meet.

In the last three decades the export volume of non-industrial
countries other than those exporting petroleum has increased by
about 25 per cent.[2] Over the same period the economically active
population in these countries has increased by about 50 per cent
in numbers alone. From such indications as are available it
seems possible that their capital stock has increased by even
more.[3] Not only is there some domestic capital creation going

[1] ECE, ECLA, FAO, GATT and the UN Secretariat, in their recent annual
reports. Special mention should be made of the following : GATT, *International
Trade 1955* (Geneva, 1956) ; UN, *World Economic Survey 1955* (New York,
1956), Chap. 2 ; FAO, *The State of Food and Agriculture 1956* (Rome, 1956) ;
ECE, *Economic Survey of Europe in 1957* (Geneva, 1958), Chaps. 4 and 5 ;
GATT, *Trends in International Trade,* A Report by a Panel of Experts (Geneva,
Oct. 1958).

[2] This is based on the GATT index for 1956 (1928 = 100), which is the latest
available, and which Dr. H. Staehle, Chief of GATT's Trade Intelligence Section,
has kindly communicated to me. The index covers exports of non-industrial
countries to each other as well as their exports to the industrial countries. The
value of the former, though still relatively small, has increased in importance
compared with that of the latter. If this is taken into account, it appears that,
leaving aside the petroleum countries, the volume of primary-commodity exports
from non-industrial to industrial countries has increased by just about 20 per cent
from 1928 to 1956.

[3] The problem of measuring capital is a notoriously hard nut to crack, conceptually as well as statistically. Nevertheless, we may note that the Economic
Commission for Latin America has compiled estimates showing that the aggregate
stock of real capital in that area, valued at constant prices, has increased by over
70 per cent in only 12 years (see *Economic Survey of Latin America 1956,* p. 7,
and earlier issues).

on, but also capital imports are coming in from abroad in substantial volume, mostly in the form of governmental transfers unrelated to any investment incentives in primary production for export.

This emphasis on the continual increase that is going on in the productive—or potentially productive—resources in underdeveloped countries may seem surprising, but is in my opinion entirely realistic. No useful purpose is served by continuing to discuss matters of trade and development on the classical assumption of a constant stock of productive factors. The problem in some of the poorer countries may be that capital resources are not expanding as fast as the labor force; or that skills and education are not improving at the same rate as health, or as fast as numbers alone are increasing. These are serious problems relating to progress in income per head. But in reality all these factors of production are continually increasing in quantity and improving in quality in underdeveloped countries today, though naturally at varying rates.

If primary production for export, though of vital importance so far as it has gone, does not offer attractive opportunities for expansion, the question is what to do with the growing labor force, and capital resources. In these circumstances it might seem best for the movable factors of production to emigrate from the less developed countries to the centers of growth, the industrial economies. This is, we must admit, a rather academic solution. Nevertheless, where it is possible, some migration of working people and even of capital funds on private account does take place nowadays from the poorer to the richer areas. The migration of labor from Puerto Rico and Jamaica to the United States and the United Kingdom respectively is a well known example. Transfers of capital remain usually invisible but, until recently at any rate, private funds from such countries as Egypt and Thailand, for example, are believed to have leaked out fairly steadily to certain financial centers for safekeeping and investment. But on the whole such movements are severely restricted, either by the would-be receiving countries, as far as labor is concerned, or by the sending countries, in the case of capital.

The more realistic alternative is, of course, industrialization.

Ten or twenty years ago development problems used to be discussed largely if not exclusively in terms of industrialization. This approach has gone out of fashion. Progress in agriculture is nowadays receiving equal emphasis. All the same, let us provisionally start with the old-fashioned concern with industrialization. I hope we can agree that it is in this general direction that the solution to the growth problem must be sought. It is largely in the building and operation of industrial production facilities that the increase in the labor force and in the other resources accruing in low-income countries will have to be employed.

Next it is essential, however, to distinguish between two types of industrialization: that which aims at producing manufactured goods for export to the industrial countries and that which caters mainly for domestic markets in underdeveloped countries. The significance of this distinction will become clearer later on. At this stage let me merely assert that the second type of industrialization generally requires, while the first does not require, a complementary advance in domestic agriculture. This is a basic, though not the only, reason for separating the two types. It is something that makes manufacturing for export much easier than manufacturing for home markets in the underdeveloped world. On the other hand manufacturing for export is vitally dependent on commercial policies in the older industrial countries, while industrialization for home markets is free from any such hazard and so in this respect easier.

Before dealing with the two development patterns in turn, let us note that they have one thing in common. Neither demands the abandonment or contraction of exports of the primary commodities which a country is naturally well suited to produce. To the extent that external demand for such commodities is growing there is even a *prima facie* case for expanding the traditional exports. It is to make use of growing resources which cannot with comparative advantage be absorbed by expansion in the traditional sectors that industrialization becomes really necessary. We therefore envisage industrial activities, whether for export or for home use, as being set up on top of the existing export sectors, so long as in these sectors a country still enjoys a high 'established' comparative advantage even though, as a consequence of sluggish expansion of external demand, its 'incremental' comparative advantage in these lines may be low.[1]

INDUSTRIALIZATION FOR EXPORT MARKETS

If demand conditions for a wide range of primary products are not conducive to growth in underdeveloped countries, is it not possible and desirable for at least some of these countries to start exporting manufactured goods in addition to their primary export staples ? There is indeed an influential school of thought which sees the main road to progress in the poorer countries in the establishment of manufacturing activities working for export to the great mass markets of the advanced economies. Professor W. A. Lewis in particular has stressed this as a solution suitable especially for densely settled areas where labor is the most abundant factor of production in relation not only to capital but also to land. Similarly the recent report of four leading experts sponsored by GATT regards it as ' a natural and economic development that relatively poor countries with high population densities like India and Hong Kong should export cheap labor-intensive manufactures in order to import foodstuffs like wheat from developed countries such as Australia, Canada and the United States which are rich in land and capital. '[2] The theory of factor proportions in international trade, which is based on the pioneering work of Heckscher and Ohlin, seems strongly to suggest that the ' incremental ' comparative advantage of over-populated countries poorly endowed with natural resources lies in increased exports of the simpler kinds of manufactured consumer goods such as textiles. This conclusion fits in well with the views of economic geographers who find that the most promising sources of increased food supplies in the world are still the temperate regions of recent settlement rather than the tropics.[3]

---

[1] The distinction between ' established ' and ' incremental ' comparative advantage, which becomes necessary as soon as we apply the central concept of traditional trade theory to the problem of economic growth, is clearly set out in A. J. Brown's *Industrialization and Trade* (London 1943), pp. 5–6, though the terms used are not the same.

[2] *Trends in International Trade: A Report by a Panel of Experts* (Professors G. Haberler, J. Meade, R. de Oliveira Campos and J. Tinbergen), GATT, Geneva, October 1958.

[3] See especially Dudley Stamp, *Our Underdeveloped World* (London, 1953).

Industrialization for export would seem an attractive solution in that it avoids the need for carrying out any drastic and painful reform or 'revolution' in domestic agriculture, under physical conditions that may be in any case unpropitious for agricultural improvement. The manufactured goods would be sold in foreign markets where there is no shortage of purchasing power, and would serve to pay for basic foodstuffs imported from regions better endowed to produce them. It seems for these reasons a relatively easy solution. Moreover, it does not necessarily depend on expansion of total demand abroad for the type of goods to be exported. It could displace high-cost suppliers in the older industrial countries, who would shift over to more productive and more rewarding lines of activity such as skilled services, engineering and chemistry. This is indeed what could and should happen, but some obvious difficulties arise in this connection.

A word should be said first about possible difficulties on the supply side. Even in densely populated areas labor may not be really cheap for the purposes of industrialization, when it is illiterate, unskilled and undisciplined. The factor-proportions analysis was never meant to be applied without reference to quality. Just as land may not be really plentiful where it consists of marsh or desert, so even in an overpopulated country we should guard against the misplaced concreteness of concluding from the teeming numbers of people that labor is relatively cheap and plentiful. All we can say perhaps is that it is potentially cheap and abundant. It must be made cheap by raising it to a minimum level of economic efficiency. This is not easy. In fact, the history of the older industrial countries shows that the creation of an industrial labor force is a task of formidable difficulty. It requires a lot of social overhead investment, especially in education and health, quite apart from investment in public utilities such as power and transport.

Today the showcase example of industrialization for export is Puerto Rico, an island which, fortunately for this purpose, lies within the United States customs area. Puerto Rico benefited from a great deal of social investment in the 1930s and the early 1940s (partly as a by-product of the war effort). It is only since then that Puerto-Rican labor has tended to become cheap for industrial uses. Earlier, though numerically plentiful, it offered no strong attraction for industries to come from the mainland, and partly for the same reason, was handicapped in migrating to the mainland, though free to do so. The importance of social overhead investment is one of the chief lessons of Puerto Rico's recent development boom. But then, we should remember that investment in education, health and public utilities is necessary for *any* pattern of development. So the need for it should not be counted as an obstacle to manufacturing for export in particular. The difficulty is none the less real.

Industrialization for export markets may encounter other difficulties on the supply side. In the scale of comparative advantage there may be a wide gap, or at any rate a certain discontinuity, between the traditional primary products and the new manufactured goods which a country would seek to export. But let us now abstract from such impediments which, however serious, may perhaps be overcome with the help of export subsidies.

Equally serious are the obstacles which industrialization for export is liable to encounter on the side of external demand. This pattern of development depends for its success on a lenient commercial policy in the older industrial countries. From general considerations as well as from recent experience it would seem that such lenience can hardly be relied upon with certainty. The significance of the Puerto-Rican success story is after all limited by the fact that Puerto Rico is a United States possession and, besides, is small enough to ' get away with it '. Moreover, Puerto Rico's industrialization is based in the main on American capital and enterprise, with a strong interest in the maintenance of free access to the American market.[1]

In the more general case of underdeveloped countries industrializing for export, the reaction of the advanced industrial centers does give cause for concern. The problem would not be so difficult if the manufactured goods which the poorer countries would start exporting were goods with a rapidly rising total demand (such as television sets or jet aircraft). Then these exports could

---

[1] This point should not be exaggerated. The predominance of American capital and enterprise in the Puerto-Rican sugar industry has not prevented the restriction, by means of a quota, of access to the American market for Puerto-Rican sugar.

find markets in the industrial states without hurting any existing producers there. It is true that existing producers may insist on a certain proportion of the growing market being reserved to them by protective measures of commercial policy. If so, the newcomers might not derive any great advantage from the fact that the demand for the goods they would wish to export is rising. But the main trouble is that in producing goods of this sort the advanced industrial centers themselves are likely to have an overwhelming comparative advantage.

The newcomers must therefore generally be content to export the cruder and simpler kinds of manufacture such as textiles. Now for these, as a rule, total demand is not rapidly expanding, so that existing producers in the advanced economies must of necessity be injured and displaced if such exports are to increase considerably in volume. The fact that export markets are found by displacement of existing high-cost suppliers in the older centers turns out to be, not an advantage, but a source of trouble, resistance and frustration.

Just as textiles are usually the first manufactures to be started in the poorer countries, so also textiles are among the first to become sick industries in the more advanced countries, where workers as well as managers are quick to raise protests against ' unfair ' low-wage competition from backward areas. The ' pauper-labor ' argument, that great standby of protectionists, is brought forward again. Charges of ' social dumping ' are heard, even though the newcomers are only trying to make use of their one advantage: ample labor and cheap efficiency wages, an advantage which, as just observed, can be hard enough for them to make effective. When their low-wage competition is furthermore promoted by export subsidies conforming essentially to the accepted infant industry argument, the protests in the established centers of manufacture become even more indignant.

In any case there is a possibility of protective countermeasures being adopted in the older industrial countries. Such measures may force underdeveloped countries to export crude and simple manufactures to each others' markets instead of the mass markets in the advanced countries. In that case the solution turns out to be output expansion for *internal* consumption in the underdeveloped world, which we are proposing to treat as a different development pattern, to be considered in a moment.

Recent experience illustrates the risks and difficulties in the way of manufacturing for export to the advanced industrial countries. The United States early in 1957 secured an agreement by which Japanese exporters ' voluntarily ' restricted their exports of certain textile products to the American market. Britain did not take long to follow this convenient example, and managed to persuade the textile manufacturers of India, Pakistan and Hong Kong similarly to curb their exports to the British market. In another predominantly industrial country, Canada, the government is pledged to give higher protection to domestic textiles. The Commonwealth Economic Conference held in Montreal in September 1958 stressed that ' obstacles should not be placed in the way of the exports of manufactured goods from underdeveloped countries '. The practical effect of this resolution will be watched with considerable interest.

It cannot be denied that industrial countries in these circumstances have some economic justification for protective measures, if labor mobility is low and if the alternative is wasteful unemployment in the industries injured by low-wage competition from less developed areas. Even Professor Haberler has admitted the validity of this argument for protection.[1] But it should be treated as an essentially short-term argument.

The industrialization-for-export pattern of development depends on a high degree of internal mobility and adaptability in the older industrial countries. These countries themselves would gain in real income by shifting out of industries where their comparative advantage is low or declining. Yet it is also natural that, for their own immediate comfort, they should wish to avoid or to cushion such adjustments at some cost in terms of their income growth. They feel they can afford to pay the cost.

Western Europe in particular is being urged to switch from consumer-goods production more and more to capital goods and chemicals.[2] This is in fact what is happening. In Great Britain the contraction of the Lancashire cotton industry has recently

---

[1] *Survey of International Trade Theory* (Princeton, 1955), p. 16
[2] ECE, *Economic Survey of Europe in 1956* (Geneva, 1957).

been described as a 'catastrophic story'.[1] In a sense it represents, on the contrary, a remarkable success story of drastic readjustment. Was it catastrophic for many individuals engaged in that industry? Surely in an otherwise active and expanding economy individuals, or their offspring, shift to other occupations and *improve* their lot in the process.

The United States tends to regard itself as a natural importer of primary commodities and to think of the less developed countries as natural exporters of such commodities. Perhaps this reflects the continuing influence of the 19th century trade model. What has happened within the United States has served to show that imports of manufactured products from poorer into richer areas are not necessarily against the laws of nature. On the whole the American economy, like the European, is moving in the direction of capital goods, chemicals and other goods and services requiring much capital and skill. Is it prepared, however, to suffer a contraction in output of the simpler types of consumer goods? From this point of view it is particularly unfortunate that American trade policy has accepted the prevention of injury to domestic industries as one of its essential tasks. This concern with injury-prevention will not stop the United States industrial structure from changing in the right direction. Yet it does tend to slow down the change. The development needs of the backward economies may demand a faster rate of adaptation than is likely to be practicable in the advanced economies.

Critics of American trade policy have been pointing out for years that it makes no sense to restrict U.S. imports from countries which the United States is helping with free grants and other forms of foreign aid. From the business interests affected, however, one often hears the argument that the United States should help these countries precisely by means of governmental grants *instead of* by admitting imports which have bad effects on local employment conditions and possibly also on domestic income distribution. But this argument, which sounds curiously like a variant of the compensation principle in trade and welfare theory, leads to an awkward question. What are the receiving countries to do with the resources put at their disposal? If, first, their

[1] A. J. Brown, *Introduction to the World Economy* (London, 1959), p. 167.

exportable primary products face a low rate of expansion in external demand and if, secondly, their exports of manufactured goods encounter obstacles, there remains only a third possible opening: output expansion for home consumption.

THE PATTERN OF HOME-MARKET EXPANSION

Industrialization for domestic needs in low-income areas runs from the very start into a difficulty well known to practical men and of great interest to economists. The trouble is this: there is not a sufficient market for manufactured goods in a country where peasants, farm laborers and their families, comprising typically two-thirds to four-fifths of the population, are too poor to buy any factory products, or anything in addition to the little they already buy. There is a lack of real purchasing power, reflecting the low productivity in agriculture. The other side of the same coin is that the local economy cannot supply the food needed to sustain the new industrial workers.

Therefore industrial development for domestic markets requires a complementary advance on the farm front, a rise in agricultural productivity. It is impossible to push domestic industrial development in isolation. This is now universally realized. It has become a platitude. Even the term ' industrialization ', still fashionable in the 1940s, is seldom found in the development literature today. This is not to say that the relation between agricultural and industrial advance is a new discovery. It is an ancient truth well known to economists in the 18th century.[1] But even the most ancient truths have to be rediscovered from time to time.

What modern economists have added to this notion is a simple application of the concept of income elasticity of consumer demand (a concept which, implicit in Engel's law, is itself over a hundred years old). Farming and manufacturing must move forward together, but not necessarily at the same rate. In a very

---

[1] Its essence may be found, for example, in Adam Smith's chapter on the Natural Progress of Opulence : ' It is the surplus produce of the country only, or what is over and above the maintenance of the cultivators, that constitutes the subsistence of the town, which can therefore increase only with the increase of this surplus produce. ' Sir James Steuart is another 18th century author who liked to harp on this theme.

poor country a given increase in manufacturing is likely to require a greater agricultural advance than in one that is not so poor. Conversely, a given increase in food output is likely to support a larger increase in manufacturing in an area where income per head is already fairly high than in one where it is still very low. The equilibrium relation between the two rates of advance may vary in the course of time as well as between countries. But this does not alter the basic principle of ' linked progress' in the two broad sectors, farming and manufacturing.

As soon as agricultural improvement is recognized as an indis- pensable condition of it, industrialization for domestic markets appears as a much more formidable task. The difficulty stems largely from the fact that agriculture in most underdeveloped areas is a conservative, sometimes feudal, always tradition-bound, passive and non-capitalist sector of economic activity. Innova- tion in this sector cannot be relied upon to happen in response to market incentives alone. Even in the United States the agri- cultural extension service has long been a classic example of a non-market method of development policy in a progressive and predominantly market-oriented economy. In backward econo- mies the necessary improvement and reorganization may demand a revolution in the countryside, affecting the lives of the great mass of the people. That is why industrialization for export markets would be so much more convenient, if only it were prac- ticable to the requisite extent.

Another cause of difficulty may lie in the somewhat dubious physical potentialities of agricultural improvement in the tropics compared with the world's temperate zones. Nevertheless, there is surely ample scope for improvement through irrigation, new techniques of cultivation, and reform of the farm fragmentation that wastes so much land as well as labor in certain areas.

If the two-sector view of linked progress in agriculture and manufacturing is accepted, the question arises whether the same principle does not apply within the manufacturing sphere also. My own inclination is to think that it does, though this extension of the principle is not acceptable to some economists. Just as it is possible for manufacturing as a whole to fail if peasants can produce no marketable surplus and are too poor to buy anything

from factories, so it is possible for a single branch of manufacturing to fail for lack of support from other sectors in industry
as well as agriculture; that is, for lack of markets. To be sure,
an expansion of one industry will have effects on income and
expenditure tending to induce other industries also to expand.
But if the others are only passive receivers of the external stimulus their expansion may be slow and uncertain. And their slow-
ness and passiveness will in turn slow down and discourage the
industry that first started expanding. In short, while it is true
that the active sectors will tend to pull the passive ones forward
(and this is what some advocates of ' unbalanced growth' have
in mind), it is equally true that the passive sectors will tend to
hold the active ones back. Would it not be better if every sector
were in some measure ' active ' in the sense of advancing spontaneously, imbued with some expansive élan of its own instead
of waiting for signals from others ? Price incentives and restraints would then be needed merely to keep each sector's rate
of advance in line with the community's pattern of demand. The
principle of balanced expansion can be looked upon as a means
of accelerating the overall rate of output growth.

The trouble of passive sectors holding the active ones back is
suggested by the drag which a primitive agriculture can impose
on the advance of manufacturing, but is probably not so serious
within the manufacturing field where the various sub-sectors are
likely to be more alert and progressive than the tradition-bound
farm sector is apt to be. Within the manufacturing sector in
particular it is of course not invariably true that output expansion in any single line depends on expansion elsewhere. A single
industry might go ahead on its own if by reducing costs it can
displace older and more primitive production methods in handi-
craft and village industries. In this case no increase in total
demand for its product would seem to be needed. However, the
existing volume of demand must be adequate to make the introduction of factory methods profitable; and in a low-income area
this is not always the case. In the face of technical discontinuities such as the one represented by a transition from handicrafts
to factories, output expansion elsewhere—implying demand expansion for the given product—may therefore be essential even

for cost-reducing as distinct from output-increasing investments in the manufacturing field.[1]

These considerations need to be elaborated, and no doubt also qualified, on a number of points into which we cannot enter. They do seem to me a necessary ingredient of the international economics of growth. They boil down essentially to a simple point. If in an underdeveloped country the stock of productive factors is growing, but if development through increased exports to the advanced industrial centers is for one reason or another retarded or blocked, there arises a possible need for promoting increases in output that are *diversified in accordance with domestic income elasticities of demand* so as to provide markets for each other locally, in contrast to output expansion for export, which is *specialized in accordance with international comparative advantage*. That the increase in production for the home market in these circumstances must ultimately conform to the pattern of domestic demand expansion is indeed a platitude if not a tautology.

This view of the pattern of home-market expansion does not in the least belittle the role of relative price changes in the efficient allocation of resource increments in the process of economic growth. Changes in relative prices are an essential means whereby in a market economy the pattern of output expansion is guided along an equilibrium path determined by consumer's demand in conjunction with specific resource availabilities. Shortages of specific factors, among other possible causes, can produce changes in the scale of relative prices, to which consumer demand will tend to adjust itself. There is no denying that price elasticities will help to determine the community's pattern of demand. But changes in relative prices have no close or determinate connection with economic growth as such, whereas income changes are a direct reflection and measure of growth. That is why the emphasis in this context falls naturally on the notion of income elasticity of demand.

It is a mere matter of labels whether diversified output ex-

---

[1] This distinction was used very effectively by Professor Viner in his address on ' Stability and Progress : The Poorer Countries' Problem ', at the Congress of the International Economic Association in Rome, 1956. See D. C. Hague (ed.), *Stability and Progress in the World Economy* (London, 1958), p. 58.

pansion in accordance with domestic income elasticities is called ' balanced growth ', to distinguish it from ' growth through trade ' which is specialized in accordance with international comparative advantage. This would be in some ways a convenient terminology, but ' balanced growth ' may mean different things to different people, and can have wider connotation not relevant to our special theme. The term is one we can easily dispense with.

Needless to say, there are limits to the diversification of output expansion. The minimum size of efficient plant is an important practical consideration which often limits the diversification of industry in any single country. This leads us at once to the crucial point that the case for diversified output growth for domestic consumption cannot be confined to national limits. Manufacturing for home markets in the less developed countries must include also production in these countries for export to *each others' markets*.[1] This is particularly important for the smaller countries, and it constitutes a strong argument for liberalization of trade policies, leading up to customs unions if possible, among groups of countries in the underdeveloped class. The result of intra-trade in manufactured consumer goods among such countries may be a reduction in their purchases of such goods from the older industrial countries, just as manufacturing for home consumption in a single country may lead to a fall in that country's imports of manufactured consumer goods. These results, however, are in my opinion not inevitable in the long run.

Industrial production for home consumption in underdeveloped countries is usually regarded as resulting in ' import substitution '. One objection to this description is that domestic output expansion can occur in the wide area of purely domestic goods which do not normally enter into foreign trade, as well as in the sphere of directly import-competing industries.

Moreover, ' import substitution ' can mean not only (a) the substitution of home-produced goods for imported goods, but also

[1] Following the chart we used earlier, there is a tendency in a sketch such as the present to treat the advanced and backward economics respectively as all consolidated into two ' countries ', reducing the problem under discussion to the traditional two-country model of trade theory. This is a convenient simplification but cannot be long maintained without appropriate ' frontier adjustments ' between the two groups of countries and without a good deal of attention being paid to intra-trade in each group.

(b) the substitution of capital goods imports for consumer goods imports. In a more comprehensive sense, as well as commonly in fact, the two substitutions (a) and (b) can both occur in combination, at least to some extent. If a country cannot increase its export earnings sufficiently, it can still increase its imports of capital equipment by cutting down its imports of consumer goods.[1] In this way it can convert its own saving into imported capital goods even if it receives no capital funds from outside. But this involves the creation of additional productive capacity and hence also, sooner or later, an enlargement of the total size of the market in the country in question. With an increase in both domestic production and real purchasing power a displacement of imports by home-produced goods, though likely in the short run, appears in the end to be not at all inevitable.[2] Eventually imports of manufactured consumer goods, perhaps even of goods identical with those now made at home, may well increase above the pre-development level. Industrial expansion combined with agricultural improvement will have enlarged the size of the market.

On the export side similarly, the development pattern we are considering has some cheerful possibilities. When industrialization for the home market has taken root, it becomes easier to increase exports of manufactured goods to the more advanced economies. In discussing the policy of industrialization for export markets, we found that since the advanced centers themselves usually have a high comparative advantage in producing the articles for which their demand is rapidly expanding, the industrial newcomers are generally limited to exporting crude and simple manufactures for which demand is relatively stagnant, so that the result is injury to existing suppliers and strong resentment on their part. But once the less developed countries have established a certain minimum volume and variety of manufacturing for home

[1] We should not forget, of course, that import restrictions on consumer goods cannot lead to a net increase in capital formation without an increase in saving.

[2] One of the conclusions of Hilgerdt's celebrated study runs as follows : ' To the extent that domestic industrial production is ... accompanied by a corresponding increase in the total amount of manufactures that can be marketed in the country, it obviously does not encroach upon the market for imported manufactures. ' (*Industrialization and Foreign Trade,* League of Nations, 1945, p. 116). This is a truly dynamic view and, as Hilgerdt's study shows, an entirely realistic one, too. But it has never found a comfortable place in the traditional framework of trade theory.

consumption, they are likely to develop ways and means of producing more of the ' progressive ' products which can be exported to the mass markets of high-income countries without displacing any existing producers there. After all, the vigorous expansion that has been going on in trade among the advanced economies is also a result, not so much of any mutual displacement of manufacturing activities in these countries, but rather of expanding total demand for a wide and growing range of manufactures.

Japan, for example, has now reached a stage in which she has started exporting such items as optical goods and engineering products to the United States without meeting the same obstacles as in the case of her textile exports to the American market. Japan is often thought of as having developed her industry for export markets from the start. Recent research has made it clear, however, that the first stage of Japan's industrialization, in the latter part of the 19th century, was mainly based on production for domestic consumption.[1] And the indispensable condition for the enlargement of the domestic market for manufactures was a remarkable advance in agricultural productivity during that period.[2] Japan profited greatly from an export boom in those early days, but that was in raw silk ; and she made good use of it in financing imports of capital goods.

At any rate in the early stages of home-market industrialization there is usually a shift (relative if not absolute) away from imports of manufactured consumer goods in favor of capital-goods imports. An increase in food imports is possible, but is not an essential characteristic of this development pattern since, unlike industrialization for export markets, industrialization for home consumption necessarily involves an increase in domestic farm productivity and food output as well. The diversification of output expansion which we have discussed concerns the ' horizontal ' composition of final output in its consumable form. From the

[1] ' The idea that the drive for foreign markets was *the* motor force of Japanese industrialization is nothing but a literary invention. It has little relationship to the facts ... The home demand for Japanese manufactures ... absorbed continuously most of the output of industry ... ' W. W. Lockwood, *The Economic Development of Japan ; Growth and Structural Change, 1868–1938* (Princeton, 1954), pp. 309 and 369.
[2] B. F. Johnston, ' Agricultural Productivity and Economic Development in Japan ', *Journal of Political Economy,* December 1951.

need for industrialization we cannot in any simple manner deduce a need for establishing capital-goods industries in under-developed countries, unless conditions for their establishment are favorable.[1] In general it is hard for any such country or group of countries to capture through domestic production the tremendous economies of scale that arise from the mass production of steel, machinery and transport equipment in the advanced industrial countries. Over 90 per cent of the total investment going on in the world (outside the Soviet area) now takes place in the industrial countries.[2] It is there that capital goods embodying the advances of modern technology can be produced on a large scale.

The less developed countries, if they wish to benefit from the economies of large-scale production of modern equipment, must for the present import the greater part of their capital-goods requirements. It is not surprising that capital-goods have come to form a steadily increasing share, now early one-half, of their total imports from the industrial world. This is one of the most conspicuous features of 20th century trade. Whereas in general the advanced countries export manufactured goods mostly to each other, in the capital-goods category their exports go mostly to the less developed countries. Whereas a hundred years ago trade between the center and the outlying parts of the world economy consisted predominantly of an exchange of textile manufactures against foodstuffs and fibers, it now consists increasingly of capital equipment going out and of minerals coming in. The international division of labor, which used to be largely ' horizontal ', has become more and more ' vertical '.

SUMMARY AND CONCLUSION

Let us quickly take a backward glance before closing. We have discussed three patterns of advance in less developed coun-

---

[1] Public utilities deserve in general a higher priority than the capital-goods industries for the simple reason that capital goods are importable, while basic services such as inland transport, water supply and electric power cannot physically be imported or, like electricity, cannot be brought from any great distance. If these services are to be had at all, the facilities for producing them must be installed on the spot. Their absence can be an absolute barrier to development while lack of home-produced equipment is not.

[2] ECE, *Economic Survey of Europe in 1957*, Chap. 4, p. 2.

tries: (i) growth through exports of primary products; (ii) growth through exports of manufactured consumer goods; and (iii) expansion of output for domestic markets. This is in some ways an arbitrary division, but most divisions in economics have an element of arbitrariness, being made for convenience of communication and analysis. More important is the fact that in the real world we seldom find a single pattern in isolation, but usually a mixture of two or more. The three main patterns can easily be combined. Even an individual country may conceivably seek to follow all of them at once. The weight given to each of them will naturally vary in different parts of the world in accordance with a country's domestic resources and external demand conditions.

Besides, the relative weight of development patterns can change over time. We have seen that Pattern I, which works through expanding for primary products, provided in the 19th century the principal opening for economic growth in outlying areas of the world economy. Advance is still possible along this line. But for reasons discussed earlier it now seems to offer relatively limited opportunities to the majority of countries in the lower income brackets. The petroleum countries are a rather special case.

Manufacturing for export to more advanced countries—our Pattern II—is being tried to some extent, in some places with success, and there are experts who predict great things for it in the near future. But it can hardly be described as a major factor at present. India, though she has less than 5 per cent of her labor force working in factories, has emerged as an exporter of textile manufactures, but even before she encountered obstacles in the United Kingdom these exports went mostly to other underdeveloped countries; and this is a different story.

More is happening along the lines of Pattern III, the pattern of home-market expansion. The local basis for it, in the form of food production in the less developed countries (outside the Soviet area), has expanded by some 25 per cent in the last ten years, though on a *per capita* basis the increase is less than 10 per cent.[1] Industrialization for home markets is undoubtedly spreading.

The continuing and perhaps widening gap in income levels between the poorer and the richer countries should not blind us to

[1] FOA., *The State of Food and Agriculture 1958* (Rome, 1958), pp. 12-13.

the fact that economic growth in aggregate terms, if not *per capita*, is probably more widespread and, in the world as a whole, perhaps more rapid today, in the 1950's, than ever before.[1] But outside the lively intra-trade of industrial centers, how much of it could be classed at ' growth through trade '? If we found it to proceed largely along Pattern III, should we be surprised and disappointed? International specialization is an essential foundation of our material civilization. The case for it is firmly based on considerations of economic efficiency; and the world is not rich enough to despise efficiency. But why should we expect international trade to solve all problems of *development*, in any and all circumstances? Unfounded expectations may be due to the influence of a certain historical association.

In the 19th century economic growth was so closely linked with international trade not only because countries previously isolated by high transport costs as well as other barriers, now came to specialize. This was a very important factor, but it was not all. On top of it, economic development was diffused to outlying areas through trade, because the pattern of advance in the rising industrial centers happened to be such as to cause a rapidly growing demand for crude products of the soil which those areas were well fitted to supply.

In the changed conditions of the present time expansion of primary production for export—our Pattern I—still has a part to play. Even if we leave out petroleum, the volume of primary products imported from the less developed areas into the industrial centers, at roughly the same terms of trade, is now about 20 per cent greater than in 1928. There are countries, apart from those exporting petroleum, for which conditions of growth through staple exports have of late been quite adequate. And Japan in the late 19th century has demonstrated how effectively this type of growth can be used as a spring-board for industrialization as well.

But in considering the picture as a whole it is hard to avoid the impression that for a great many countries under present conditions Pattern I, though excellent as far as it goes, does not go far enough. Let us keep in mind especially the rate at which productive factors in the underdeveloped countries are growing

[1] Cf. A. J. Brown, *Introduction to the World Economy* (London, 1959), p. 93.

all the time, through the increase in population numbers, health, education and capital, home-made as well as imported. On the other side there is no doubt that world demand for a wide range of primary products is, for well-known reasons, relatively slow in expanding. In these circumstances any exclusive emphasis on the traditional pattern of growth through trade would be out of place, and could be interpreted as a hang-over from bygone days. We should try to understand the need for other patterns of development and the many new problems which they involve.

DYNAMIC ASPECTS OF TRADE THEORY*

APPENDIX

No attempt can here be made to deal with the theory of international trade in general terms. We concentrate on a particular situation: the lag in the export trade of less developed countries. We should remember that this situation concerns a relatively minor portion of world trade. Far larger is the volume of trade conducted among the advanced industrial centers. It may be that the conventional trade theory, a product of advanced countries, is best applicable to the intra-trade of countries already fairly well developed. In view of the quantitative weight of this trade such a basis would in fact be natural and legitimate. Nevertheless the situation on which we choose to concentrate is one that should not be neglected, and may have implications for trade theory generally.

I

The expansion of external demand for the primary commodity exports of the poorer countries appears in recent years, as we have seen, to have lagged behind the rate of increase in both the exports and national incomes of the industrial countries.

In the theory of comparative advantage, when a country experiences unfavorable demand conditions for its existing exports, certain forces operating through the monetary mechanism come into play that bring about two types of adjustment to these circumstances. At the export end of the scale of comparative costs, new commodities—the next in the scale—begin to be exported. At the import end of the scale, goods hitherto imported are displaced from the import list and begin to be produced at home. Two development patterns discussed earlier (patterns II and III respectively) correspond to these theoretical alternatives, though

---

* This appendix summarizes certain remarks presented for discussion in a seminar at the Stockholm School of Economics on April 13, 1959, insofar as they bear upon the subject of the preceding lectures.

the correspondence is not exact. If we are to keep in touch with the classical model we must modify it by making it dynamic and translating it into rates of change.

Static theory does not exclude change, but the type of change it deals with is of the once-for-all variety. The gains from trade which the classical theory of international specilization analyses are of this character. Once trade has been opened up and factors appropriately re-allocated, a higher level of real income is attained. The theory can accommodate without difficulty the ' optimum-tariff ' modification, supporting the terms-of-trade argument for trade restriction, which is similarly static in nature.

This type of trade theory is absolutely basic; it can be extremely useful. It is, however, limited in scope; and the more clearly we recognize its limitation the better for the realism and relevance of international economics.

Dynamics, by contrast, is concerned with effects of continuing changes and with rates of change.[1] The nineteenth-century type of growth transmission from an advancing economic center is an essentially dynamic story, in which a rising demand for crude products is a decisive feature which in turn may generate outflows of productive factors to the peripheral areas to supply this demand. The case for international specialization as such is as strong as ever. But the engine of growth transmission from advanced to less developed countries is, in relative terms,[2] less powerful than it once was.

In a dynamic interpretation of the classical model as applied to the present situation we must take into account two rates of change in particular: the rate of expansion of external demand for primary products and the rate of increase in productive resources in underdeveloped countries. On the one hand, we do not have a once-for-all downward shift in external demand for exports of primary products. What we have is typically a lag, in relation

---

[1] R. F. Harrod, *Towards a Dynamic Economics* (1949), p. 8.

[2] These are the terms that matter if we admit that the international ' problem ' of development has to do with income disparities and differential rates of advance. An excellent outline of this problem was given by Professor Erik Lundberg in his address on ' International Stability and the National Economy ' at the 1956 Congress of the International Economic Association (see *Stability and Progress in the World Economy*, ed. D. C. Hague, op. cit., especially pp. 223-26).

to the exports and incomes of advanced countries, in the rate at which external demand is shifting upward.

Moreover, if we adhere to the usual distinction between shifts of the demand schedule and movements along a given schedule, we may say that external demand for primary commodities is generally price-inelastic as well as sluggish in shifting upward (to the right). This does not contradict the fact that, if price is increased, a demand schedule cannot remain inelastic for ever, and that any country trying to apply optimum-tariff argument should actually, like a monopolistic firm, be operating on the elastic portion of the demand schedule with which it is confronted. It does mean that cost reductions and output increases in the face of such demand conditions may not do any good to primary producing countries. (If one of several countries exporting the same primary commodity were to cut its export costs and prices, its export earnings might well increase, but only at the expense of a fall in the other countries' earnings. The balance-of-payments adjustment mechanism alone, whether through exchange rate variations or domestic price changes, would force the latter to cut their export prices too, and all would be worse off at the end than they were at the start.) Price-inelastic demand is not an obstacle to growth through primary commodity exports if the demand schedule itself is vigorously upward-shifting. Trouble begins only when such demand expansion does not occur.

So much for external demand. On the other hand, we must give up the constancy of factor supplies commonly assumed or implied in the classical trade model. In the typical case in reality, even a poor country's stock of productive factors is continually increasing, through growth of population and therefore its labor force, through improvements in health, education and skills, and through capital creation at home as well as capital imports from abroad. Indeed we can interpret the poorer countries' export lag in its most significant sense as *a lag in the rate of growth of external demand in relation to the rate of growth of domestic factor supplies.* This statement leaves, however, a good many loose ends, some of which we must try to examine.

II

An increase in numbers alone may constitute ' growth ' in aggregate productive capacity, but not necessarily ' progress ' in terms of *per capita* output and income. As a rule progress must involve an advance in the factors other than numerical size of the labor force. While this should be kept in mind, we must concern ourselves generally with growth in factor supplies whether or not it involves progress.

Factor supplies must be treated as a variable, but they can be dependent, an independent, or a policy variable. (1) They can be incorporated as a dependent variable in a general equilibrium system of international trade, such as the one constructed by Professor Ohlin. This is a substantial advance, but not necessarily in the direction of dynamics. A given functional relationship between factor supplies and factor prices still need not take us outside the realm of static analysis. (2) It may be more realistic to treat certain factor supplies as an independent variable. This fits to some extent the growth of manpower, the spread of knowledge and perhaps even ' official ' capital imports, which may happen regardless of price incentives or domestic government policies. (3) Factor supplies may become a policy variable in development planning. The problem of ' resource mobilization ' is : how to get additional factors of production? It is here that special attention must be paid to increasing skills and material capital in relation to population numbers. The use of surplus farm labor for capital building is one example of resource mobilization. It may be that nothing can be done about the quantity of natural resources, which are said to be ' the most permanent and powerful factor governing comparative costs. '[1] But physical permanence need not be economically relevant. What matters is the amount of *useful* natural resources.[2] This depends on human knowledge. And knowledge is a variable.

On the other side we have the problem of ' incremental resource allocation ': what to do with additional factors of production? Allocation of resource increments is a central concern of dynamic trade theory.

[1] A. J. Brown, *Industrialization and Trade,* op. cit., p. 16.
[2] A point stressed by Viner, op. cit., p. 45.

But first, is it not somewhat arbitrary to keep resource mobilization and additional resource allocation in separate compartments (or separate paragraphs)? Admittedly in some cases the one may in fact be directly linked with the other. In business investment financed out of profits the link is particularly close. There are other possibilities of interrelation. In general terms the growth of factor supplies may depend to some extent on whether or not attractive or profitable openings exist for the employment of additional factors. When external demand expansion is relatively sluggish, and no attractive domestic opportunities come into being either, the growth of at least certain kinds of factors, including capital, may be slower than it would otherwise be. It may not be unrealistic then to think of external demand as an initiating force to which the stock of capital in an underdeveloped country will in some degree adapt itself. The most conspicuous instance of such resource adaptation is the international migration of private capital to countries enjoying a rapid rise in world demand for their export products (the new countries of the 19th and the oil countries of the 20th century). All this amounts to saying that factor supplies may be a dependent variable in dynamic contexts as well as in static systems of analysis. Besides, it still remains true that factor changes may be, and perhaps increasingly are, an autonomous variable or one subject to policy action. And conceptually, in any case, it *is* a separate question to consider to what use additional productive resources should be put if and when they become available.

III

Is there a presumption that they should be channelled into the existing export sectors because these are the lines in which, for the time being, the country is comparatively most efficient? There is not. If external demand conditions are unfavorable the result could be worsening of the terms of trade such as actually to reduce the country's total real income. This possibility has attracted some attention recently under the label of ' immiserizing growth '. It is a conceivable—and analytically very interesting—case, but, as will be seen, there is no need for it to happen.

Nor is there, on the other hand, anything to be gained by pulling resources out of the traditional export activities.[1] Since in the typical situation there is no absolute fall in demand for the traditional export staples, there is everything to be said in favor of at least maintaining production of these staples. And yet, to put *additional* resources into the existing export sectors might be of little or no use if export demand is inelastic as well as sluggish in expanding. Thus we see that while a country's established comparative advantage in the current export products may be high indeed, its incremental comparative advantage in these lines may be zero or actually negative. The only question, then, is whether the increment in the stock of productive factors should be utilized for developing new export activities, or whether it should be used to establish industries catering for home consumption and tending at least initially perhaps to displace existing imports.

Once more we face the two alternatives corresponding to the two possible adjustments to an adverse change in foreign demand under the classical trade model. In the classical model it is normally the shape of the comparative cost scale at both the export and the import ends of the scale that determines the proportions in which the adjustment occurs through increased exports and decreased imports respectively. If, for example, the scale of comparative costs has a kink at the import end but is smoothly ascending at the export end, the adjustment may come mostly through new exports rather than diminished imports; and vice versa.

Similar considerations may apply to our ' dynamic ' situation. It was argued earlier that even in densely populated countries labor is not necessarily cheap for purposes of industrial production for export markets.[2] In such a case indeed a country may have no very marked incremental comparative advantage in any line on the export side. Yet the stock of resources may be growing. Is not this a situation in which the bulk of the factor increase would have to be employed for output expansion for

[1] Unless previously unused opportunities exist for ' optimizing ' the country's barter terms through trade restriction. We may assume that such opportunities are being fully and continuously exploited.

[2] Lecture II, section 2.

domestic markets? In any event this is a solution that needs more consideration that it commonly receives. It may be obvious in general terms but it demands attention in the particular framework of international economics as well.

From the very fact that output expansion is for domestic markets it follows that it must to some extent be diversified in accordance with domestic income elasticities of demand.[1] The process of domestic output growth must of necessity observe a certain ' balance ' in its horizontal composition if the additional supply of goods and services is to create its own demand or, concretely, if the extra outputs are to find adequate markets. This is perhaps a mere tautology. The more substantive content of this view may be its ' instrumental ' (as distinct from its teleological) aspect which concerns itself with the mechanics of the process and looks upon concerted expansion of a range of sectors actively pushing ahead, as a means to accelerated growth.

Output expansion for home markets is of interest in the present setting as an escape from Immiserizing Growth.[2] This concept, as already mentioned, envisages growth in the factor stock as leading to impoverishment through bad effects on the terms of trade produced by output expansion for export in the face of unfavorable external demand conditions. As a theoretical scarecrow it undoubtedly has its uses, but it need not be accepted as an inevitable necessity in a spirit of economic determinism. It is not incompatible with the classical trade model; the immiserezation is by comparison with the pre-growth and not, of course, the pre-trade situation. But what is it that is supposed to produce the immiserizing growth? Obviously not the price system; if the terms of trade are falling why should additional resources crowd into the export sectors? Immiserizing growth seems to rest on the novel concept of ' output elasticity of sup-

[1] Let it be recalled once more that the argument is not necessarily confined to national limits, which are arbitrary and accidental, but is applicable to a group of countries—or all countries—affected by the situation under consideration.

[2] For an ingenious formal presentation of the theory of immiserizing growth, see the two remarkable papers by J. Bhagwati, ' Immiserizing Growth : A Geometrical Note ' (*Review of Economic Studies,* Vol. XXV, No. 3, June 1958) and ' International Trade and Economic Expansion ' (*American Economic Review,* December 1958).

ply ',[1] which does not operate through relative price changes but assumes instead something like a fixed propensity of factor increments to go into certain predetermined limes of activity. If the output elasticity of supply of traditional export sectors is high, the fall in the terms of trade can more than offset the real income gains from output expansion in other sectors.

Output elasticity of supply is not an easy concept to accept. It is evidently constructed by analogy with the income elasticity of demand. Is the analogy a valid one? Although it has its difficulties too, the income elasticity of aggregate as well as individual demand is firmly based on the diversity of wants and the ' limited capacity of the human stomach '. Is there anything comparable on the production side? Is there any reason, independent of demand considerations, why factor increments should seek to distribute themselves along certain predetermined patterns? Institutional connections between factor creation and factor allocation do not provide a reason. Insofar as factor creation depends on attractive openings for factor allocation, one would not expect adverse demand conditions for exports to attract factor increments into export industries. It is no doubt a pedestrian question to ask, but what then is the empirical rationale of the concept?

Classical trade theory assumed domestic mobility of existing labor and capital. Actually there may be circumstances in which neither geographical nor occupational mobility of existing factors is necessary, as e.g. when the Indonesian peasant switches from rubber (for export) to rice (for home consumption) or vice versa. Flexibility in the structure of output is, after all, what matters.

' Immiserizing growth ' would seem to deny the mobility of factor increments, whereas general considerations suggest that increments in factor supplies are as a rule, and in the very nature of the case, ' mobile ' even if the factors already existing and employed are not. Transformation of output structure is in any case essential to development, as Professor Svennilson's work has

---

[1] This notion appearing in Harry G. Johnson's powerful taxonomic investigation, ' Economic Expansion and International Trade ' (*Manchester School*, May 1955, now republished as Chap. 3 in Johnson's *International Trade and Economic Growth*, 1958) and has been extensively used since then, notably in J. Bhagwati's papers just cited.

emphasized. It is perhaps only natural that a concept which implicitly denies capacity for transformation should point a way to impoverishment rather than development.

IV

If, by contrast, some mobility of resources and more especially of resource increments is accepted as generally plausible, a different approach suggests itself. It will be remembered that in Professor Hicks's celebrated analysis of trade and growth,[1] a balance-of-payments problem—the dollar shortage—resolves itself elegantly into a terms-of-trade problem. Aside perhaps from inevitable transitory difficulties in the foreign-exchange accounts, any country can normally restore its payments balance by accepting a worsening in its barter terms.[2] In this model external equilibrium is maintained by changes in the terms of trade.

Can we not go a step further? Although there are good reasons for the prominence which the terms of trade receive in the theory of international trade, there has been a tendency, in Britain and elsewhere, to exaggerate the actual extent and the economic significance of changes in the terms of trade in the study of long-term growth. One is too apt to think of these changes as if in each country resources were forever committed to the existing export industries or as if newly created resources were somehow predestined in certain proportions for these same industries. In the short and even the medium run resources are indeed more or less fixed, and accordingly changes in the terms of trade are notoriously wide and disturbing in the business cycle. But in the longer run labor and capital within each country can and do move to other occupations. If the relationship of export prices to import prices undergoes a marked decline or increase, factors of production will tend to move from export industries to home-market industries

---

[1] J. R. Hicks, ' An Inaugural Lecture, ' *Oxford Economic Papers,* June 1953.

[2] This tends to happen as a byproduct of price adjustment either through exchange rate variation or through the ' gold standard ' mechanism of internal price reduction. Import restriction in these circumstances might be preferred on terms-of-trade grounds, but this would seem to assume that unused opportunities in the optimum tariff direction exist; which may be contrary to fact and is in any case contrary to our assumption.

(including directly or indirectly import-competing industries) or vice versa. In a growing economy this will involve changes in the allocation of increases in factor supplies rather than movements of existing factors. The effect on foreign trade will be a decrease or increase in the volume of both exports and imports, or quite possibly just a change in the rate of increase in trade.

In this way a change in the terms of trade tends to induce shifts in production and in the distribution of resources which will tend to reverse or counteract the change in the terms of trade.[1] In other words, changes in the terms of trade are apt to be ' washed out ' in the long run. What remains is growth or decline in the volume of productive activity, in the export and the home-market sector respectively, induced through international trade by external demand conditions. On this view changes in the terms as well as in the balance of trade are a transient element in the mechanism by which processes of economic growth (or decline) may be transmitted from one country to others. What may be a payments problem in the short run becomes a terms-of-trade problem in the medium run and a development problem in the long run.[2]

Because of the possibility of internal factor shifts in response to varying price relationships, long-term trends in external demand conditions need not be reflected fully, if at all, in changes in the terms of trade. This does not imply that shifts in external demand do not matter. They can have a crucial influence on the directions of growth. Fortunate indeed is the country with an expanding export demand for the commodity in whose production

[1] If, for instance, a devaluation restores the payments balance but causes for the present worsening in the terms of trade, in the longer run factors will respond to the change in price relations by moving from export to import-competing industries. This movement need not disturb the balance but will at least tend to repair the terms of trade.

[2] The present discussion is not concerned with the balance of payments, and there is no implication here that the troubles we are considering must start with a payments imbalance. Our starting point is not an absolute fall in export demand. Our purpose here is to view the terms of trade in long-term perspective. If we had to deal specifically with balance-of-payments problems in the present context, we would start from the ' absorption approach ' in which such problems appear as essentially monetary in nature, reflecting ' excess ' expenditure, and not as the result of development as such or of development in one direction rather than another. An excellent statement of this approach is given in H. G. Johnson's book, op. cit., Chap. 6, though some of his earlier studies (especially Chap. 4 and even parts of Chap. 3) seem not entirely consistent with this position.

it has a comparative advantage. For then it can find comparatively advantageous employment for the growth in its stock of productive factors; and it can then draw increasing supplies of goods in wide variety from the outside world.

By comparison with this, output expansion for home markets does not present itself as an ideal, but as a *pis aller*. It may be better than any other possible line of action; better than immiserizing growth; better also than leaving factor increments unemployed. But it reduces the relative degree of international specialization and, for the time being, the efficiency of factor allocation compared with the traditional pattern of growth through trade. It calls for the creation, which is likely to be difficult, of a greater diversity of specific resources. It is likely to necessitate import restrictions, though these may be justifiable in the short or medium run on terms-of-trade grounds in view of the ' immiserizing growth ' alternative. In the longer run there are the hopes held out by the infant-industry and infant-economy arguments for protection. We may indeed expect that in the longer run the scale of comparative costs will change as the infants grow up.

Leaving aside these more distant prospects, we must look upon output expansion for home markets not as a substitute for international specialization but rather as a substitute for the traditional mechanism of growth transmission through trade. This mechanism may not be as vigorous as it used to be, but we should remember the increased importance of other means of diffusion, including official capital transfers, technical assistance, the spread of knowledge, and demonstration effects on the production as well as the consumption side.[1] Besides, we have no way of predicting the future. Conditions of transmission through trade may change in the future as they have changed in the past.

[1] This implies no judgment as to whether even the combined forces of diffusion are strong enough to offset those making for concentration, which are of course formidable. Just look, for example, at the way in which, in capital-rich economies, *capital improvement* goes on easily and continuously in the mere course of capital *replacement* financed from depreciation funds, whereby the fruits of ' research and development ' expenditure are promptly applied to the productive structure ; whereas in poorer areas the introduction of modern techniques generally involves the painful necessity of *new* capital creation.

V

It is curious to note that, in the light of preceding observations, a relative slackening of certain dynamic forces in world trade has made a dynamic extension of trade theory more rather than less necessary. In the past dynamic considerations have been brought into international economies mainly through a side entrance: the theory of commercial policy. They should come in by the front door. My neglect of commercial policy is partly deliberate, though none the less regrettable.

I hope that no apologies are needed for the concern with development and underdevelopment which these remarks have introduced into a discussion of trade matters. If it happens to be the fashion, we can cheerfully go along with it in the belief that this concern may enrich the general body of economics just as the concern with employment did in the thirties. An economics unaffected with real-world problems would court the danger of sterility.

The developmental aspects of trade theory bring out the need to take account of the economic environment of international trade relations. This was a lesson taught by the income approach to international economics. Still earlier it was a dominant theme of Professor Ohlin's classic work, *Interregional and International Trade*. It is not good enough to watch the things that move across national boundaries; trade must be viewed in its context. The current preoccupation once again is forcing us to look at that this concern may enrich the general body of economics just thing for international trade theory.

INDEX OF AUTHORS

Bhagwati, J., 221, 222
Brown, A. J., 197, 202, 212, 218
Cairncross, A. K., 176, 185
Campos, R., 197
Daly, R. F., 185
Engel, E., 203
Faaland, J., 185
Fabricant, S., 185
Haberler, G., 197, 201
Hague, D., 206, 216
Harrod, R. F., 216
Heckscher, E., 197
Hicks, J. R., 187, 223
Hilgerdt, F., 173-4, 208
Hobson, J. A., 177-8
Imlah, A. H., 179
Jevons, S., 189
Johnson, H. G., 222, 224
Johnston, B. F., 209
Lederer, W., 184
Lewis, W. A., 182, 197
Lockwood, W., 209
Lundberg, E., 216
MacDougall, D., 185

Malthus, R., 178, 189
Marshall, A., 174, 177
Meade, J., 197
Mill, J. S., 189
Myint, H., 186, 193
Myrdal, G., 176
Ohlin, B., 179, 197, 218, 226
O'Leary, P. J., 182
Paley, W., 184, 185
Perroux, W., 190
Ricardo, D., 172
Robertson, D. H., 172, 177
Robinson, E. A. G., 173
Schultz, T. W., 184, 185
Smith, A., 203
Staehle, H., 194
Stamp, D., 197
Stern, R. M., 175, 190
Steuart, J., 203
Svennilson, I., 176, 222
Tinbergen, J., 197
Viner, J., 206, 218
Wicksell, K., 176